SOCIOLOGY IN FOCUS

for AQA AS Level

Edited by
Michael Haralambos and Peter Langley

Written by
Michael Haralambos, John Richardson, Paul Taylor, Alan Yeo, with Pam Law

Dedication
To our mothers from Michael and Peter

Acknowledgements

Cover and page design	Caroline Waring-Collins (Waring-Collins Ltd)
Graphic origination	John A. Collins (Waring-Collins Ltd)
Graphics	Tim Button (Waring-Collins Ltd)
Author index and typing	Ingrid Hamer
Reader	Mike Kidson

Picture credits

Advertising Archives 50(r), 54, 67(tl), 110(bl); Andrew Allen 114 (l), 163(mr and r), 181; Associated Press 6(bl and br), 21(tl), 26, 32(bl), 45(r), 57(t), 60(l), 74, 75(r), 85(l), 104; Axel Poignant Archive 34; BBC Photograph Library 6(t), 18; BHS 20; British Library 45(ml and bl); Bridgeman Art Library 86(l and r); Camera Press 145(l), 168(r); David Hoffman 75(bl), 144(tr), 148(bl and br), 170; Digital Vision 48(bl); Ethnological Museum, Berlin/World Trades Publishing 46(b); Eye Ubiquitous/James Davis Worldwide 35(l); Format (and Jacky Chapman) 177; Glenbow Archives 85(r); Hulton Deutsch 52(r); Institute of Agricultural History and Museum of English Rural Life 49(ml); John Collins 24, 88, 152; Kate Haralambos 57(mr), 78; Lancashire Museum Service 52(tl); Oxo 52(bl); Peter Newark's American Pictures 90(r); PhotoDisc 48; Photofusion (and Martin Bond) 4, (and Paula Solloway) 9(tl and tr), 12(tl), 123, 188, (and Jacky Chapman) 9(br), 10(t), 12(bl), 16(b), (and Julian Martin) 9(bl), 119, (and Ulricka Preuss) 15(br), (and Ray Roberts) 89, (and Robert Brook) 101, 112, (and Joanne O'Brien) 112, (and David Tothill) 113, (and Louis Quail) 117; popperfoto.com 12(tr), 21(tr), 65 (t and b), 129, 144(mr), 174(bl); Rex Features 10(m), 14(tl and tr), 15(bl), 56(t and m), 50 (r), 70(r), 80(b), 90(l), 91, 139, 145(r), 149, 167, 168(l), 179; Robert Estall Photo Agency 35(r); Sally and Richard Greenhill 31, 32(tl), 32(bl), 48(ml), 49(mr), 80(t), 122, 163(l and ml); Smithsonian Institution 7; Topham Picturepoint 12(br), 16(t), 32(tr), 37(l), 70(l), 75(ml), 84, 110(tr), 120, 132(l), 178(l), 184.

Cartoons
The cartoons in this book have been specially drawn by BRICK www.brickbats.co.uk

Cover picture
Hundertwasser
RANGITOTO-TARANAKI-RAKINO, 1973
© J. Harel, Vienna

Every effort has been made to locate the copyright owners of material used in this book. Any omissions brought to the attention of the publisher are regretted and will be credited in subsequent printings.

British Library Cataloguing in Publication Data
A catalogue record for this book is available from the British Library.

ISBN 1 902796 15 2

Causeway Press Limited
PO Box 13, Ormskirk, Lancs L39 5HP

© Michael Haralambos, Peter Langley, John Richardson, Paul Taylor, Alan Yeo

First impression 2003
Printed and bound by Scotprint, Haddington, East Lothian.

Contents

1 People and society

Introduction

Is there anybody else exactly like you? You'll probably answer 'no'. We like to think of ourselves as individuals and to see ourselves as unique.

Sociology does not deny this individuality. It does not claim that everybody is the same. However, it does argue that many of us have certain things in common. For example, members of a particular society share the same language. In this respect, we are not unique.

Most people live in social groups – in families, communities and nations – rather than as isolated individuals. As the poet John Donne said, 'No man is an island' (nowadays he would say that goes for women too). In other words, we are constantly coming into contact with other people. We are affected by them, we develop bonds with them. Indeed, we only become fully 'human' by participating in society.

Sociology has sometimes been described as the study of people in social groups. In this chapter we shall explore the fascinating story of how individuals are not isolated 'islands' but active members of society. We shall see how we learn certain values and ways of behaving, and how our membership of social groups gives meaning to our lives and shapes our identities.

Sociologists do not always agree on how and why things happen. But they help us to see more clearly how we are both 'individuals' and members of 'society'. And they help us see the connections between the two.

Unique individuals with many things in common

chaptersummary

▶ **Unit 1** identifies the main components of culture.

▶ **Unit 2** identifies the main components of social structure.

▶ **Unit 3** looks at socialisation – how people learn culture and their roles in society.

▶ **Unit 4** outlines some of the ways sociologists have explained social life.

▶ **Unit 5** looks at how society has changed.

Unit 1 *What is culture?*

keyissues

1 Are humans ruled by instincts?
2 How does culture shape human behaviour?
3 What are the main components of culture?

1.1 Becoming human

Instincts vs culture

Why do human beings behave the way they do? One view is that it is a matter of *instincts* – biological predispositions that tell us 'instinctively' what we should do. Instincts are something we are born with rather than something we learn. A great deal of animal behaviour seems to be ruled by instincts. For example, birds seem to follow fairly fixed patterns of behaviour as if they were a set part of their 'nature'.

Nowadays, a popular explanation for human behaviour is to look for the answer in our genes. People vary in their genetic make-up and this might explain why they behave differently. Some scientists claim there is a gene for crime, one for alcoholism, even a 'gay' gene. Some have offered genetic explanations for why men are unable to find butter in the fridge, or why women can't read maps!

Sociologists accept that humans have natural *reflexes* – for example, we automatically flinch when someone strikes us. They also accept that we have certain biological *needs* that must be met – for example, the need for food and drink. But sociologists believe human behaviour is too

activity1 genes or society?

Item A *Nappies and planes*

There is no gene or brain pattern which makes men incapable of ironing, shopping, changing nappies or expressing their emotions. And there is none which stops women running governments or multinational corporations, flying fighter planes, abusing children or committing murder. It is culture which explains why women do more of some things and men do more of other things.

Adapted from MacInnes, 1998

Item B *A woman's place*

questions

1 What view does Item A take on the genes versus culture debate?

2 Look at Item B.

   a) Why are the passengers reacting like this?

   b) Is there any justification for their reaction?

---

complex and diverse to be explained in simple biological or genetic terms. Rather, they see our actions as the result of our social and cultural environments. We *learn* to think and act in certain ways. And it is our *culture* which teaches us how we should think and act.

Feral children

People become fully human only when they are socialised into the culture of a society – when they learn the way of life of that society. It is culture which allows them to develop their human potential. We can see this in the case of so-called feral children – children raised in the wilds or in prolonged isolation from human company. Some reported cases are pure fantasy but the few authentic cases show that when these children are discovered and enter human society they encounter serious problems. They often seem stupid, unresponsive and animal-like. Deprived of the stimulation of human company, stripped of the opportunity to acquire human language early in life, these children are sometimes barely recognisable as human.

Cultural diversity

If human behaviour really is dictated by our genes or instincts, we would expect to find people behaving in much the same way all over the world. But what is regarded as normal behaviour varies from one culture to another. If we lived in Victorian Britain or in modern China, we would follow different customs, have different lifestyles. So human behaviour is flexible and diverse. It varies according to the culture we live in. Even the way we display our bodies in public changes over time and from place to place.

The social body Norbert Elias (1978) provides a detailed account of changing cultural attitudes towards the body. In sixteenth century Europe there was little sense of shame or delicacy about bodily matters. People would happily wipe snot on their sleeve or blow their nose on the tablecloth. They usually ate with their hands, and belching, farting, scratching, and even urinating or defecating in public were commonplace. But Elias describes how in the succeeding centuries people gradually became more sensitive to the 'shame' and 'disgust' of bodily functions as they developed 'good manners' and disciplined their bodies to act in a 'civilised' way.

Becoming human – conclusion

The long-running debate over whether human behaviour is largely the result of 'nature' (genes, biology) or 'nurture' (culture, environment) shows no sign of coming to an end. Nature and nurture always interact in complex ways. Even if we have a biological inclination to behave in certain

activity2 *from monkey boy to choir boy*

Walking through a Ugandan forest, a woman spotted a group of monkeys. To her astonishment, she realised that one member of the group was a small boy. Local villagers 'rescued' this 'monkey boy' and identified him as John Ssabunnya who had been abandoned as a two-year-old.

For the past three years, John had lived with a troupe of colobus monkeys. He had learned to communicate with them – with chatters, shrieks, facial expressions and body language. He shared their diet of fruit, nuts and berries, he became skilled at climbing trees and, like those who adopted him, he walked on all-fours. He was terrified of his 'rescuers' and fought to remain with his family of monkeys.

John, aged 14

John was washed and clothed – much to his disgust – and taken to an orphanage. He gradually learned to behave like a human being. Slowly but surely, he began to sing, laugh, talk, play, dress and walk like children of his age.

Today, John is a member of the Pearl of Africa Choir which has successfully toured the United Kingdom.

Adapted from the *Daily Mail*, 23.9.1999

question

How does the case of John Ssabunnya illustrate the importance of learned behaviour for human beings?

activity3 *the body*

Afghanistan

Rome

question

What do these photographs suggest about culture and attitudes towards the body?

ways, this will be channelled by society – the aggressive individual could become a violent criminal or a successful boxer, depending on social circumstances.

Whatever our underlying nature, it is clear that culture has a huge effect on our behaviour. We saw this in the case of feral children. Also, human behaviour is enormously diverse, showing wide variations over time and between societies. Norbert Elias demonstrated how even our intimate body habits are a product of society.

Sociologists suggest that if we want to explain social behaviour, then most of the answers can be found at the social and cultural level.

1.2 Looking at culture

Shared meanings and values

Sociologists usually define culture as the shared meanings, values and norms of a society or group.

Meanings Stuart Hall (1997) describes some of the key features of cultural meanings. First, it is largely thanks to *language* that humans are able to create meanings and make sense of the world. It is through language and other symbols, for example visual images, that people express their emotions and thoughts and communicate with one another. Second, culture is about *shared* meanings. People produce meanings together and so over time each social group builds up shared understandings of the world. Third, humans are constantly creating new meanings and revising old ones – so culture can be seen as a process or activity.

Values are things we regard as important, the most significant standards or principles in our lives. Love is an obvious example. Other examples are religious convictions and political loyalties. In everyday life, most people subscribe to the values of honesty, consideration towards others, justice and fairness – although we are not so good at living up to these values!

Norms are social expectations or rules about how people should or should not behave – for example, you should hold the door open for others, you should not grab the last biscuit. There are different rules for different situations – you can let your hair down at an end-of-term party, but the same behaviour would be frowned upon during normal class time. Norms also vary in their degree of seriousness. Committing murder will result in severe legal punishment but bad table manners might only provoke irritation in others.

activity4 meanings, values, norms

Item A Meanings

Item B Values

The Cheyenne lived on the Great Plains of North America. This account describes their traditional culture.

The Cheyenne believe that wealth, in the form of horses and weapons, is not to be hoarded by the owner. Instead it is to be given away. Generosity is highly regarded and people who accumulate wealth and keep it for themselves are looked down upon. A person who gives does not expect an equal amount in return. The greatest gift they can receive is prestige and respect for their generous action.

Bravery on the battlefield is one of the main ways a man can achieve high standing. Killing an enemy, however, does not rank as highly as a number of other deeds. Touching or striking an enemy with the hand or a weapon, rescuing a wounded comrade or charging the enemy alone while the rest of the war party looks on are amongst the highest acts of bravery.

Adapted from Hoebel, 1960

Cheyenne photographed in 1889

Item C Norms

Culture defines appropriate distances between people when they hold a conversation. In *The Silent Language*, Edward Hall observed that these distances in North and South America are different. This can cause problems when North meets South. In Hall's words, 'The result is that when they move close, we withdraw and back away. As a consequence, they think we are distant or cold, withdrawn and unfriendly. We, on the other hand, are constantly accusing them of breathing down our necks, crowding us and spraying our faces.'

Adapted from Hall, 1959

questions

1 What meanings does the symbol in Item A communicate?

2 a) Identify the values of the Cheyenne described in Item B.

   b) How do they indicate that values vary from culture to culture?

3 Norms are important. Discuss briefly with reference to Item C.

Whole way of life

Anthropologists specialise in studying whole societies, especially small-scale, less technologically developed societies. Perhaps, as a result of this, they tend to adopt a sweeping definition of culture. Clyde Kluckhohn (1951) described culture as the distinctive 'way of life' of a group of people. This way of life includes their typical patterns of behaviour – their common lifestyles, the skills and techniques they use to make a living, and all their routines, customs and rituals.

Subcultures

As societies grow larger and more complex, it becomes increasingly difficult to talk about one culture which everybody shares. For example, in Britain today, there are groups who share many aspects of mainstream culture, but who also have certain beliefs, attitudes and ways of behaving of their own. In other words, they have their own *subcultures*.

Groups with distinctive subcultures include some ethnic minority groups, social class groups, regional groups and some age groups. This subcultural diversity has lead to the term *multicultural society* being used to describe many large-scale industrial societies.

The death of a princess

We can see how the different elements of culture operate by looking at the public response to the tragic death of Diana, Princess of Wales. Diana died in 1997 when her chauffeur-driven car crashed in a Paris tunnel while racing away from pursuing photographers. The reaction to Diana's death demonstrates the importance of values, symbols and norms in our lives.

Values Humans place high value on life and so they feel threatened and troubled by death. But they do not have to work out the meaning of life and death from scratch, alone and unaided. Their culture supplies them with ways of making sense of it all. In Diana's case, the funeral service in Westminster Abbey brought spiritual comfort to many people.

Symbols Many mourners used cultural symbols as a way of expressing their feelings. Some wrote poems, some hung flowers or ribbons on trees and others collected souvenirs of Diana. Music was another popular form of expression and Elton John's re-worked version of *Candle in the Wind*, played at the funeral, quickly shot to the top of the record charts.

Norms Cultural norms provide mourners with guidance on how to think, act and feel. In Victorian times people were

activity5 ethnic subcultures

Serving food, Pakistani wedding, Bradford

Bhangra dancing, Pakistani wedding Bradford

Steel band

Celebrating the Holi Festival, Norwood Green Nursery

question

With reference to the pictures, identify some of the ways in which ethnic minority groups may have their own subcultures.

expected to keep a tight control over their emotions (the 'stiff upper lip'). But cultural norms change and by the time of Diana's death it had become more acceptable to display emotions openly.

Cultural diversity Cultural guidelines are learned rather than innate and so there are differences between societies in their funeral customs. Nigel Barley (1995) reports that the Nyakyusa tribe ritually insult the dead and the bereaved – the relatives and close friends – who are not permitted to take offence. But in Britain, people are expected to speak respectfully of the recently dead. In Diana's case this rule was observed even by newspapers which had previously raked over her life for scandal and gossip.

Subcultures Various ethnic groups responded to Diana's death in terms of their own subcultures – for example, the expression of their grief was directed by their particular religions.

activity6 the death of Diana

The reaction to the news of Princess Diana's death was immediate. A sea of flowers appeared outside the royal palaces. Crowds of mourners waited up to six hours to sign books of condolence. On the day of the funeral, as a mark of respect, the National Lottery draw was postponed, shops closed and football matches were cancelled. People appeared with sleeping bags outside Westminster Abbey days before the funeral – the vigil had begun.

At 9.08 am on September 6, 1997, the bells at Westminster Abbey began to toll for the funeral procession. Diana's coffin, draped in the Royal Standard and covered in lilies, emerged from Kensington Palace to begin its two-hour journey to the Abbey. Along the route, the procession was greeted with silence and tears. After the service, there was a minute's silence when the entire nation came to a halt in an expression of grief and loss.

Adapted from *Chronicle of the Year 1997*

Mourners created their own shrines to Diana

A floral tribute at the gates of Kensington Palace, Diana's former home

question

Using the pictures and text, suggest how culture defines appropriate responses to death.

Looking at culture – conclusion

Culture is essential to the operation of human society. Without shared meanings, people would be unable to communicate. Without shared values, they would be pulling in different directions. And without norms directing behaviour, there would be no order in society.

From a sociological viewpoint, human behaviour is primarily organised and directed by culture. We are not ruled by instinct, governed by our genes, or directed by biological needs and impulses. If we were, then human behaviour would be much the same in different times and in different societies. It isn't, as can be seen from the wide variation between cultures in different time periods and places.

key terms

Culture The values, norms, meanings, beliefs and customs of a society; its whole way of life.

Meanings Things which give sense and significance to people's experiences.

Norms Social expectations; detailed guides to behaviour.

Rituals Actions regularly performed on special occasions.

Symbols Things – words, sounds, images – which stand for something else.

Values General standards or ethical principles which are highly prized.

Subculture Certain norms, values and meanings which are distinctive to a particular group within society.

summary

1. Although animals sometimes learn new ways of behaving, they are largely controlled by more or less fixed biological instincts.

2. Human behaviour is too complex and too diverse to be explained solely by biologically-based instincts, needs or drives.

3. From a sociological view, human behaviour is largely directed by culture. Culture is learned rather than biologically based.

4. The example of feral children shows the importance of culture in making us fully human. Culture provides us with language, values and a sense of our human identity.

5. Culture varies from society to society.

6. Culture provides meanings, norms and values to guide our conduct and shape our emotions.

7. As societies become larger and more complex, there are growing numbers of groups with their own subcultures.

Unit 2 *Social structure and social control*

key issues

1 What are the main components of social structure?

2 How are culture and structure related?

3 What are the main methods of social control?

2.1 Building a society

We have already seen what we mean by culture. But culture is not the only aspect of society of interest to sociologists. They also study the way societies are organised – their *social structure*.

Lego land

It is easy to be dazzled by the sheer complexity of society. So many different things seem to be going on at once, and nothing seems to stand still for long. Yet if we follow all this activity for long enough we can detect some regular patterns. There seems to be a recognisable shape to social life. We can also see how the various parts of society are related to other parts.

These patterns and relationships are called social structure. We can think of it as like a giant Lego model, assembled by putting all the component parts together. The basic building blocks consist of *social roles* which cluster into *social institutions* and together these make up the overall structure of society.

Social roles A role is a set of expectations that is applied to a particular *social status* or position in society. We expect a nun to be 'holy' and unselfish. A soldier is required to be brave and disciplined.

Each of us occupies a number of different statuses and so sometimes we have to juggle with competing expectations – this is called *role conflict*. For example, a father who is expected to put in long hours at work will find this clashes with his ability to spend time with his children.

The notion of role is borrowed from the stage. Shakespeare likened society to the theatre:

All the world's a stage
And all the men and women merely players
And one man in his time plays many parts
His acts being seven ages.

(Shakespeare – *As You Like It*)

Social institutions Social roles tend to arrange themselves in clusters, with each role having a strong connection with related roles. For example, the roles of patient, nurse, general practitioner and hospital consultant are interlinked. When roles group together like this they make up social institutions – economic, political, legal and other kinds of institutions. The family, too, can be considered as an institution – there are established conventions about the responsibilities and roles of parents, children and partners.

Social structure Just as social institutions are one level up from roles, so social structure is the next step up from social institutions – see Figure 1. The social structure of a society is the collection of social institutions in a society. These institutions are interrelated. For example, the education system trains people in literacy, numeracy and knowledge and this ensures a supply of educated workers for the economy. The economy, in turn, creates wealth and some of this is used to finance the education system.

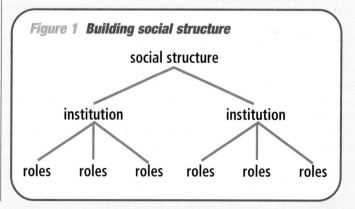

Figure 1 Building social structure

social structure

institution   institution

roles roles roles   roles roles roles

activity7 roles and institutions

Item A Roles

Policewoman

Doctors

Item B Institutions

School

Prison

questions

1   What are the role expectations of the people shown in Item A?

2   In what sense can the school and prison shown in Item B be seen as institutions?

Connecting culture and structure

Sociologists usually describe society as consisting of both culture and structure (see Figure 2). Certainly it is easy to separate them on a chart. However, in real life they always interact with each other. For instance, roles are both cultural (based on norms – cultural expectations) and structural (based on social statuses – structural positions). This can get confusing.

To avoid getting tied in knots, maybe it's simpler just to think of two separate spheres – culture and structure. And then think of the effect they have on each other.

Cultural norms and values shape how people behave –

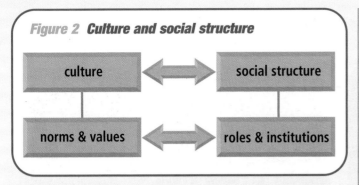

Figure 2 *Culture and social structure*

culture ⟷ social structure

norms & values ⟷ roles & institutions

and this creates the roles and institutions of society. For example, a society with strong religious values will encourage religious roles (priests) and religious institutions (churches, mosques, temples). It will also ensure that religious values are reflected in other institutions (eg, media, education).

In turn, the culture of a society is shaped by that society's social structure. For example, a society with a private enterprise (market) economy is likely to promote values which support that system – values such as individualism and competition. It is unlikely to preach the values of equality and cooperation.

Building a society – conclusion

Everyday life often seems to be a mixture of chaos and constant motion. But behind this buzz of activity it is possible to make out a shape or pattern. Sociologists call this social structure. It is a way to recognising that social behaviour is not totally random or a matter of mere chance. Rather, there is a pattern of relationships between people, roles and institutions, and this lends some consistency and stability to social life.

Sociologists find it useful to break society into two parts – culture and structure. Each of them has an effect on the other. No society first creates culture then social structure, or the other way round. They are both essential components of society. They are always interacting.

2.2 Regulating social life

From the ancient Greeks to the present day, philosophers have puzzled over how societies manage to hold things together. How on earth do complex societies succeed in maintaining stability and social cohesion among their populations? This section looks at some of the more common methods of *social control*.

Social control

Social control refers to the methods employed to ensure that people comply with society's rules and regulations. It is a way of checking that *deviance* – breaking of norms – is kept to a minimum. Peter Berger (1966) identifies some of the more common methods of social control:

Physical violence Sometimes people use violence against those who offend them. But it is the government and its

agencies which claim the authority to exercise legitimate or lawful violence in society. The police and the military back up society's rules with the threat of physical force or imprisonment. Violence is very much a last resort – usually the mere threat of it is enough to ensure that people conform.

Economic pressure People may conform because it is in their economic interests to do so. Workers who misbehave may be sacked, people who refuse to take jobs can have their welfare benefits withdrawn. Strikers are often forced to return to work when they find they cannot manage without a wage.

Social acceptance One of the most common things that keeps us in line is the desire to be accepted by others. When we are tempted to break rules we often ask ourselves 'What will people say if I get caught?'. We fear ridicule or gossip and we dread being excluded or shunned by others.

Socialisation This is perhaps the main method of social control. We are taught society's rules through the process of *socialisation* – the transmission of norms and values. People are socialised into society's mainstream values by parents, schools and the media. We *internalise* cultural expectations and they become part of our own code of values. This reduces the likelihood that we will wish to break the rules.

key terms

Social status A position in society, eg father, nurse, teacher.
Social role A set of expectations attached to a particular social status.
Role conflict When one role prevents the effective performance of another role.
Social institution A cluster of social roles; an established pattern of roles.
Social structure The overall network of roles and institutions in society.
Social control The methods used to ensure that people comply with society's rules and regulations.
Deviance Breaking social norms.
Socialisation The process by which norms and values are transmitted and learned.
Internalise Learning to the extent that it becomes a part of the individual's normal way of thinking. It becomes a part of them.

activity8 social control

Item A Paedophiles out!

Item B Gossip

question

What forms of social control are represented in Item A and Item B?

summary

1. The various parts of society are related to each other. This forms the social structure.

2. Each social status is accompanied by a social role which provides guidelines for acting in terms of that status.

3. Roles tend to cluster together. These clusters form social institutions.

4. Social institutions are often interlinked, eg economic and educational institutions.

5. Roles and institutions form the structure of society.

6. Culture and social structure are interrelated – they interact and shape each other.

7. Society has a number of methods to maintain social control. These include physical violence, economic pressure, social acceptance and socialisation.

Unit 3 Socialisation

keyissues

1 What is socialisation?

2 How do people learn social roles?

3 Who are the main agents of socialisation?

3.1 The learning game

In this unit we turn to the question of how individuals adopt cultural values and roles. The answer is that we *learn* the culture through a process of *socialisation*. Since culture is not an innate thing, something we are born with, it has to be passed down from one generation to another.

So we have to be taught the norms and values of our society or group. Over time we *internalise* many of these – they become part of our personal set of norms and values.

But socialisation is not a simple one-sided process of instruction in which we passively accept what we are told. We are not empty vessels into which culture and customs are poured. Each of us actively participates in our own cultural learning, trying to make sense of society's values and beliefs, accepting some of them but rejecting others.

Types of socialisation

Primary socialisation The early years of life are important in the learning process. This is the stage of *primary socialisation*, when we are normally in intimate and prolonged contact with parents. Our parents are *significant* others – they have a great influence on us and we care about their judgements of us. Significant others play a key part in teaching us basic values and norms.

Secondary socialisation This refers to the socialisation we receive later in life, from a wide range of people and agencies. They include peer groups, teachers, media and casual acquaintances. Sometimes they play a supportive role, adding to the primary socialisation of earlier years. But teachers also introduce us to new and more complex knowledge and skills. And friends sometimes introduce us to values and lifestyles which wouldn't win the approval of our parents!

Re-socialisation We usually have to learn new ways when our roles change. This may be a gradual process, for example, growing into adulthood. At other times it can be dramatic and abrupt. For example, army recruits experience the shock of basic training, when they have to abandon their civilian identity and submit to strict discipline and humiliating obedience tests.

Anticipatory socialisation In many cases we have already 'rehearsed' roles before we take them on. We imagine ourselves in them, we read about them, we learn something about them beforehand. For example, the young person who enters medical school already knows a bit about the life of a doctor from personal experience as a patient and from watching television shows such as *ER* or *Casualty*.

3.2 Agents of socialisation

The *agents of socialisation* are the people or groups who play a part in our socialisation. Sometimes they play an important role without us realising it. Sometimes we overestimate the influence they have on us. For some views on this, see Table 1.

Table 1   Survey of young people aged 11-21

'From whom do you think you have learned the most about sex and growing up?'

Parents	7%
Teachers	22%
The Internet	7%
Friends	27%
Brothers and sisters	4%
Newspapers and magazines	12%
TV and radio	13%
Church/clergy	0%
Don't know	9%

The Observer, 21.07.2002

Parents

The majority of children still grow up in a family headed by both their natural parents. But over the last thirty years there has been an increase in the numbers of lone-parent

activity9 learning the drill

US army recruits during basic training

Getting married

question

What kinds of socialisation apply to the people in these photographs?

activity10 learning

Pledging allegiance to their country

Playtime in a London primary school

question

What do you think these pupils are learning from the activities shown in these photographs?

families and also a rise in step-families. So family life has become more diversified. But whatever the particular family set-up, parental figures remain the main agents of primary socialisation. A sense of security in the early years of life is often seen as crucial for developing a stable personality and for effective learning of norms and values.

In the early years of our lives, most of our time is spent with parents and we are highly dependent on them. We learn by *imitating* what they do and we use them as *role models* for our own behaviour. We also learn by responding to the rewards and punishments parents have at their command. Even later in life, when school and peer groups take on increasing importance, parents continue to guide us – although nowadays young people sometimes have to teach their parents about things like computers!

Schools

Modern Western societies are too complex for young people simply to 'pick up' their culture as they go along. Rather, they are required to undergo a long period of formal education. In school they are formally taught the cultural heritage of their country – its history, geography, language and religions. They also learn technical knowledge, such as maths and science, that often has practical applications in daily life.

School pupils also learn from the unofficial *hidden curriculum* – the background assumptions, expectations and values that run through the school system. For example, through the exam system they learn about the importance of competition, hard work and success.

School is also a setting where children's social horizons are widened. They may mix with people from different social classes, ethnic groups and cultural backgrounds. They also become more aware of the different identities of people from various ethnic, gender and social class groups.

Peer group

A *peer group* is a friendship group formed by people of roughly the same age and social position. They meet each other as equals rather than being supervised by adults. In the early years of life, children like to play with one another for fun and amusement. But play is also a valuable learning experience. In play situations they learn about social norms (eg, treating others properly) and they develop social skills (eg, negotiating over toys). They can also experiment with social roles (eg, playing shop assistants and customers).

When children become teenagers, they spend increasing amounts of time away from their families and in the company of their friends. Parents often worry that peer group pressures will encourage their children to steal, take drugs, or engage in sex. Young people themselves often worry about their popularity within the peer group. Nevertheless, these groups perform valuable functions for their members. Within them, young people begin to develop independence from their parents. This prepares them for taking on adult roles themselves.

*activity*11 *peer groups – the good and the bad*

Item A *Talking*

'I can talk to my friends about things I can't really talk to my parents about, because well – they seem to understand me more, and my parents don't really listen to me, and my friends do, because they've been in the same situation as me'.

Young girl, quoted in Tizard & Phoenix, 1993

Item B *Messing up*

It isn't your parents who mess you up, it's your peers. After all, it isn't your parents who ridicule your cheap trainers, or your miserable choice of music, or who force you to drink a bottle of tequila and pass out in a dog basket, or who destroy you for looking wrong or talking wrong or being interested in things that you shouldn't be interested in. It isn't your parents who give you sexually transmitted diseases or who ply you with drugs.

Adapted from Bathurst, 2002

Item C *Friends*

questions

1 What do Items A and B reveal about peer groups?
2 Why is *Friends* so popular with young people?

Mass media

Mass media consume an enormous amount of our time – just think of all those teenagers locked away for hours on end in their bedroom with their own music centre, TV, game console and computer. We seem in constant danger of being overwhelmed by the sheer volume of print (newspapers, magazines, books) and electronic messages (TV, radio, the Internet). So it seems only reasonable to assume that the media have some effect on our attitudes, values and behaviour.

Admittedly, media seldom have a direct *hypodermic effect* – they do not inject their content into us and make us immediately accept what they tell us. But they help to create the cultural climate within which we live. They give us a sense of what values and behaviour are acceptable in the modern world. They provide us with role models – they hold up certain sports stars or showbiz celebrities for us to admire and copy.

The view of the world we get from the media is often highly stereotyped. For example, magazines such as *Cosmopolitan* seem to project an image of women as obsessed with sex and fashion. Likewise, men's magazines such as *Maxim* have been criticised for celebrating a crude 'lad culture' of lager louts, football and 'babes'. However, some people say these magazines are just escapist fun, and most people have little difficulty in separating media stereotypes from the 'real' world.

Religion

Religions deal with the deepest meanings and core values of life. They provide a set of moral values. Although religions put us in touch with the supernatural, they also prescribe a code of ethics (eg, the Ten Commandments) to regulate our earthly behaviour. We can see this when people undergo a religious conversion – it usually means far-reaching changes in their values and lifestyles.

The symbols, rituals and ceremonies of religion have traditionally been seen as a major force for social unity in Britain. But the long-term decline in church attendance suggests the country is becoming more secular – non-religious. Yet this does not necessarily mean that people have abandoned religious ideas and beliefs. Over 70% of the population still say they believe in God. Also, religion plays a significant role among Britain's minority ethnic communities of Muslims, Sikhs and Hindus.

Socialisation – conclusion

Socialisation is an essential element in any society. There are a variety of agents who perform socialisation tasks, but

activity 12 soaps

Item A Distortion

Most parents rely on television soaps such as *EastEnders* to trigger discussion of 'difficult' personal subjects with their children, according to research by the National Family and Parenting Institution. Many parents believed the storylines help children and young people to understand family life.

But the portrayal of family life in the soaps bears little relation to real life. Eighty per cent of the parents complained that the soaps do not promote positive images of the family. They claim that soaps consistently over-represent broken families, and place too much emphasis on sex and violence, cheating on partners, and alcohol abuse.

Adapted from *The Guardian*, 17.10.2002

Item B An affair

Ricky and Natalie having an affair in EastEnders

question

What do these items suggest about the ways in which TV soaps help children to 'understand' family life?

---

experts disagree on which ones exercise the most influence. Traditionally it was thought that parents, and perhaps the church, had the greatest effect. In modern society the school, peer group and mass media seem to have growing influence.

There is also disagreement about whether these agents have a sufficiently 'responsible' attitude to their socialisation tasks. For example, parents are sometimes accused of simply putting their kids in front of the TV rather than talking to them. Peer groups offer us friendship but they also introduce us to dangerous temptations. Mass media inform us about the world, but sometimes they distort that world.

summary

1. Socialisation is a key feature of any society – it transmits the cultural heritage from one generation to the next. It is the way in which people learn social norms, roles and values.

2. Socialisation is not a one-way street in which people passively accept society's norms and values. They participate in internalising, modifying or rejecting these norms and values.

3. There are different forms of socialisation. Primary socialisation is often thought of as the most important and influential. But secondary socialisation is increasingly significant in fast-changing modern societies.

4. Socialisation is performed by different agents – parents, school, peer group, mass media and religion. These agents come into play at different stages of our life, and they have different effects.

key terms

Primary socialisation Intimate and influential socialisation (usually from parents) in the early years of life.
Secondary socialisation Socialisation that comes later in life, from various sources.
Agents of socialisation The individuals, groups and institutions which play a part in the socialisation process.

Unit 4 *Theories of society*

keyissues

1 What are the main sociological theories?
2 What are their strengths and weaknesses?

4.1 Structure and action

What shapes our behaviour? Do we control our own destiny or do social pressures determine our actions? Are we largely moulded by the wider society and forced to behave in certain ways or do we have the freedom to decide our own actions?

Social systems Some approaches in sociology emphasise the power of society over the individual. They are sometimes called *social systems* or *structuralist* approaches.

From this viewpoint, the individual is largely controlled by society. We are what we are because of the expectations and pressures of the social groups to which we belong. Society is in us, moulding our thoughts and directing our actions. We are socialised in terms of the culture of society, our behaviour is shaped by the social structure, we are kept in line by mechanisms of social control, we learn roles, norms and values and act accordingly.

Social action Other approaches emphasise the ability of individuals to direct their own actions. They are sometimes called *social action* or *interpretivist* approaches.

From this viewpoint, individuals actively create their own social world. They give meanings to social situations, interpret the behaviour of others, and they take action on the basis of these meanings and interpretations.

Social action approaches do not necessarily deny the existence of roles, norms and values. However, they tend to see them as flexible guidelines rather than inflexible directives. For example, each doctor interprets his or her role somewhat differently. Some tend to see illness as a physical problem. As a result, they are unlikely to spend much time discussing patients' personal lives. Others believe that illness often results from problems in patients' relationships. They will be more likely to discuss these problems in order to deal with the illness.

The role of doctors is also affected by interaction with patients. To some degree, it is worked out or negotiated with patients, each with their own views and expectations of behaviour appropriate for a doctor. The role of doctor is not simply acted out from a standard script.

Systems versus action Although we can differentiate between social systems and social action approaches, neither is quite so extreme as suggested here. Systems approaches do not see people as totally controlled by society, nor do action perspectives view people as totally

activity13 views of society

question

Which of these cartoons illustrates a) a social systems approach and b) a social action approach?

Give reasons for your answer.

free agents. Rather it is a matter of emphasis.

Social systems approaches place more emphasis on the structure of society and its power to determine individual behaviour. Social action approaches place more emphasis on the freedom of individuals to direct their own actions.

4.2 Consensus and conflict

How would you describe society? Is it based primarily on *consensus* – agreement between people about social norms and values? Or is it based on *conflict*?

A brief glance through the newspapers, a review of family life, or a quick read through history books might well suggest that conflict prevails. But consider how we go about our daily lives. Most of us seem to agree with the rules of society, and we work together in terms of those rules. So although conflict might grab the headlines, it could be argued that social life is largely based on consensus and cooperation, not conflict.

So far, we have distinguished between social systems and social action perspectives. The distinction between consensus and conflict allows us to make a further division. Social systems approaches can be divided into those which characterise society as based on conflict and those which see society as based on consensus.

Consensus Consensus approaches see agreement or consensus as the basis of social life. Without it, society would collapse into chaos with its members being unable to agree on rules and norms of behaviour. Consensus provides the basis for cooperation and social unity. Unless there was general agreement about what is important and worthwhile – in other words, shared values – there would be no cooperation and unity in society. It would be replaced by conflict and division as individuals pursued their own interests which would often directly conflict with those of others. *Value consensus* provides a harmony of interests in society.

Conflict Conflict approaches see conflict as the main characteristic of society. This does not mean that members of society are constantly at each other's throats or on the brink of civil war. Rather it means that there are basic conflicts of interest in society with some groups gaining at the expense of others.

Some groups are more powerful than others – usually as a result of their stronger economic position. In this situation, norms and values are not freely agreed by everyone but are imposed on the weaker sections of society by the more powerful groups. What appears on the surface as consensus is in fact *coercion* – an 'agreement' based on force. What seems to be cooperation is in fact *exploitation* – one group gaining at the expense of others.

4.3 Functionalism and consensus theory

So far, we have distinguished between a number of broad perspectives or approaches within sociology. Social systems perspectives have been contrasted with social action perspectives. Consensus approaches have been compared with conflict approaches.

The rest of this unit looks at *sociological theories* which derive from these broader perspectives. A sociological theory is a set of ideas which claims to explain the social behaviour of human beings. This section looks at a sociological theory known as *functionalism*.

Consensus Functionalism sees society as a social system based on consensus. It begins from the assumption that society has certain basic needs which must be met if it is to survive. First and foremost is the need for social order – for a smooth-running, well-ordered society in which social life is predictable and people know what is expected from them.

Social order requires a certain degree of cooperation and *social solidarity* (social unity). This is made possible by shared norms and values. This in turn requires some means of socialisation to ensure that norms and values are learned, plus mechanisms of social control to ensure that norms and values are conformed to. In particular, value consensus is seen as essential since without it people would be pulling in different directions and the result would be conflict and disorder.

Society as a system Functionalists see society as a system – a set of parts which work together to form a whole. These parts are the institutions of society – for example, the family, the education system and the political system. Based on the assumption that society is a system, the questions now become: 'How do the various parts work together to maintain social order?' and 'What is the contribution of each part to the maintenance and wellbeing of the social system?'

*activity*14 *contrasting views*

Item A **Who gains?**

Consensus From a consensus perspective, successful business people deserve high rewards. They have made important contributions to society by building up efficient and productive companies and providing employment. High rewards motivate them and everybody benefits from their success.

Conflict From a conflict perspective, the wealth and lavish lifestyles of the rich and powerful are paid for by exploiting workers. Wealth is produced by the workers but their wages are small change compared with the extremely generous salaries, bonuses and dividends which business owners pay themselves.

Item B **Top of the pay list**

In 2002, Philip Green paid himself over £157 million, making him the highest paid person in the UK. He is a very successful businessman with a 'hands on' approach and a reputation for turning round failing businesses. For example, he bought the ailing BHS (British Home Stores) for £200 million – it is now valued at £1 billion.

Philip Green works hard and plays hard. In 2002, he spent £5 million on his 50th birthday party, flying 200 friends in a private 747 to Cyprus where Rod Stewart and Tom Jones sang to toga-wearing guests in a Roman amphitheatre.

Philip Green   Adapted from the *Sunday Times Magazine*, 3.11.2002

question

Explain Philip Green's wealth from a) a consensus perspective and b) a conflict perspective.

*activity*15 *social solidarity*

Item A *Golden Jubilee*

Queen Elizabeth on her way to St Paul's Cathedral to celebrate her Golden Jubilee, June 4, 2002

Item B *9/11*

Ceremony marking the first anniversary of the attack on the World Trade Center, ground zero, New York, September 11, 2002

question

Functionalists see celebrations, ceremonies and rituals as very important for creating social unity or social solidarity. Using the photographs in Items A and B, suggest how this is done.

Let's look at some simple answers to these questions. When looking at any part of society, functionalists often ask, 'What is its function?' By *function* they mean its contribution to the maintenance of the social system. Thus a simple answer to the question 'What is the function of the family?' is that the family socialises new members of society and teaches them the norms and values which are essential for social life. Assuming that the various parts of the social system work together for the benefit of society as a whole, the next question is: 'What is the relationship between the family and other institutions such as the education system?' Again very simply, the educational system continues the process of socialisation begun in the family. In this way, the institutions of family and education work together to maintain social order.

Social disorder It appears from this brief outline that society is a smooth-running, well-oiled system. What about conflict and social disorder? Functionalists obviously recognise their existence but see them as a temporary disturbance to the social system rather than inbuilt and permanent aspects of society. Functionalists accept that social groups have certain differences of interest but this usually results in competition rather than conflict. And these differences are minor compared to the values and interests they have in common.

Criticism Functionalists have been criticised for presenting a deterministic view of social behaviour. This refers to the tendency of some functionalists to picture human beings as shaped by the social structure, and directed by society's norms and values. As such, they appear to lack free will, initiative and creativity. Hence Peter Berger's criticism that society is sometimes portrayed as a prison or a puppet theatre with people as prisoners of the system or puppets on the end of a string (Berger, 1966).

4.4 Conflict theory

This section provides a brief introduction to conflict theory and to Marxism, the best known and most influential version.

Conflict theory has a number of similarities to functionalism. It sees society as a system and human behaviour, to some extent, as a response to that system. Some of the questions asked are similar, for example: 'How is social order maintained?' However, the type of social system and the kind of social order are very different. Conflict rather than consensus is the primary characteristic of society. Social groups are in conflict since their interests are fundamentally opposed. And social order tends to be imposed by the powerful rather than based on a consensus freely agreed by all.

Ideology Many conflict theorists replace the idea of value consensus with the concept of *ideology*. Used in this sense, ideology is a set of beliefs and values which disguises the truth and distorts reality.

Ideology is transmitted by the agents of socialisation. For example, the mass media may present a picture of a reasonable and just society – a false view of the situation.

activity 17 looking at gender

Item A Barbie

Every girl in America owns an average of eight Barbies. Over 500 million have been sold worldwide. And for Christmas 1995, Barbie was the bestselling girls' toy in the UK. Sun Jewel Barbie, the new fuschia-bikinied and diamond-necklaced model, is the bestselling Barbie ever. Other new models include 'Dance 'n' Twirl', a radio-controlled Barbie who flounces across the dance floor, and a horse and carriage set to take Barbie and Ken (her boyfriend) to the ball.

According to Michelle Norton, PR person for Mattel Toys who created Barbie, 'She's a wonderful role model for little girls. She does everything they want to do and dream of. She's got lovely fashions and a boyfriend. It's a friendship sort of thing.' And it has to be – sex is out as Ken lacks the appropriate parts.

Adapted from *The Observer*, 22.12.1995

Item B Gender and maturity

In 1972, a fascinating study was published which explored the way mental health professionals thought about men and women (Broverman et al., 1972). The researchers asked a large number of applied psychologists (both men and women) to describe the qualities of:

1 The mature, healthy, socially competent adult
2 The mature, healthy, socially competent man
3 The mature, healthy, socially competent woman.

The descriptions of the 'mentally healthy man' and the 'mentally healthy adult' were virtually identical. Both were capable, independent, objective, stable and well adjusted.

But the description of the 'mentally healthy woman' was quite different. She was characterised as more submissive, more easily influenced, as excitable in minor crises, concerned with her appearance and more likely to have her feelings hurt. She was less independent, less dominant, less aggressive, less objective and less adventurous.

Adapted from Stainton Rogers & Stainton Rogers, 2001

question

How might a feminist sociologist analyse Items A and B?

---

marriage. A functionalist analysis looks at marriage in terms of the social system. The emphasis is on the roles of husband/father, wife/mother which are seen as largely given by the system and shaped to meet the requirements of the system. Thus, these roles are structured – for example, to provide a unit for the production and socialisation of children.

Social action theory would not reject the idea of roles. However, it would argue that when two people get married they have only a vague idea of how a husband and wife should behave. Should they share household chores, should they always go out together, should they kiss 'hello' and 'goodbye'? As a result of their day-to-day interaction, they gradually construct their own reality of married life.

They give meanings to marriage, they define and redefine what it means to be a husband and wife, and develop a shared view of their relationship.

From a social action perspective, marital roles are not prescribed by the social system, they develop from negotiated meanings during the process of interaction. This is a creative process with individuals directing their own actions rather than being constrained by the social system.

Symbolic interactionism

Symbolic interactionism is an example of social action theory. It starts from the idea that people interact in terms of symbols, the most important of which is language. To understand human action it is necessary to discover the meanings which people use to guide, interpret and make sense of their own actions and those of others.

Presentation of self Typical of the interactionist approach is the work of Erving Goffman. In *The Presentation of Self in Everyday Life (1969)* he analyses the techniques we use in order to influence how others see us. This process, which we all employ, he calls *impression management*. As social actors, we give more-or-less continuous 'performances' in that we present an 'appearance' of 'keen student', 'hard working, professional lecturer' or 'caring parent'. Our facial movements, body language, speech content, style and so on are coordinated in an attempt to convey a particular impression. We create the proper 'setting' of office, classroom, doctor's surgery or whatever, equipping it with appropriate 'props' (desks, white coats, medical books etc) to reinforce this impression.

As everyone else is also engaged in impression management, we become very skilled in interpreting the actions of others and at watching for discrepancies in their performances. For example, when cooking a meal for a friend, their polite response of 'what a lovely meal' will be checked by looking to see how much they've eaten, whether there are any facial signals of distaste or any whispered comments of a negative nature.

Definition of the situation The American sociologist W.I. Thomas captured one of the main insights of symbolic interactionism when he wrote, 'If men define situations as real, they are real in their consequences'. By this he meant that people act in terms of the way they define situations. To give a rather flippant example – a person walks down a street swathed in bandages. This situation may be interpreted in a number of ways – fancy dress (the Invisible Man), a practical joke, a 'dare', a bet, someone who has serious injuries, or even a sociologist conducting an experiment. Each of these definitions is real in its consequences. People will act towards the bandaged figure depending on their interpretation of his or her behaviour. Whether or not their definition is 'really correct' is not the point. The point is that to understand their response, we have to understand their *definition of the situation*.

Criticism Criticisms of symbolic interactionism and social action theory as a whole are in some ways a reversal of those of systems theory. Because they focus on small-scale interaction situations, social action theorists tend to ignore the wider society. Critics argue that to some extent this wider social framework influences and even constrains interaction. They claim that social action theorists have gone too far – human action is not as free, creative, spontaneous and flexible as they appear to suggest.

key terms

Value consensus An agreement about values.
Social solidarity Social unity.
Function The contribution made by a part to the maintenance of the system as a whole.
Infrastructure In Marxist theory, the economic base of society which shapes the superstructure.
Superstructure The rest of society – the political, legal and educational systems, the family, religion, beliefs and ideas.
Ruling class Those who own the means of production.
Subject class Those who do not own the means of production and are subject to the power of the ruling class.
Means of production This includes the land, raw materials, machinery and buildings used to produce goods.
Ruling class ideology A set of beliefs and values which supports the position of the ruling class by distorting reality. For example, it presents the relationship between the ruling and subject classes as just and reasonable.
False consciousness A false view which prevents people from seeing the reality of their situation.
Patriarchy A system of male domination which permeates the whole of society – from norms and values to roles and institutions.
Negotiation A process where the outcome is not fixed or predetermined. Instead, it is open to discussion and modification – it is negotiable.
Impression management A process used in social interaction designed to manage the impression others have of ourselves.
Definition of the situation The way people define, interpret and give meaning to situations. People then act in terms of their definition of the situation.

summary

1. Social systems perspectives look at society as a system. They tend to see human behaviour as shaped by the system.

2. Some social systems perspectives see consensus, others see conflict, as the primary characteristic of society.

3. Social action perspectives place more emphasis on the freedom of individuals to direct their own actions.

4. Functionalism sees society as a social system based on consensus. It sees the various parts of society working together to maintain social order.

5. Marxism sees society as a social system based on conflict. It sees a basic conflict of interest between the two main classes, since one gains at the expense of the other.

6. Feminists see gender inequality as the basis of conflict in society.

7. Social action approaches focus on small-scale interaction situations. They see social life as directed by negotiated meanings. Human action is not prescribed by the social system, it is a creative process directed by individuals in interaction situations.

activity 18 negotiating justice

How is a person charged with breaking the law? The following American study of delinquency – the criminal activity of young people – shows it is not a straightforward process.

When a young person is arrested, he or she is handed over to a juvenile officer who decides whether or not to prosecute. This decision is based on a process of negotiation between the juvenile officer, the person arrested and his or her parents. Crucial to the outcome of this negotiation is the picture juvenile officers have of the 'typical delinquent'. In their eyes the 'typical delinquent' is male, from a low-income household in an inner-city area, belongs to an ethnic group, comes from a broken home, rejects authority and is a low achiever at school. If the suspect fits this picture, they are more likely to be charged with an offence.

Becoming a delinquent involves a process of negotiation between the young person, their parents and the juvenile officer.

Middle-class parents are often more skilled at negotiation than their working-class counterparts. They start with an advantage – their child does not fit the picture of a 'typical delinquent'. They present their child as coming from a stable home, as having a good background and a promising future. They promise cooperation, express remorse and define the 'offence' as a 'one-off' due to high spirits, emotional upset, or getting in with the wrong crowd, all of which tends to remove blame from the young person.

As a result, the statistics show that delinquency is mainly a working-class problem as young people from middle-class backgrounds are typically 'counselled, cautioned and released'. Thus 'what ends up being called justice is negotiable'. And what ends up as delinquency is a label attached to a person whose social characteristics are seen to fit the picture of a 'typical delinquent'.

Adapted from Cicourel, 1976

Stop and search in Brixton, South London

question

In what ways does this study illustrate a social action approach?

Unit 5 Social change

keyissues

1 What are the main developments in human society?
2 How have they affected people's lives?

A number of sociologists have tried to identify the main developments in human society. Some distinguish between *premodern* society and today's *modern* society. Others believe we have moved beyond modernity and are now living in *postmodern society*.

These distinctions are important. They point to major changes in human society. They help to explain the behaviour typically found in each type of society.

5.1 Premodern society

Anthony Giddens (2001) identifies various types of society that developed in the premodern era.

Hunting and gathering societies Numbering between 40 and 100 people, hunting and gathering bands were the earliest form of human society. They had a simple division of labour – typically the men hunted and the women gathered nuts, roots and berries. There was little social inequality, though elders tended to have more power and status than younger members of the band.

Pastoral societies Developing around 20,000 years ago, pastoral societies were based on domesticated animals – cattle, sheep, goats, camels – which provided milk and meat. Like hunting and gathering bands, they were usually nomadic, moving in search of pasture for their herds and flocks. Compared to hunting and gathering bands, there was more social inequality since people could accumulate wealth in the form of animals.

Agrarian societies These societies were based on the cultivation of crops, often alongside domesticated animals. People usually lived in settled villages since crops needed tending over several months. Grain was often the main crop and one of the main forms of wealth. Since people could accumulate large stocks of grain, this sometimes led to considerable social inequalities.

Non-industrial civilisations Emerging around 6000 years ago, these civilisations were often based on the rule of kings and emperors at the head of a highly developed system of local and national government. Ultimately, they depended on an efficient agrarian economy which freed many people from food production, allowing them to specialise in a variety of roles in art, science and administration. These societies often had widespread inequalities of wealth, power and status.

Non-industrial civilisations include Ancient Greece and Rome, Ancient Egypt, the Aztecs and Mayas of Central America and the early Chinese and Indian civilisations.

5.2 Modern society

Although there were significant changes in premodernity, many sociologists see the move to modernity as *the* major change in human history. Here are some of the key features of modern society which sociologists have identified (Lee & Newby, 1983; Giddens, 2001).

- **Industrialism** Beginning in the 18th century in Britain, industrialism involves the production of goods using non-human sources of power (eg, electricity) and machinery (eg, conveyor belts and robots).
- **Urbanism** The movement of most of the population from rural areas to towns and cities.
- **Social classes** New social classes developed – a wealthy class whose members owned businesses and a working class whose members worked for wages.
- **Military power** The rise of professional armed services and the ever-increasing power of military technology.
- **The nation-state** This is a fairly recent development – a community with clearly defined boundaries which has power over many areas of its citizens' lives. For example, it has the right to tax them and imprison them for breaking national laws.
- **Liberal democracy** A system of government in which adult citizens have the right to elect those who govern them. This usually involves political parties and a legislature which makes laws, eg the UK Parliament.
- **Change** Compared with premodern society, the pace and scale of change is much greater in modern societies – mass movements of people from rural to urban areas, world wars, major changes in technology (eg, production by robots) and in communications (eg, the Internet).

New ways of thinking and acting In the premodern era, thought and action were more likely to be guided by:

- tradition – it's always been done this way
- emotion – it feels right to do it this way
- religion – the gods say it should be done this way.

In modern society, these guidelines are increasingly replaced by rational thought and action. Problems are solved by the application of reason – for example, a building is designed for a specific purpose rather than simply following tradition.

Technology and science are increasingly seen as a means of solving problems – they can be tried and tested and judged by results.

Late modernity

Some sociologists believe that Western industrial societies are now entering *late modernity*. This is a phase rather than a new era, the development of an existing type of society rather than a new type of society. Various dates have been given for the onset of late modernity, with the early 1970s being a popular choice.

Here are some features of late modernity.

- **Risk and uncertainty** The German sociologist Ulrich Beck sees risk and uncertainty as the key features of late modernity (he calls this phase 'the second modernity') (Beck, 1992, 1997). Traditional norms and values are breaking down at an increasingly rapid rate, often leaving uncertainty in their place. And the pace and scope of social change are increasing.
  There are risks at every turn. Here are some examples.
  - **In employment** There are no longer jobs for life.
  - **In relationships** The divorce rate is approaching 50% in several societies.
  - **With new technology** Nobody really knows the risks involved with genetically-modified food.
- **Choice and individualisation** People have greater individual choice to select their own identity, construct their own roles and design their own lifestyle. For example, they have greater freedom to choose and design their relationships – to marry, to cohabit, to divorce, to live in a heterosexual or a gay or lesbian relationship and so on. People are less likely to be forced to conform to traditional marital, family and gender roles.
- **Social reflexivity** This term is used by the British sociologist Anthony Giddens (1991, 2001). In earlier phases of modernity, people were more likely to follow traditional norms and to take those norms for granted. Now they are more likely to be *reflexive* – to reflect on what they are doing, to assess and question their behaviour, to examine what was previously taken for granted.
  What was once standard is now questioned and assessed. Should I marry given the declining marriage rate and the high divorce rate? Should I cohabit given its popularity? Should I divorce and remarry? Should I call it a day and live on a desert island?!! What's best for me in my present situation?

activity 19 late modernity

question

How do these cartoons illustrate some of the features of late modernity?

5.3 Postmodern society

Some sociologists disagree that the present age is simply an extension of modernity. Instead, they argue that we are moving into a brand new era – *postmodernity* – and a brand new type of society – *postmodern society*.

Symbols and images

Postmodern society is dominated by electronic communication and media – by TV, films, DVDs, videos, websites, e-mails, chat rooms, computer games, adverts and recorded music. We are bombarded with symbols and images from around the world. They expose us to an increasingly diverse range of ideas and values, many of which have little connection with our present lives or past histories. This can cut us off from our past and make our lives feel rootless and empty.

Media symbols and images are constantly changing. TV channels multiply, new styles of music are here and gone, adverts for new perfumes, new shampoos and new drinks appear with monotonous regularity. Everything seems to be in a state of flux – nothing seems permanent or solid.

Symbols and images are enormously important in our lives. They help us build our sense of identity. For example, we buy brand name goods – Nike trainers, Levi jeans, Rayban sunglasses – for their stylish qualities and advertising image. They say something about who we are. Style is everything, and people shift from one brand or fashion to another without any great sense of commitment or loyalty. Sometimes, different styles are combined in unusual and unpredictable ways. The mood is one of novelty, irony and playfulness. Instead of a dominant or mainstream culture, there is a wide diversity of lifestyles. People choose their own values and lifestyles from the thousands on offer, rather than simply following the cultural traditions of their society.

Postmodern identities

The drift towards postmodern culture is seen as having all sorts of consequences for people's identities.

First, the diversity of postmodern society has multiplied the *number* of social identities which people can adopt. Competing identities exist within each person's head. For example, one person can combine the identities of a forceful business executive *and* a caring mother *and* a Sikh and a British patriot *and* an enthusiastic hang-glider.

Second, postmodern identities are typically based on *choice* rather than tradition or birth.

Third, postmodern identities are becoming increasingly *decentred* – more unstable and fragile. These new identities may be exciting and offer choice but they do not provide a firm sense of roots.

Loss of faith

Postmodernity has seen a loss of faith in science and technology. The threat of weapons of mass destruction, the risks of genetic engineering, the negative side-effects of using drugs to treat psychological problems, the dangers of global warming and the damage cause by pollution all point to science and technology gone wrong.

There has been a similar loss of faith in rational thinking. People are increasingly turning to the supernatural – to New Age religions, traditional healers and alternative therapists – in their search for answers, cures and solutions to problems.

A new reality

Some sociologists believe that our whole view of reality in postmodern society is shaped by the flood of images from the media. Images we experience from the media become as, if not more, real and significant than things we directly experience in everyday life. For example, the death of Princess Diana resulted in an outpouring of grief across the world – but for the vast majority she existed only through the media. And, going one step further, a death, a divorce or a marriage in a soap opera glues millions to the screen and is talked about next day as if it were real.

Postmodern society – conclusion

There are different versions of postmodern theory. Some are optimistic and welcome the new freedoms. Others are more pessimistic and point to the shallowness of postmodern life. Leaving these differences aside, what does the arrival of postmodern society mean in broad terms?

If postmodern theorists are correct, society will splinter into fleeting, unstable and fragmented cultures. And instead

of a few major identities, people will move restlessly between a long list of alternative identities – and these will be superficial and give little sense of roots.

Of course, postmodernists may have greatly exaggerated current trends. They are right to point to the greater diversity of contemporary life, but many sociologists argue they over-state their case.

key terms

Premodern society The society before modern society.
Modern society According to many sociologists, the type of society which developed during the 18th century and continues today.
Late modern society According to some sociologists, a development within modern society rather than a new type of society.
Postmodern society Some sociologists believe that a new type of society, which follows modern society, has developed.
Social reflexivity People reflecting on what they are doing, assessing and questioning their behaviour, and examining what was previously taken for granted.

summary

1. A number of sociologists have tried to identify the main developments in human society.
2. Some have identified premodern and modern societies. And some believe that a new phase, late modernity, has developed within modernity.
3. Features of late modernity include:
   - Risk and uncertainty
   - Choice and individualisation
   - Social reflexivity.
4. Other sociologists claim that a new type of society – postmodern society – has emerged.
5. Features of postmodern society include:
   - Dominance of electronic communication and the media
   - The importance of symbols and images
   - Multiple identities based on choice
   - A loss of faith in rational thought, science and technology
   - A new reality largely shaped by media images.

activity20 postmodern identity

Item A *Identity cards*

SUPERMODEL

SCRATCH HERE

POP STAR

SPORTS STAR

Dream Identity Card

FILM STAR

Will it ever come to this? The Government is planning to sell Identity Scratch Cards. Scratch off the special square and you may win a year's worth of free identity. The winner gets to chose a dream identity, for example, a pop star or a major sports personality.

Adapted from Iannucci, 1995

Item B Symbols and style

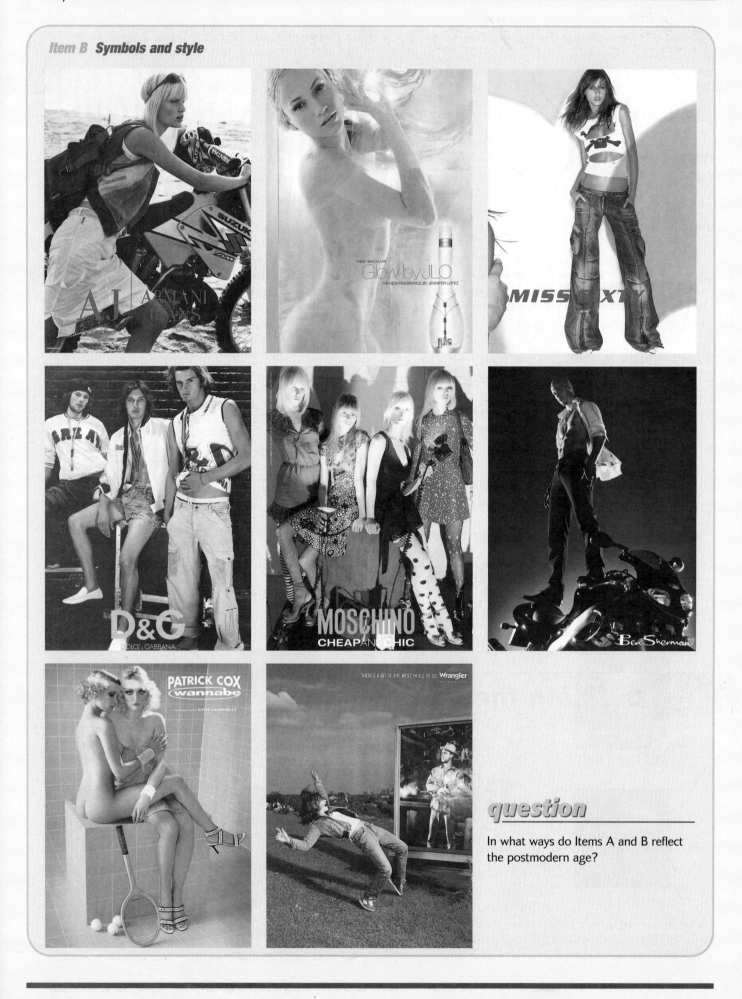

question

In what ways do Items A and B reflect the postmodern age?

2 Families and households

Introduction

Picture the family. Does the image on the right come to mind – mum, dad and the kids? This is the usual picture presented by advertisers. But, for more and more of us, it no longer reflects the reality of family life.

Families are changing. Married women who devote their lives to childcare and housework are a dwindling minority. Marriage itself is declining in popularity. More and more couples are living together without getting married. And more and more marriages are ending in separation and divorce. Families have become increasingly diverse.

What do sociologists make of all this? Some believe that the family is in crisis, and that this threatens the wellbeing of society as a whole. Others welcome change. They see the diversity of family life as an opportunity for choice. No longer does the old-fashioned idea of the family restrict women to the home, keep unhappy marriages going, and maintain destructive family relationships.

This chapter looks at these different views. It investigates changes in family life and examines the causes and effects of these changes.

chaptersummary

▶ **Unit 1** looks at the problem of defining the family and shows how families vary from society to society.

▶ **Unit 2** outlines the main sociological theories of the family and considers government policy towards the family.

▶ **Unit 3** examines the relationship between family life and industrialisation.

▶ **Unit 4** outlines and explains changing patterns of marriage, cohabitation, childbearing, divorce and separation.

▶ **Unit 5** looks at family diversity, focusing on lone-parent families, reconstituted families and gay and lesbian families.

▶ **Unit 6** examines changes in the division of domestic labour and the distribution of power in the family and asks to what extent they are linked to gender.

▶ **Unit 7** focuses on children and asks how ideas of childhood have changed.

Unit 1 Defining the family

keyissues

1 How has the family been defined?
2 What are the problems with definitions of the family?

1.1 What is the family?

In 1949, the American anthropologist George Peter Murdock provided the following definition of the family.

'The family is a social group characterised by common residence, economic cooperation and reproduction. It includes adults of both sexes, at least two of whom maintain a socially approved sexual relationship, and one or more children, own or adopted, of the sexually cohabiting adults.'

Spelling out this definition:

- Families live together – they share the same *household*.
- They work together and pool their resources – to some extent they share domestic tasks and income.
- They reproduce – they have children.
- They include an adult male and female who have a sexual relationship which is approved by the wider society – for example, they have a marital relationship.
- This heterosexual couple have at least one child – either their biological offspring or an adopted child.

The nuclear family

George Peter Murdock based his definition of the family on a sample of 250 societies ranging from hunting and gathering bands, to small-scale farming societies to large-scale industrial societies. Although he found a variety of family forms within this sample, Murdock claimed that each contained a basic nucleus consisting of a husband and wife and one or more children, own or adopted. This is the *nuclear family*. Murdock believed that the nuclear family is 'a universal social grouping' – in other words, it is found in all societies.

activity1 defining the family

Item A Lone-parent family

A single mother and her children

Item B Extended family

An American extended family

Item C Nuclear family

A heterosexual married couple and their children

Item D Gay family

A gay married couple and their adopted childen

questions

1 Which of these 'families' fit/s Murdock's definition? Explain your answer.

2 Do you think those that do not fit should be regarded as families? Give reasons for your answer.

Extended families

Murdock saw the other family forms in his sample as extensions of the nuclear family. These *extended families* contain *kin* – relatives based on 'blood' or marriage – in addition to the nuclear family. The nuclear family can be extended in various ways.

Polygamy Marriage in the West is *monogamous* – it involves one wife and one husband. In many societies, marriage is *polygamous* – a person is permitted additional wives or husbands. Men may have more than one wife – a system known as *polygyny*. Or, in a small number of societies, women may have more than one husband – a form of marriage known as *polyandry*.

Other forms of extension Apart from additional marital

*activity*2 *polygamy*

Item A Polygyny

Adama is a wealthy man. He lives in a village called Sobtenga in Burkina Faso, a country in northwest Africa. Ten years ago he had two wives.

Zenabou, his first wife, thought polygyny was a good idea. It provided her with a 'sister' to share the burdens of domestic work and childcare. Now she is not so sure. Adama has taken two more wives, the youngest of whom, Bintu, is only 16. He is besotted with Bintu and she clearly enjoys the attention. Despite grumbling, his other wives accept the situation, for marriage is seen primarily as an economic affair. Adama's 12 oxen are proof that he can provide security for his wives and children.

Polygyny is much more common than polyandry. It is found in many small-scale traditional societies, particularly in Africa. As the example of Adama suggests, polygyny is a privilege of the wealthy. Not every man can afford two or more wives and in any case there aren't enough women for this. Census figures from 1911 for the Pondo of South Africa show that 10% of men had two wives and only 2% had more than two.

Adapted from Mair, 1971 and Brazier, 1995

Adama's wives – Zenabou, Bintu, Meryan and Barkissou

Item B Polyandry

The Nyinba people of Nepal practice fraternal polyandry – two or more brothers are married to one wife. They inherited this custom from their Tibetan ancestors who migrated to Nepal centuries ago. They also inherited a love for trading and herding which, together with cultivating the meagre soil, make up the traditional Nyinba economy. Polyandry suits this economy. 'With one or two husbands always on herding or trading trips, one husband will always be at home to care for the wife,' explained Maila Dai, a trader from the village of Bargaau. 'We think polyandry is just like insurance for the wife. If one husband is no good or leaves his wife, there's always another brother.'

Polyandry among the Nyinba of Nepal. The 12 year old girl on the right is engaged to five brothers, three of whom are pictured here.

Polyandry has been explained as a way of preventing land from being divided up into less profitable units when a family of sons inherits from the previous generation. It also concentrates the wealth of each household by maintaining a large population of working adult males under one roof.

To the Nyinbas, its advantages are obvious. 'All our brothers work together,' explained Dawa Takpa, 'so we can be wealthy people. If we all go our own way, how can we survive? We have to study, do agricultural work, take care of animals and trade, so we have to work together.' 'For me,' said Tsering Zangmo, who at 21 is the wife of three brothers (the youngest of whom is seven), 'polyandry is fine. If I had only one husband, I would be very poor.'

When asked about jealousy between her husbands, Tsering Zangmo replied, 'But they are brothers. They are never jealous.' However when pressed she giggled and blushed, admitting, 'Well, they only have a very little jealousy. If you like one husband very much, you have to be secret so the others don't know. We make love in the middle of the night, lying naked in sheepskins. We'd never do it just before going to sleep or just before waking up as the others might hear us.'

Adapted from Dunham, 1992

questions

1 How can polygamous families be seen as extensions of the nuclear family?
2 Judging from Items A and B, what are the advantages and disadvantages of polygyny and polyandry?

partners, families can be extended in a variety of ways. For example, a three-generation extended family may include grandparents within the family unit. Similarly, uncles and aunts (brothers and sisters of the married couple) may form part of the family unit.

1.2 Diversity in family systems

Many sociologists and anthropologists have seen the nuclear family, either in its basic or extended form, as universal, normal and natural. Others have rejected this view. For example, Felicity Edholm (1982), in an article entitled 'The unnatural family', argues that there is nothing normal and natural about the nuclear family. She claims that family and kinship relationships are *socially constructed*. They are based on culture rather than biology. The links between husband and wife, parent and child, are constructed very differently in different societies. In Edholm's words, 'Relatives are not born but made'. Here are some examples Edholm gives to support her argument. They are taken from traditional cultures and may not apply today.

Parent-child relations – genes Ideas about the biological relationship between parents and children vary from society to society. For example, the Lakker of Burma see no blood relationship between mother and child – the mother is simply a container in which the child grows. As a result, sexual relationships between children of the same mother are permitted – because they are non-kin, such relationships are not seen as incest.

Parent/child relations – adoption Most sociologists consider the tie between mother and child as basic and inevitable. However, in some societies, many children do not live with their biological parents. For example, in Tahiti, in the Pacific Ocean, young women often have one or two children before they are considered ready to settle down into a stable relationship with a man. They usually give these children for adoption to their parents or other close relatives. Children see their adoptive mother and father as 'real' parents and their relationship with them as far closer than with their natural parents.

Marriage and residence Some sociologists argue that 'marriage' varies so much from society to society that it makes little sense to use the same word for these very different relationships. For example, the basic social group amongst the Nayar of Northern India is made up of men and women descended through the female line from a common ancestor. Brothers and sisters, women and children live together – children are members of their

A Tahitian family

mother's group, not their father's. Nayar girls 'marry' a man before puberty and later take as many lovers as they like. Her 'husband' may or may not be one of these lovers. Children are raised in their mother's social group. 'Husbands' and fathers do not share the same residence as their 'wives' and have little to do with their children.

According to Edholm, examples such as these show that the family is socially constructed. Rather than seeing the family as a natural unit created by biological necessities, it makes more sense to see it as a social unit shaped by cultural norms. And as culture varies from society to society, so do families. In view of this diversity, Edholm rejects the claim that the nuclear family is universal.

Family diversity today

Edholm's research focused on family diversity in non-Western societies. There is evidence that family diversity is steadily increasing in modern Western societies. In Britain, 26% of families with dependent children were headed by lone parents in 2000 (*Social Trends*, 2002). This was partly due to divorce, partly to never-married mothers, and, to a much smaller extent, to the death of one partner.

Reconstituted families – families in which the adult couple bring children from a previous relationship – are steadily increasing. There has also been a rapid growth in *cohabitation* – unmarried couples living together, often in a long-term relationship. And, in recent years, a small but growing number of lesbian and gay families have appeared.

This diversity in today's Western societies will be examined in later units.

1.3 Defining the family revisited

Where does this diversity of so-called families leave us? Is it possible to come up with a definition which covers this diversity? David Cheal (1999) summarises some of the responses to this problem.

We don't know Faced with the diversity of family forms, some sociologists frankly admit that no one really knows what a family is. This is not a useful state of affairs. For example, how can different family forms be compared if a 'family' cannot be identified?

Extensions and reductions Following Murdock, some sociologists have seen all families as extensions or reductions of one basic and elementary form – the nuclear family. So, extended families are extensions, lone-parent families are reductions. Not everybody agrees that the variety of family forms can be seen as extensions or reductions of the nuclear family. For example, if a woman decides to produce a child by *in vitro* fertilisation and rear the child herself, can this be seen as a 'reduction' of the nuclear family?

Abandon the idea One solution is to stop using the term family and replace it with a concept such as *primary relationships* (Scanzoni et al., 1989). Primary relationships are close, longlasting and special ties between people. There is no problem placing the wide diversity of 'families' under this heading. But, it does away with the whole idea of family – an idea which is vitally important to individuals, to the 'family group', and to the wider society.

Ask people From this point of view, families are what people say they are. If families are socially constructed,

activity3 family diversity

Item A The Ashanti

The Ashanti of West Africa are a matrilineal society (descent is traced through the mother's line). While a child's father is important, he has no legal authority over his children. This rests with the wife's family, particularly her brother. It is from the mother's brother that children inherit, though the father is responsible for feeding, clothing and educating them. Many Ashanti men cannot afford to set up a household of their own when they first marry. Since men never live with their wife's brothers, and children are the property of the wife's family, couples often live apart. Only about a third of married women actually live with their husbands.

Adapted from Fortes, 1950

An Ashanti puberty ritual at which a girl becomes a woman. She belongs to her mother's family.

Women and children in the Trobriand Islands

Item B The Trobriand Islanders

Some matrilineal cultures, such as the Trobriand Islanders, think that the father's role in the conception of a child in minimal. He simply 'opens the door' or, at most, shapes the growing embryo through intercourse.

Adapted from Beattie, 1964

question

The family is a social construction shaped by cultural norms and beliefs. Discuss with reference to Items A and B.

then sociologists should discover how people in society construct, define and give meaning to families. This approach may lead to a bewildering diversity of families. But, if this is the social reality within which people live, then this may well be the reality which sociologists should investigate.

key terms

Household A group of people who share a common residence.

Nuclear family A family consisting of an adult male and female with one or more children, own or adopted.

Extended family A family containing relatives in addition to the nuclear family. An extension of the nuclear family.

Kin Relatives based on marriage or genes.

Monogamy A system of marriage involving two adults, one of each sex.

Polygamy A system of marriage involving two or more wives, or two or more husbands.

Polygny A system of marriage involving two or more wives.

Polyandry A system of marriage involving two or more husbands.

Reconstituted family A family in which one or both partners bring children from a previous relationship.

Cohabitation Living together as a partnership without marriage.

Primary relationships Close, longlasting and special ties between people.

summary

1. According to Murdock, the nuclear family is the basic form of family. He sees all other family forms as extensions of the nuclear family.

2. Murdock claims that the nuclear family is a universal social grouping – that it is found in all societies.

3. Edholm argues that the family is a social construction based on culture rather than biology. She rejects the view that the nuclear family is universal.

4. Cross-cultural evidence indicates that family forms vary considerably. Recent evidence from Western societies indicates increasing family diversity.

5. Sociologists have responded to the problem of defining the family in the following ways.
   - By admitting that they don't really know what the family is
   - By seeing all family forms as extensions or reductions of the nuclear family
   - By rejecting the concept of family and replacing it with the concept of primary relationships
   - By accepting the definitions of the family used by members of society – the family is what people say it is.

Unit 2 The family and social structure

keyissues

1 What are the main sociological theories of the family?

2 How have government policies affected the family?

2.1 Functionalist theories of the family

Functionalist theories see society as made up of various parts, each of which contributes to the maintenance and wellbeing of the system as a whole.

Some functionalist theories are based on the idea that societies need *consensus* – agreement about norms and values – in order to survive. As a result, they are also known as *consensus theories*.

Functionalists often assume that if a social institution such as the family exists, then it must have a *function* or purpose – it must do something useful. As a result, the family is usually seen to perform functions which benefit both its members and society as a whole.

George Peter Murdock

According to Murdock (1949), the family is a universal institution with universal functions. In other words, it is found in all societies and it performs the same functions everywhere. These functions are vital for the wellbeing of society. They are:

Sexual In most societies, there are rules limiting or forbidding sexual relationships outside marriage. This helps to stabilise the social system. Without such rules, conflict may result.

Economic In many societies, the family is a unit of production – for example, a 'farming family' producing food. In the West today, the family acts as a unit of consumption – buying goods and services for the family group. These economic functions make an important contribution to the wider society.

Reproduction The family is the main unit for the reproduction of children. Without reproduction, society would cease to exist.

Educational The family is largely responsible for *primary socialisation*, the first and most important part of the socialisation process. Without socialisation, there would be no culture. And without a shared culture, there would be no consensus about society's norms and values.

Murdock believes that the nuclear family, either alone, or in its extended form, performs these 'vital functions'. He cannot imagine a substitute. In his words, 'No society has succeeded in finding an adequate substitute for the nuclear family, to which it might transfer these functions. It is highly doubtful whether any society will ever succeed in such an attempt.'

Talcott Parsons

The American sociologist Talcott Parsons focuses on the nuclear family in modern industrial society. He argues that the family has become increasingly specialised. Functions for which families were responsible in pre-industrial societies, for example, looking after the elderly or educating children, have been taken over in industrial societies by specialised institutions such as social services and schools (Parsons & Bales, 1955).

However, Parsons claims that the family retains two 'basic and irreducible' functions. These are:

1 the *primary socialisation* of children
2 the *stabilisation of adult personalities.*

Primary socialisation This is the first and most important part of the socialisation process. Parsons argues that every individual must learn the shared norms and values of society. Without this there would be no consensus, and without consensus, social life would not be possible.

For the socialisation process to be really effective, shared norms and values must be 'internalised as part of the personality structure'. Children's personalities are moulded in terms of society's culture to the point where it becomes a part of them.

The stabilisation of adult personalities This is the second essential function of the family. Unstable personalities can threaten the stability and smooth-running of society. According to Parsons, families help to stabilise adult

activity4 functionalism and the family

Item A *Family shopping*

Item B *The 'warm bath theory'*

Item C *'The bottle'*

The drunken husband – a 19th century view of domestic violence

questions

1 Functionalists often argue that the family's economic function as a unit of production has been replaced by its function as a unit of consumption. Explain with some reference to Item A.

2 Look at Items B and C.

   a) Parsons' theory is sometimes known as the 'warm bath theory'. Why?

   b) Critically evaluate this theory. Refer to Item C in your answer.

personalities in two ways. First, marital partners provide each other with emotional support. Second, as parents, they are able to indulge the 'childish' side of their personalities – for example, by playing with their children.

Family life provides adults with release from the strains and stresses of everyday life. It provides them with emotional security and support. This helps to stabilise their personality and, in turn, the wider society.

Conclusion Although the functions of the family have become fewer and more specialised, Parsons believes they are no less important. He cannot imagine an institution other than the family performing these 'basic and irreducible' functions.

Criticism of funtionalism

The following criticisms have been made of functionalist views of the family.

- Functionalists assume that on balance families perform useful and often essential functions both for their members and for society as a whole. Married couples are pictured as living in harmony, as good in bed, and as effective socialisers of the next generation. Critics argue that this does not reflect the realities of family life.
- As a result of this picture of happy families, functionalists tend to ignore the 'dark side' of family life – conflict between husband and wife, male dominance, child abuse, and so on. They give insufficient attention to the *dysfunctions* of the family – the harmful effects it may have on the wider society.
- Functionalists tend to ignore the diversity of family life in industrial society. For example, there is little reference to lone-parent families, cohabiting families and reconstituted families. Nor do they pay much attention to variations in family life based on class, ethnicity, religion and locality.
- Parsons' view of the family has been criticised as sexist since he sees the wife/mother as having the main responsibility for providing warmth and emotional support, and for de-stressing her hardworking husband.

key terms

Functionalism A theory which sees society made up of various parts, each of which tends to contribute to the maintenance and wellbeing of society as a whole.

Consensus theories Functionalist theories based on the idea that societies need consensus or agreement about norms and values.

Function The contribution a part of society makes to the wellbeing of society as a whole.

Dysfunction The harmful effects that a part of society has on society as a whole.

Primary socialisation The first and most important part of the socialisation process whereby young people learn the norms and values of society.

2.2 New Right perspectives

Like functionalists, New Right thinkers see the family as a cornerstone of society. They also see a 'normal' family as the nuclear family unit. For example, John Redwood, a Conservative MP, stated in 1993 that the 'the natural state should be the two-adult family caring for their children'. And for him, the two adults are a male and a female.

In recent years there has been growing concern about the state of the family. It is 'in decline', 'under threat', 'fragmenting', 'breaking down'. This view of the family was put forward by New Right thinkers from the 1980s onwards.

Evidence They point to the following evidence to support their claims. There has been an increase in:

- Lone-parent families
- Fatherless families
- Divorce rates
- Cohabitation
- Gay and lesbian couples.

As a result of these changes, the two-parent nuclear family headed by a married couple is steadily decreasing as a proportion of all families.

Causes The following have been seen as causing these changes.

- A breakdown of 'traditional family values'.
- Over-generous welfare benefits to single mothers which allow fathers to opt out of their responsibilities for raising and providing for their children.
- The influence of feminism which has devalued marriage, domesticity and childrearing, and encouraged women to seek fulfilment outside the home.
- Increased sexual permissiveness.
- Greater tolerance of gay and lesbian relationships as alternatives to heterosexual marriage.

Consequences According to the New Right, these changes have serious consequences. The 'fragmented family' is no longer performing its functions effectively. In particular, it is failing to provide adequate socialisation. This can result in children and young people underachieving at school and behaving in anti-social ways ranging from rudeness to crime.

Over-generous welfare benefits can lead to welfare dependency. Lone mothers become dependent on state benefits and, in effect, are 'married to the state'.

Solutions For the New Right, there are two main solutions to these problems. First, a return to traditional family values – life-long marriage and a recognition of the duties and responsibilities of parenthood. Second, a change in government policy – redirecting welfare benefits and social service provision to support and maintain two-parent families and penalising those who fail to live up to this ideal.

Sociology and the New Right New Right thinkers have tended to be journalists and politicians rather than sociologists. However, a few sociologists have developed similar arguments. For example, Norman Dennis and George Erdos make the following points in *Families Without Fathers* (2000).

Increasing numbers of children are born outside marriage and raised by single mothers. This places the children at a disadvantage. On average, they have poorer health and lower educational attainment than children from two-parent families.

Dennis and Erdos's main concern is the effect on boys. They grow up without the expectation that adulthood involves responsibilities for a wife and children. This can result in irresponsible, immature, anti-social young men.

According to Dennis and Erdos, families without fathers are not an adequate alternative to the standard nuclear family. Families are not just changing, they are 'deteriorating'.

activity5 New Right perspectives

Item A Fatherless families

According to the American sociologist Charles Murray, increasing numbers of 'young, healthy, low-income males choose not to take jobs'. Many turn to crime (particularly violent street crime) and regular drug abuse.

Many of these boys have grown up in a family without a father and male wage earner. As a result, they lack the male role models of mainstream society. Within a female-headed family dependent on welfare benefits, the disciplines and responsibilities of mainstream society tend to break down. Murray believes that work must become the 'centre of life' for young men. They must learn the disciplines of work and respect for work. And they must learn to become 'real fathers', accepting the responsibilities of parenthood.

Murray believes that the socialisation and role models required to develop these attitudes are often lacking in female-headed, low-income families. He claims that, 'Over the last two decades, larger and larger numbers of British children have not been socialised to norms of self-control, consideration for others, and the concept that actions have consequences'. In Murray's view, when it comes to effective socialisation, 'No alternative family structure comes close to the merits of two parents, formally married'.

Adapted from Murray, 1990, 2001

Item B Welfare dependency

Item C A typical Victorian image

'The abandoned mother'

questions

1 Read Item A. Why does Murray see the nuclear family as superior to other family structures?

2 What points is the cartoon in Item B making?

3 How does Item C question the idea that welfare dependency has led to the breakdown of the family?

Criticisms of New Right views

Blaming the victims Critics argue that the New Right tends to 'blame the victims' for problems that are not of their own making. Many of these problems may result from low wages, inadequate state benefits, lack of jobs and other factors beyond the control of lone parents.

Value judgements The New Right sees the nuclear family consisting of husband, wife and children as the ideal. Other family arrangements are considered inferior. Critics argue that this reflects the values of the New Right rather than a balanced judgement of the worth of family diversity in today's society. Who is to say that families without fathers are necessarily inferior? Why should everybody be forced into the nuclear family mould?

An idealised view of the past New Right thinkers may be harking back to a golden age of the family which never existed. Even in Victorian times – supposedly *the* era of traditional family values – lone parenthood, cohabitation and sexual relationships outside marriage were by no means uncommon.

2.3 Marxist theories

Marxists reject the view that society is based on value consensus and operates for the benefit of all. Instead, they see a basic conflict of interest between a small powerful ruling class and the mass of the population, the subject class. The family is seen as one of a number of institutions which serves to maintain the position of the ruling class.

Modern industrial societies have a capitalist economic system. Capitalism is based on the private ownership of economic institutions, for example, banks and factories.

In capitalist economies, investors finance the production of goods and services with the aim of producing profits. These investors form a ruling class. The subject class – the workers – produce goods and services and are paid wages for their labour. The ruling class are seen to exploit the subject class – they gain at the workers' expense since their profits come from the workers' labour.

Marxists argue that the economy largely shapes the rest of society. Thus, a capitalist economic system will produce a certain type of society. Institutions such as the family, the education system and the political system are shaped by the requirements of capitalism and serve to support and maintain it.

Inheritance and private property In *The Origin of the Family, Private Property and the State*, first published in 1884, Friedrich Engels argued that the modern nuclear family developed in capitalist society. Private property is at the heart of capitalism and it was largely owned by men. Before 1882 in Britain, married women could not own property – it passed to their husband on marriage.

A key concern of the capitalist was to ensure that his property passed directly to his legitimate heirs – those he had fathered. According to Engels, the monogamous nuclear family provided the answer. It gave men greater control over women – until the late 19th century wives were seen as chattels, as their husband's property. With only one husband and one wife, doubts about the paternity of children are unlikely. And with only one wife, there are no disputes about which wife's children should inherit. Within the nuclear family, a man could be fairly sure that he had legitimate children with a clear right to inherit his wealth.

activity6 the next generation

question

Give a Marxist interpretation of the role of the family illustrated in this cartoon.

Maintaining capitalism In some respects, Marxist views of the family are similar to those of functionalists. For example, both see the family as a unit which reproduces and socialises children. In other respects, their views are very different.

Marxists see the family as a means for:

- Reproducing 'labour power' – reproducing future generations of workers
- Consuming the products of capitalism
- Providing emotional support for workers, so helping them to cope with the harsh realities of capitalism
- Socialising children to accept the inequalities of capitalist society.

From a Marxist viewpoint, the family helps to maintain an unjust and exploitative system.

Criticisms of Marxism

Marxist views of the family follow logically from Marxist theory. If, for example, the family provides emotional support for workers, then this helps them to accept the injustices of the capitalist system. This makes sense if capitalism is seen as essentially unjust. However, many sociologists reject this view of capitalism and, as a result, Marxist views of the family.

Sociologists generally agree that the economic system has some influence on the family. However, most would disagree with the view that the family is shaped by the needs of that system.

> ## key terms
>
> **Marxism** A theory which sees a basic conflict of interest between those who own the economic institutions and those who are employed by them.
> **Capitalism** A system of production in which the economic institutions, eg banks and factories, are privately owned.

2.4 Feminist theories

Feminists start from the view that most societies are based on patriarchy or male domination. *Radical feminists* see patriarchy as built into the structure of society. *Marxist feminists* see it as resulting from class inequalities in capitalist society. Both see the family as one of the main sites in which women are oppressed by men.

Domestic labour Within the family most of the unpaid work – housework and childcare – is done by women. This applies even when women are working full time outside the home. Women make the main contribution to family life, men receive the main benefits (Delphy & Leonard, 1992).

Marxist feminists argue that the wife's unpaid domestic labour is invaluable to capitalism. She produces and rears future workers at no cost to the capitalist. And she keeps an adult worker – her husband – in good running order by feeding and caring for him (Benston, 1972).

Emotional labour The inequalities of domestic labour also apply to 'emotional labour'. Radical feminists claim that it's wives rather than husbands who provide emotional support for their partners. Wives are more likely to listen, to agree, to sympathise, to understand, to excuse and to flatter (Delphy & Leonard, 1992).

Marxist feminists take a similar view, seeing the emotional support provided by wives as soaking up the frustrations produced by working for capitalism.

Economic dependency Married women are often economically dependent on their husbands. In most couples, it is the wife who gives up work to care for the children. Mothers often return to part-time rather than full-time employment in order to meet their childcare and domestic responsibilities.

Male domination Feminists see the family as male dominated. As noted above, wives are usually economically dependent. Men often control key areas of decision-making such as moving house and important financial decisions. And they sometimes use force to maintain control. Domestic violence is widespread and the majority of those on the receiving end are women. Around 570,000 cases are reported each year in the UK and probably a far larger number go unreported (Hopkins, 2000).

Criticisms of feminism

Ignores positive aspects of family life Critics argue that feminists are preoccupied with the negative side of family life. They ignore the possibility that many women enjoy running a home and raising children.

Ignores trend to gender equality There is evidence of a trend towards greater equality between partners (see Section 6.2). Critics argue that rather than celebrating this trend, feminists remain focused on the remaining inequalities.

> ## key terms
>
> **Feminism** A view which challenges the power of men over women.
> **Patriarchy** A social system based on male domination.
> **Radical feminists** Feminists who see patriarchy as the main form of inequality in society.
> **Marxist feminists** Feminists who see patriarchy as resulting from class inequalities.
> **Domestic labour** Unpaid work such as housework and childcare, within the home and family.

activity7 housewives

Magazine cover from 1955

Magazine cover from 2003

question

How might a feminist analyse these magazine covers?

2.5 Social policy and the family

In recent years, governments have been increasingly concerned about families. And government policies have reflected this concern.

These policies are influenced by values. Should government policies be shaped by 'traditional family values' which see the nuclear family as the ideal? Or, should they recognise the increasing diversity of family life and support *all* family types?

The New Right

The New Right comes down firmly on the side of the nuclear family (see Section 2.2). It's the best kind of family and should be encouraged. The rest are second-best and should be discouraged. How does this translate into social policy?

Encouraging nuclear families Governments should 'explicitly *favour* married parenthood over all other choices for raising children' (Saunders, 2000). Taxes and welfare benefits should be directed to this end. The marriage contract should be strengthened and married couples should have special legal rights and safeguards.

Discouraging family diversity According to the New Right, over-generous welfare benefits have supported the rapid increase in lone-parent families. These benefits should be reduced so lone-parenthood becomes a less attractive option. Cohabitation should be discouraged by denying unmarried couples the legal rights and privileges given to married couples. And divorce should be made more difficult to discourage marital break-up (Morgan, 1999; Saunders, 2000).

Supporting all families

Critics of the New Right argue that governments should not

attempt to impose one type of family and force everybody into the same mould. Instead, they should recognise that families are diverse and the trend is towards increasing diversity. Government policy should therefore support *all* families (Bernardes, 1997).

It is not the job of government to force couples to stay together by making divorce more difficult. Nor should rights and privileges be denied to those who cohabit simply because they aren't married. Governments should not make judgements about which form of family is best and base policy on such judgements. They should accept the decisions people have made about *their* form of family life and develop policies to support all families.

Family policy in the UK

Conservative policy This section looks at family policy from 1990. The Conservative Party under John Major was in government from 1990 to 1997. It showed a clear preference for the married, two-parent nuclear family. Lone parents were denounced in what one writer described as 'an orgy of lone-parent bashing' (Lister, 1996). John Major himself heralded the virtues of 'traditional family values' in

*activity*8 *party manifestos 2001*

Item A *The Labour Party*

Ambitions for Britain
Labour's manifesto 2001

new Labour new Britain

Strong and stable family life offers the best possible start to children. And marriage provides a strong foundation for stable relationships. The government supports marriage. But it has to do more than that. It must support families, above all families with children. Our vision of the tax and benefits system for families with children is to provide help for all families; to give most help at the time families need it most; and to give more help to those families most in need.

We will create an integrated Child Credit of cash support for children, built on the foundation of universal child benefit.

Item B *The Conservative Party*

time for **common sense**

Conservatives

Conservatives will help families bringing up children. We will let families keep more of what they earn. We will support marriage.

Despite all the evidence that marriage provides the best environment for bringing up children, married couples do not fit into Labour's politically correct agenda. That is why they have penalised millions of families by abolishing the Married Couple's Tax Allowance.

The arrival of children often puts a family under particular pressure. One parent may give up work for a while, reducing the couple's income just when their expenses are greatest.

A Conservative government will support families coping with these pressures. We will introduce a new Married Couple's Allowance which will give a tax cut worth £1,000 to many families when they need help most.

Item C *The Liberal Democrats*

We will establish a scheme for the civil registration of partnerships. This will give two unrelated adults who wish to register a settled personal relationship legal rights which are at present only available to married couples.

questions

To what extent do these manifesto statements support

a) the traditional nuclear family

b) family diversity?

his Back to Basics campaign. However, this campaign was quietly brushed under the carpet, not least because many Cabinet members were divorced – hardly a reflection of traditional family values.

Talk rather than action characterised the Major years. There were only two major pieces of legislation directed at the family. In 1991, The Child Support Act was passed which led to the formation of the Child Support Agency. The main aim was to force absent fathers to pay maintenance for their children in the hope of reducing welfare payments to lone mothers. Although the government claimed this would help lone mothers, any money received from the fathers was deducted from the mothers' benefits.

The Family Law Act of 1996, introduced a one year waiting period before a couple could divorce. The intention of the act was to support the institution of marriage. Couples were encouraged to take every possible step to save their marriage. However, the act was never implemented as judges saw it as unworkable.

Labour policy The tone of Labour's words on family policy was milder than those of the Conservatives. There was an attempt to steer a middle course between supporting both marriage and the nuclear family and providing help for other forms of family. There was no 'back to basics' but no 'anything goes' either. Labour has been careful not to condemn alternatives to the nuclear family (Lewis, 2001).

This can be seen from *Supporting Families* (1998) – a discussion document which suggested ways of providing 'better services and support for parents'. The emphasis is on *all* families. The government doesn't want to 'interfere' in family life, to 'pressure people' into a preferred family form, or to 'force' married couples to stay together. It accepts that many lone parents and unmarried couples raise children successfully. But, at the end of the day, 'marriage is still the surest foundation for raising children'.

This is what Labour said. What have they done?

Labour's family policy has formed part of its welfare policy. Summed up in Tony Blair's statement, 'Work for those that can, security for those that can't', this policy seeks to move those who can work from welfare into work and to improve benefits for those who can't.

Labour's New Deal schemes are designed to help people find paid employment. One of these schemes is aimed at lone parents, most of whom are lone mothers. Since April 2001, all lone parents are required to attend an annual interview about job opportunities. The Working Families Tax Credit tops up the wages of parents moving from benefits to low paid jobs.

Various childcare schemes have been introduced. For example, the Sure Start programme provides health and support services for low-income families with young children.

One of Labour's stated aims is to take all children out of poverty. Various benefits have been increased with this in mind. For example, Child Benefit has been increased by 26% in real terms from 1997 to 2001 (Page, 2002).

Labour's policies focus on money and work – children need money, parents have a responsibility to work (Lewis, 2001).

Conclusion Government policies are increasingly recognising the realities of family life – that family diversity is here to stay. Politicians are realising that the clock can't be turned back, that they have a responsibility to support all families. Alternative family forms are no longer condemned. But despite this, both Labour and Conservative Parties see marriage and the nuclear family as the ideal.

This can be seen clearly from David Willetts' speech at the Conservative (Tory) Party Conference in October 2002. He announced, 'Let me make it absolutely clear: the Tory war on lone parents is over'. He admitted that families come in all shapes and sizes, and that the state had a duty to support them all. Talking about lone parents, he said, 'We'll support them and value them and, above all, we'll back them'. Yet, despite this, Willetts' claimed that the evidence was 'overwhelming' that it was better for children to be brought up by two parents in a stable marriage.

summary

1. Functionalists argue that the family is a universal institution. It performs functions which are essential for the maintenance and wellbeing of society.

2. Parsons argues that the family performs two 'basic and irreducible' functions in modern industrial society – primary socialisation and the stabilisation of adult personalities.

3. The New Right sees the nuclear family as the ideal family form. They believe the nuclear family is under threat. Alternative family forms, particularly lone mother families, fail to provide adequate socialisation.

4. Marxists argue that the modern family has been shaped to fit the needs of capitalism. It helps to maintain an economic system based on exploitation.

5. Feminists see the family as patriarchal – it is dominated by men and serves the needs of men.

6. According to the New Right, government policy should favour marriage and the nuclear family.

7. Others argue that governments should recognise family diversity and support all family forms.

8. In practice, governments have seen the nuclear family as the preferred family form. However, there is increasing acceptance of family diversity and a recognition that government should support all families.

Unit 3 *The family and social change*

keyissues

1 What is the relationship of the family to industrialisation and urbanisation?

2 Has there been a trend towards nuclear families?

3.1 The family in pre-industrial society

Farming families

Before the industrial revolution, most people lived on the land. Family members worked together to produce goods and services – the family unit was a *production unit.* Activity 9 Item A shows people working together in Medieval England. The people working together are probably from the same family.

In many developing countries today, the farming family continues as a production unit. This can be seen from Activity 9 Item B which describes a farming family in Manupur, a village in India.

Cottage industry

Before the industrial revolution, many goods were produced by craftsmen and women in their homes and in

activity⁹ *farming families*

Item A *Farming in Medieval England*

Harvesting

Milking sheep to make cheese and butter

Item B *Farming families in India*

Husband and wife picking crocuses to make saffron in Kashmir, India

The day begins early for a farmer in Manupur, around four in the morning. He must first feed the animals (oxen, cows, buffalo) and give them water.

The oxen are tied to the cart at around five o'clock in the morning and the men are ready to go to the fields and work. Meals are brought to the field by the son, or, if necessary, by the daughter. The distance between the house and the farm is sometimes over a mile, and it would be a waste of precious time to go home.

During sowing and harvest times, work may go on as late as 10:00pm. Once home, the animals must be tended. If the farmer has a young son, grass has already been cut; if not, he must employ someone to do it. It remains for him to prepare the fodder, and to feed, wash, and clean the animals.

The farmer's wife has an even greater burden of work. She must prepare the meals (breakfast, lunch, and dinner) and tea (early morning, mid-afternoon, and late night). Meals are made for the husband and the children and, if there are few children, for the labourers who have to be hired. The buffalo must be milked twice a day, morning and evening. The milk is used to make lassi, a yoghurt drink for warm mornings, and to make butter late in the evening. Dishes must be washed after every meal.

Adapted from *New Internationalist*, May 1974

questions

1 How might the people in each of the pictures in Item A be related?

2 Why is a family essential for the farmer in Item B?

activity 10 cottage industry

Around 1720, Daniel Defoe (author of *Robinson Crusoe*) journeyed to Halifax in West Yorkshire. This is what he saw.

'People made cloth in practically every house in Halifax. They keep a cow or two and sow corn to feed their chickens. The houses were full of lusty fellows, some at the dye-vat; some at the loom, others dressing the cloths; the women and children carding, or spinning; all employed from the youngest to the oldest. The finished cloth was taken to the market to be sold.'

Spinning in a cottage in the early 1700s

question

What evidence does this activity provide which suggests that the family is a unit of production?

small workshops. This type of production is sometimes known as *cottage industry* as goods were often produced in cottages. As with farming, the family was the main unit of production in cottage industry. Activity 10 provides a description of families producing cloth in Halifax in West Yorkshire.

Kinship-based societies

Many small-scale, non-Western societies are organised on the basis of kinship. People's roles and the institutions of society are largely based on kinship relationships – relationships of 'blood' and marriage. Families are embedded in a wider network of kin, they are closely linked to people they are related to. Societies like this are sometimes known as *kinship-based societies*.

For example, many African societies were traditionally organised on the basis of *lineages* – groups descended from a common ancestor. Lineages often owned land and formed political units – important decisions which affected all members of the lineage were made by a council of elders.

activity 11 the economics of marriage

In many pre-industrial societies, marriage is essential for economic reasons. In traditional Inuit (Eskimo) society, men build igloos and hunt. Women gather edible plants and catch fish. Their skill in sewing animal skins into clothes is indispensable in the Arctic climate. Sewing is a skill that men are never taught, and many of the skills of hunting are kept secret from women.

Adapted from Douglas, 1964

Inuit women beating fish skin to make into 'fish leather'

question

Why was marriage in traditional Inuit society essential for both husband and wife?

The importance of marriage in kinship-based societies can be seen from the following quotation and the example in Activity 11. The French anthropologist, Claude Lévi-Strauss (1956), recalls meeting a pathetic looking man during his research among the Bororo of central Brazil. The man was 'about thirty years old: unclean, ill-fed, sad, and lonesome. When asked if the man was seriously ill, the answer came as a shock: What was wrong with him? – nothing at all, he was just a bachelor, and true enough, in a society where labour is systematically shared between man and woman and where only the married status permits the man to benefit from the fruits of woman's work, including delousing, body painting, and hair-plucking as well as vegetable food and cooked food (since the Bororo woman tills the soil and makes pots), a bachelor is really only half a human being.'

Pre-industrial families

The evidence suggests that families in pre-industrial societies were often extended beyond the basic nuclear family. The example of producing textiles in Activity 10 suggests that the family was extended to include three generations – note the old woman in the picture.

There is evidence that the family was *multifunctional* – that it performed a number of functions. For example, as a production unit it had an economic function, as part of a wider kinship group it sometimes performed political functions, and by socialising children and providing them with job training, it had an important educational function.

A person's status or position in society was often ascribed – fixed at birth – by their family membership. Daughters tended to take on the status of their mothers, sons the status of their fathers.

3.2 Industrialisation, urbanisation and families

The industrial revolution began in Britain around 1750. It brought a number of important changes in society.

- A large part of the workforce moved from agriculture and small cottage industries to industrial work, producing manufactured goods in factories.
- Manufacturing industry was mechanised – machinery was used to mass produce goods. Small home-based family businesses could not compete with this.
- Towns and cities grew in size and the majority of the population was concentrated in large urban areas rather than small villages. This process is known as *urbanisation*.

This section examines the impact of these changes on the family.

Talcott Parsons – the isolated nuclear family

The American functionalist sociologist, Talcott Parsons (1951) argued that industrialisation has led to the *isolated nuclear family*. He sees this as the typical family form in modern industrial society. Compared to pre-industrial times, the nuclear family – the married couple and their children – are isolated from the wider kinship network. Although there are usually relationships with relatives outside the nuclear family, these are now a matter of choice rather than necessity or obligation and duty.

Loss of functions According to Parsons, the main reason for this isolation is a loss of functions performed by the family. For example, the typical modern family is no longer a production unit – its adult members are now individual wage earners. In addition, local and national government has taken over, or reduced the importance of, many of the functions of the family. Schools, hospitals, welfare benefits and the police force have reduced the need for a wide network of kin (see Activity 12).

Achieved status In modern industrial society, status is achieved rather than ascribed. In other words, a person's position in society is achieved on the basis of merit – ability and effort – rather than ascribed on the basis of family membership. Children are unlikely to follow their parents' occupations. Job training is performed by the educational system and the employer rather than the family.

Geographical mobility In modern industrial society, extended family networks may be *dysfunctional* – they may be harmful to society. A modern industrial economy requires a geographically mobile workforce – workers who are able to move to places where their skills are in demand. Large extended families tend to be tied down by obligations and duties to their relatives. They are bulky and unwieldy units compared to the small, streamlined isolated nuclear family.

Summary Parsons argues that the isolated nuclear family is ideally suited to modern industrial society. Although it is slimmed down, it can still perform its essential functions – the socialisation of children and the stabilisation of adult personalities (see pages 37-38).

key terms

Production unit A group of people involved in the production of goods and services.
Cottage industry The production of goods in the home.
Kinship-based society A society in which social institutions and people's roles are largely organised on the basis of kinship relationships.
Lineage A social group made up of people descended from a common ancestor.
Multifunctional Performing a number of functions.
Industrialisation The move to the production of manufactured goods in factories.
Urbanisation The concentration of an increasing proportion of the population in urban areas – towns and cities.
Isolated nuclear family A married couple and their children who are largely independent from the wider kinship network.

activity12 loss of functions

Item A Factory production

Item B National Health Service

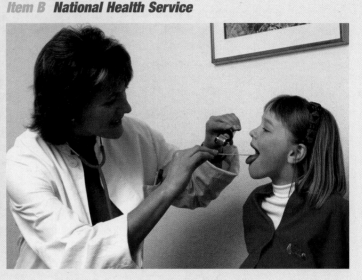

Item C Home for the elderly

question

How can these pictures be used to argue that many of the functions of the family have been reduced or lost in modern industrial society?

Peter Laslett – the family in pre-industrial England

Historical research has questioned the view that most people in pre-industrial societies lived in extended families. The historian Peter Laslett (1965, 1977) examined parish records which record the names of people living together in households – 'under the same roof'. He found that only about 10% of households in England from 1564 to 1821 included kin beyond the nuclear family. The figure for Great Britain in 1981 was similar – around 9% – but by 2001 it had dropped to under 5% (*Social Trends*, 2002).

Laslett claims that his research shows that nuclear families were the norm in pre-industrial England. He found a similar pattern in parts of Western Europe. His research was based on *households*, but people do not have to live under the same roof to form extended families. It is not possible from Laslett's data to discover how much cooperation occurred between kin who lived in different households. Extended families may have been important even though relatives lived in neighbouring households. This can be seen from Activity 13.

Michael Anderson – the working-class extended family

Historical research by Michael Anderson (1971) suggests that the early stages of industrialisation may have encouraged the development of extended families. Anderson took a 10% sample of households from Preston in Lancashire, using data from the 1851 census. He found that 23% of households contained kin beyond the nuclear family. Most of these households were working class. This was a time of widespread poverty, high birth rates and high death rates. Without a welfare state, people tended to rely on a wide network of kin for care and support. Anderson's study suggests that the working-class extended family operated as a mutual aid organisation, providing support in times of hardship and crisis.

activity13 *farming families*

Item A *Families in rural Ireland*

The following description is taken from a study of farming families in Ireland in the 1930s.

An elaborate system of cooperation had grown up between farmers and their relatives. Men often lent one another tools and machinery. Women clubbed together to make up a tub or firkin of butter or lend a girl when a family was shorthanded for the work of dairying.

Help from extended family members is especially important at harvest time when grass is mowed and collected. One farmer was helped by the sons of three others, his second cousins, and in due course he mowed their meadows. Another was helped by the son of his cousin and his nephew. He took his mowing machine to do the fields of their fathers. There were, however, five cases of farmers who although obviously shorthanded had no help. Two of these were bachelors who could not return the help, and two 'strangers' who would not be expected to.

Adapted from Frankenberg, 1966

Item B *Haymaking*

Haymaking in Berkshire in 1906

Baling hay on a modern farm

questions

1 a) What evidence of extended families is provided by Item A?

   b) How can this evidence be used to question Laslett's conclusions?

2 Judging from Item B, why are farmers today less likely to rely on extended family members?

The mid-19th century was a period of rapid urbanisation as people moved from rural areas to work in factories – for example, in the cotton mills of Preston. Overcrowding was common due to a shortage of housing and a desire to save on rent. As a result, people often moved in with their relatives.

3.3 Industrialisation, women and families

Ann Oakley (1974) argues that industrialisation had the following effects on women and family life.

During the early years of industrialisation (1750-1841)

the factory steadily replaced the family as the unit of production. Women were employed in factories where they often continued their traditional work in textiles. However, a series of factory acts, beginning in 1819, gradually restricted child labour. Someone now had to care for and supervise children, a role which fell to women. The restriction of women to the home had begun.

Women were seen by many men as a threat to their employment. As early as 1841, committees of male workers called for 'the gradual withdrawal of all female labour from the factory'. In 1842, the Mines Act banned the employment of women as miners. Women were excluded from trade unions, men made contracts with their employers to prevent them from hiring women and laws

activity14 mutual support

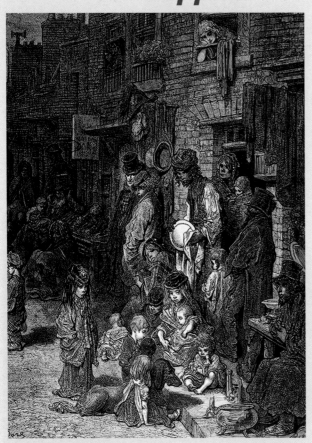

Gustav Doré's engraving of Wentworth Street, Whitechapel, London in the 1870s

question

Suggest ways in which members of the working-class extended family might help each other during the 19th century.

were passed restricting female employment in a number of industries. Tied down by dependent children and increasingly barred from the workplace the restriction of women to the home continued.

Slowly but surely women were being locked into the mother-housewife role and confined to the home. In 1851, one in four married women were employed, by 1911, this figure was reduced to one in ten. From 1914 to 1950 the employment of married women grew slowly but the mother-housewife role remained their primary responsibility. Even by 1970, when about half of all married women were employed, most saw their occupational role as secondary to their duties as a wife and mother and their responsibility for the home.

Oakley concludes that industrialisation had the following effects on the role of women. First, the 'separation of men from the daily routines of domestic life'. Second, the

'economic dependence of women and children on men'. Third, the 'isolation of housework and childcare from other work'. The result is that the mother-housewife role became 'the primary role for all women'.

Recent evidence indicates that the position of married women is changing. By 2000, 75% of married or cohabiting women of working age (16-59) in the UK were economically active (ie, either in work or seeking work). There has been a steady decline in full-time mothers and housewives. In 1991, 17% of women of working age gave their occupation as 'looking after family/home'. By 2001, this had declined to 13% (*Social Trends*, 2002).

activity15 the mother housewife role

question

How does this magazine cover from 1957 reflect Oakley's picture of the mother-housewife role in the 1950s?

3.4 Families in the 20th century

There is evidence that the working-class extended family continued well into the 20th century. Research indicates it was alive and well in the 1950s in a Liverpool dock area

(Kerr, 1958), in a Yorkshire mining town (Dennis, Henriques & Slaughter, 1956) and in the East End of London (Young & Willmott, 1957).

Bethnal Green In their study of Bethnal Green in the East End of London, Michael Young and Peter Willmott define an extended family as 'a combination of families who to some large degree form one domestic unit'. The extended family does not have to share the same household – ie, live under the same roof – as long as its members are in regular contact and share services such as caring for children and elderly relatives. Activity 16 is based on Young and Willmott's research in Bethnal Green.

Greenleigh In the second part of their research, Young and Willmott studied families from Bethnal Green who had been rehoused in Greenleigh, a new council estate in Essex. Young and Willmott describe their family life as *privatised* – it had become home-centred and based on the nuclear family. Living 30 miles from Bethnal Green, wives lost regular contact with their mothers and became more dependent on husbands for companionship and support. Husbands were cut off from social contacts in Bethnal Green, for example visiting the pub with workmates, and became more involved in domestic activities. Gardening, watching television and other home-centred leisure activities largely replaced the extended family.

Young and Willmott's findings are reflected in later studies such as John Goldthorpe and David Lockwood's (1969) research into affluent (highly paid) manual workers in Luton in the 1960s. Many had moved to Luton in search of better paid jobs. They led privatised, home-centred lives – the home and nuclear family were the focus of their leisure activities.

Stages of family life

Many sociologists have argued that there is a long-term trend towards the nuclear family. Michael Young and Peter Willmott take a similar view. In a study entitled *The Symmetrical Family* (1973), they bring together their earlier research, historical evidence, and data from a survey they conducted in London in the early 1970s. They argue that the family in Britain has developed through three stages.

Stage 1 The pre-industrial family The family at this stage is a production unit – family members work together in agriculture and cottage industries.

Stage 2 The early industrial family The industrial revolution disrupted the unity of the family as its economic function was taken over by large-scale industry. Men were increasingly drawn out of the home into industrial employment. The family was 'torn apart' – long working hours meant that men had little time to spend with their

activity16 *Bethnal Green*

Item A **Mother and daughter**

The link between mother and daughter in Bethnal Green is often strong. The following example shows how much their lives are sometimes woven together. Mrs Wilkins is in and out of her mother's all day. She shops with her in the morning and goes round there for a cup of tea in the afternoon. 'Then any time during the day, if I want a bit of salt or something like that, I go round to Mum to get it and have a bit of a chat while I'm there. If the children have anything wrong with them, I usually go round to my Mum and have a little chat. If she thinks it's serious enough I'll take him to the doctor.' Her mother looked after Marilyn, the oldest child, for nearly three years. 'She's always had her when I worked; I worked from when she was just a little baby until I was past six months with Billy. Oh, she's all for our Mum. She's got her own mates over there and still plays there all the time. Mum looks after my girl pretty good. When she comes in, I say, "Have you had your tea?", and she says as often as not, "I've had it at Nan's".'

Adapted from Young & Willmott, 1957

Item B **Contact with kin**

Contacts of married men and women with parents

	Fathers		Mothers	
	Number with father alive	Percentage who saw father in previous 24 hours	Number with mother alive	Percentage who saw mother in previous 24 hours
Men	116	30%	163	31%
Women	100	48%	155	55%

From Young & Willmott, 1957

questions

1 In view of Young and Willmott's definition, does Mrs Wilkins in Item A belong to an extended family? Give reasons for your answer.

2 Mr Sykes who lives near his mother-in-law in Bethnal Green said, 'This is the kind of family where sisters never want to leave their mother's side'. How does Item B suggest that this kind of family is widespread?

wives and children. Poverty was widespread. Kinship networks were extended, mainly by women, to provide mutual support. Extended families continued well into the 20th century in low-income, working-class areas such as Bethnal Green.

Stage 3 The symmetrical family This type of family first developed in the middle class. By the 1970s, it had spread to the working class. It has three main characteristics.

- It is nuclear.
- It is home-centred and privatised – family life is focused on the home. Husband and wife look to each other for companionship. Leisure is home-based – for example, watching TV. The family is self-contained – there is little contact with the wider kinship network.
- It is *symmetrical* – the roles of husband and wife are increasingly similar. Although wives are still mainly

responsible for childcare, husbands play a greater part in domestic life.

Stratified diffusion Young and Willmott argue that the development of the stage 3 family has occurred through a process of *stratified diffusion*, whereby new ideas of family life were started by the higher social classes and gradually filtered down to the lower classes. As the working class has come to enjoy shorter working hours, more comfortable homes and a higher standard of living, family life has become increasingly privatised and nuclear. There is less need for the traditional mutual aid network of the extended family. There is more opportunity to devote time and money to home and children.

Stage 4 Young and Willmott suggest a possible fourth stage in family life. They argue that if stratified diffusion continues, then the upper classes will be setting the trends

*activity*17 *three stages of family life*

Item A Early 20th century

A Lancashire farming family

Item C 1970s

A shot from an Oxo commercial

Item B 1954

Chatting over the garden fence

question

Match each picture to one of Young and Willmott's three stages of family life. Explain your choices.

for family life in the future. Their survey included a sample of managing directors' families. It indicates a trend away from the symmetrical family towards a more asymmetrical form. Husbands were highly involved in their work and domestic responsibilities were left mainly to their wives. Couples spent less time in joint activities than the typical privatised family.

Criticisms of Young and Willmott

1 Their theory suggests an historical 'march of progress' in which family life gets better and better. They have been criticised for failing to address the negative aspects of changes in the modern family.

2 Many sociologists are unhappy about the concept of stratified diffusion, implying as it does that the working class automatically follow norms established by the middle class. Goldthorpe and Lockwood's Luton study, while showing privatised lifestyles among affluent manual workers, showed that they still retained a distinctive working-class outlook on life.

3 Feminists have attacked Young and Willmott's concept of the symmetrical family. For example, they claim that women are still mainly responsible for household tasks such as cooking and cleaning (McMahon, 1999).

4 The extended family may be more important than Young and Willmott's picture of the largely independent nuclear family suggests.

The modified extended family

The picture presented so far is a steady march of progress blossoming into the privatised, self-sufficient, self-centred nuclear family. Kin beyond the nuclear family appear to play a minor role. A number of sociologists argue that this process has been exaggerated. Important services are often exchanged between nuclear family members and extended kin, though the ties that bind them are not as strong as those in the traditional extended family.

The term *modified extended family* is sometimes used to describe such family groupings. Members come together for important family events and provide support in times of need. Improved communications, such as email, telephones, cars and air travel, mean that contact over long distances is easier than before.

The following studies suggest that sociologists have tended to underestimate the importance of kinship beyond the nuclear family.

North London in the 1980s Peter Willmott (1986) studied married couples with young children in a North London suburb. Two-thirds saw relatives at least once a week, nearly two-thirds were helped by mothers or mothers-in-laws when a child was ill, and nearly three-quarters were helped with babysitting – again mainly by mothers or mothers-in-law. Four-fifths looked to relatives, mainly parents or parents-in-law, when they needed to borrow money.

Luton in the 1980s In 1986-1987, Fiona Devine (1992) studied Vauxhall car workers and their families in Luton. In part, this was a restudy of Goldthorpe and Lockwood's 1960s' research which pictured the working-class family as privatised and self-contained. Devine's research suggests that the degree of privatisation has been exaggerated. Most couples had regular contact with kin – especially parents and, to a lesser extent, brothers and sisters. Many had been helped by kin to find jobs and housing when moving to the area.

Manchester in the 1990s Research in the 1990s largely confirms the findings of earlier studies. A study of Greater Manchester by Janet Finch and Jennifer Mason (1993) found that over 90% of their sample had given or received financial help from relatives, and almost 60% had shared a household with an adult relative (apart from parents) at some time in their lives. In addition, many reported giving and receiving practical assistance, emotional support, and help with children. While emphasising that family relationships are based on a sense of obligation, Finch and Mason also found that help was negotiated and not necessarily given automatically.

Declining contact, 1986-1995 The above studies indicate the continuing importance of kin beyond the nuclear family. However, there is evidence of a decline in contact with kin. The British Social Attitudes (BSA) Survey is based on a representative sample of adults aged 18 and over. The 1986 and 1995 Surveys looked at frequency of contact with kin. They indicate a significant decline. The figures suggest that people are less likely to visit or be visited by anybody at all – relatives or friends. The data showing this is presented in Activity 18.

Why has contact declined? The average journey time between relatives has increased only very slightly since 1986. There is no evidence that friends have replaced relatives. The most likely explanation appears to be the increasing proportion of women working outside the home. The most marked fall in contact has been among women in full-time employment – for example, a drop of nearly 20% seeing their mother at least once a week (McGlone et al., 1999).

Social change and the family – conclusion

Functions of the family There is no simple, straightforward relationship between industrialisation and the functions of the family, the structure of family relationships and the content of family roles. Sociologists generally agree that industrialisation ended the family's role as a unit of production. However, some argue that this has been replaced by an equally important economic function – the family as a *unit of consumption*. Goods and services are increasingly bought and consumed in the name of the family – houses, family cars, home improvements, family holidays and so on. Rising living standards resulting from industrialisation have enabled the family to become a unit of consumption.

Has the family lost many of its functions? Some sociologists argue that the functions of the family have not

activity18 declining contact

Item A Contact with kin

	Frequency seeing relative/ friend at least once a week	
	1986 (%)	1995 (%)
Mother	59	49
Father	51	40
Sibling	33	29
Adult child	66	58
Other relative	42	35
'Best friend'	65	59

Adapted from McGlone et al., 1999

Item B Full-time work

	Frequency seeing non-resident mother at least once a week	
	1985 (%)	1995 (%)
Men in full-time work	49	46
Women in full-time work	64	45

Adapted from McGlone et al., 1999

Item C Keeping in touch

NOKIA HAS FAMILIES TALKING.

From grandson to grandpa, Nokia has a mobile phone for all the family. In fact, Nokia is a firm family favourite.
Could it be that our small and stylish phones fit so easily into the pocket? Or that they take so little out of it?
Could it be their handy memories, ease of use and crystal-clear clarity?

Is it simply that Nokia works on all national mobile phone networks? Or that Nokia manufactures one of Britain's best-selling portable phones? In a word, yes. Whether you're Mum, Dad, Aunt or Uncle, there's a Nokia phone for you. One that will get you talking.
For more details on Nokia mobile phones, call 0800 101 121 today.

NOKIA CONNECTING PEOPLE

questions

1 a) Briefly summarise the data in Item A.

   b) How does it indicate that friends have not taken over from family?

2 What does Item B suggest is the reason for reduced contact with relatives?

3 Items A and B refer to face-to-face contact with relatives. This may exaggerate the extent of the decline of contact. Why? Refer to Item C in your answer.

been reduced or lost. Instead, they have been supplemented and supported. For example, Ronald Fletcher (1966) claims that traditional functions such as the care and education of children have been supported rather than removed by state schools, hospitals and welfare provision.

Structure of the family Does industrialisation lead to the development of isolated nuclear families? Not necessarily, as Anderson's study of Preston in 1851 indicates. However, many sociologists believe there is a trend in this direction. Although extended family networks continued well into the 20th century, available evidence suggests that they have largely disappeared in their traditional form.

However, the picture of the privatised, self-contained nuclear family has probably been exaggerated. Contact between kin beyond the nuclear family is widespread – sufficient to use the term modified extended family to describe many families. However, there is evidence that contact declined fairly significantly towards the end of the 20th century.

Family roles Have family roles changed as a result of industrialisation? To some extent yes, though not simply in one direction. For example, women were an important part of the labour force during the early years of industrialisation, most had turned to the home by the beginning of the 20th century, then most had returned to paid employment by the start of the 21st century.

Family diversity This unit has looked at some of the changes in family life since industrialisation. However, it has not examined some of the more recent changes mentioned in Unit 2 – the growth in lone-parent families, reconstituted families and cohabitation, the rise in the divorce rate, and the increase in gay and lesbian families. These changes will now be examined.

key terms

Symmetrical family A nuclear family in which the roles of husband and wife are increasingly similar. It is home-centred, privatised and self-contained.
Stratified diffusion The spread of ideas and behaviour through the class system from top to bottom.
Modified extended family A weaker version of the traditional extended family. Members don't usually share the same household. However, contact is regular and important services are often exchanged.
Unit of consumption A group of people who consume goods and services as a unit.

summary

1 Families in pre-industrial society performed a range of functions. These included economic, educational and welfare functions.

2 Pre-industrial families were often extended – they formed part of a wider kinship network. This wider network was needed to effectively perform the family's functions.

3 Talcott Parsons saw the isolated nuclear family as the typical family structure in industrial society. He argued that family members no longer needed to rely on large kinship networks because many of the family's functions had been taken over by specialised agencies.

4 According to Parsons, an industrial economy requires a geographically mobile labour force. The small, streamlined nuclear family meets this requirement.

5 Peter Laslett's research shows that only 10% of pre-industrial households in England contained kin beyond the nuclear family. However, family members do not have to live under the same roof to form extended families.

6 Michael Anderson's research on Preston households in 1851 suggests that the early years of industrialisation may have encouraged the formation of extended families in the working class. Such families may have operated as mutual aid organisations before the days of the welfare state.

7 During the early years of industrialisation, married women often worked in factories. They were gradually excluded from the labour force and restricted to the home. The mother-housewife role became their primary role. Today, the majority of women have returned to the labour force.

8 Defined by Young and Willmott as 'a combination of families who to some large degree form one domestic unit', extended families continued well into the 20th century in many working-class areas.

9 Young and Willmott claim that the family in Britain has developed through three stages. 1) the pre-industrial family 2) the early industrial family 3) the symmetrical family.

10 Studies from the 1950s to the early 1970s claimed that the typical family structure was nuclear. Families were pictured as privatised, home-centred and self-contained.

11 Studies from the 1980s and 1990s suggested that this picture of privatisation and self-containment was exaggerated. Kin beyond the nuclear family still played an important role. Many families could be described as modified extended families.

12 However, evidence from the British Social Attitudes Survey indicates that contact with kin beyond the nuclear family declined towards the close of the 20th century.

Unit 4 Changing family relationships

keyissues

1 How have patterns of marriage, cohabitation, childbearing, separation and divorce changed?

2 What explanations have been given for these changes?

4.1 Marriage

Apart from a few ups and downs, the number of marriages per year in the UK increased steadily from 1838 (when they were first recorded) until the early 1970s. Since then there has been a significant decline, from 480,000 marriages in 1972 to 306,000 in 2000.

These figures refer both to *first marriages*, in which neither partner has been married before, and to *remarriages* in which one or both partners have been married before. The number of first marriages peaked in 1970 at almost 390,000 and steadily decreased to 180,000 in 2000 (*Social Trends*, 2003 – unless mentioned, the figures in this unit are taken from various issues of *Social Trends*).

Remarriage Remarriages increased from 57,000 in 1961 (14% of all marriages) to 126,000 in 2000 (41% of all marriages). Most remarriages involve divorced persons rather than widows and widowers. The largest increase occurred between 1971 and 1972 following the introduction of the Divorce Reform Act of 1969.

Age at marriage Over the past 30 years, people have tended to marry later. In 1971, the average age for first marriages was 24 for men and 22 for women. By 2000, it was 30 for men and 28 for women. The increase in cohabitation – living together as a couple – partly accounts for this. Many couples see cohabitation as a prelude to marriage.

key terms

First marriage A marriage in which neither partner has been married before.
Remarriage A marriage in which one or both partners have been married before.

Singlehood

Some people never marry. They either choose to remain single or fail to find a suitable marriage partner. There are increasing numbers of 'never-married' people. For example, in England and Wales only 7% of women born between 1946 and 1950 remained unmarried by the age of 32, compared with 28% of those born between 1961 and 1965. There is a similar trend for men.

Many 'never-married' people cohabit – they live with a

activity19 patterns of marriage

Item A Marriages and divorces

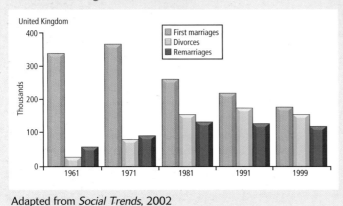

United Kingdom

Adapted from *Social Trends*, 2002

Item B Keep on marrying

Patsy Kensit with husband number three, Liam Gallagher. The marriage is now over.

Item C Wary of marriage

Sue Sharpe studied working-class girls in London schools in the early 1970s. She found their main concerns were 'love, marriage, husbands, children, jobs, and careers, more or less in that order'. A third wanted to be married by 20 and three-quarters by 25.

When she returned to the same schools in the early 1990s, she found the girls' priorities had changed to 'job, career and being able to support themselves'. In her words, 'Young people had witnessed adult relationships breaking up and being reconstituted all around them. Girls in particular were far more wary of marriage. Now, only 4 per cent wanted to be married by 20, although there was still a feeling of "A wedding day – that sounds good fun".'

Adapted from Sharpe, 1976 and 1994

Joan Collins with husband number five, Percy Gibson.

questions

1 a) Describe the trends shown in Item A.

   b) What does Item A suggest about the relationship between divorce and remarriage?

2 Why does the term serial monogamy fit Patsy Kensit's and Joan Collins's marital history?

3 How might Item C help to explain

   a) the decline in marriage

   b) the later age of marriage?

partner as a couple. There has been a steady increase in cohabitation in recent years as the following section indicates. There has also been a steady increase in singlehood – living without a partner.

Living alone Growing numbers of people are living alone. The largest increase is in the 25 to 29 age group in social class 1 – people in professional occupations, particularly women. In England and Wales in 1971, 6% of this group lived alone, in 1991 just under 20%.

In 1991, 90% of the under 30 age group who lived alone were never-married, over 50% of the 30-39 age group and 30% of the 40-59 age group. In many cases, remaining

single and living alone was the 'desired' option (Hall et al., 1999).

Creative singlehood In the past, being single was seen as a negative status, particularly for women. They had 'failed' to find a marriage partner, their situation was 'unfortunate', they were 'spinsters' and 'old maids' – terms with negative overtones.

Today, views are changing. The term *creative singlehood* is sometimes used to describe a positive view of singlehood whereby people choose to remain single as a lifestyle option.

activity20 *singlehood*

Item A *Creative singlehood*

Never-married people who live alone tend to see their situation in positive terms. They have chosen to remain single. They emphasise the importance of independence and freedom. As one single woman in her 30s put it, 'It was the freedom of it really, come and go when I like'.

Others emphasise the importance of work. One woman said, 'Until the age of 30 there was always a man in my life, but around the age of 30, it all started to change and work took over. By the age of 35, I had come to the conclusion that I should knock it on the head and concentrate on work'.

Adapted from Hall et al., 1999

Singles night in a supermarket

Item B *Single women*

Women are choosing to live alone because they have the capacity to do so. New opportunities in education and employment over the past few decades mean there is now a third way for women between living with and looking after their aged parents, or getting married. Single women tend to have much more developed and intense social networks and are involved in a wide range of social and other activities. Single men, by contrast, tend to be lonely and isolated. The signs are that living alone is good for women but bad for men.

Adapted from Scase, 2000

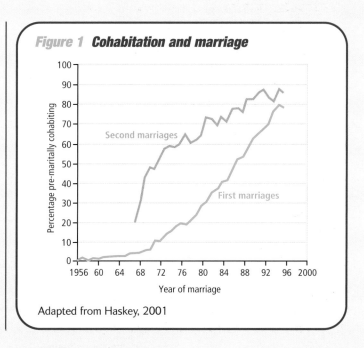

Girls' night out

questions

1 How does the term creative singlehood apply to Item A?
2 Why are more women choosing to remain single? Refer to both items in your answer.

4.2 Cohabitation

Definition Cohabitation is living together as a couple without being married. It involves a shared residence in which a couple set up home together. Love is the most common reason people give for cohabiting (McCrae, 1999).

Extent and age From 1976 to 1998, the proportion of women under 50 who were cohabiting more than trebled – from 9% to over 27%. Cohabiting couples tend to be young – nearly 40% of non-married women aged 25 to 29 were cohabiting in 1998. The picture is similar for men (Haskey, 2001).

Cohabitation and marriage Cohabitation before marriage has now become the norm. Figure 1 shows the proportions of first and second marriages in which the couple lived together before marriage. For first marriages in the 1950s the figure was less than 2%, by 1996 it was 77%. For second marriages, the figure rose from less than 20% in 1967 to 84% in 1996 (Haskey, 2001).

Figure 1 *Cohabitation and marriage*

Percentage pre-maritally cohabiting

Second marriages

First marriages

Year of marriage

Adapted from Haskey, 2001

Reasons for cohabitation The 1998 British Household Panel Survey asked people why they chose to cohabit. These are the reasons they gave.

- For most people, cohabitation is part of the process of getting married – it is a prelude to marriage, *not* an alternative to marriage.
- Over half saw cohabitation as a trial marriage – it provided an opportunity to test the relationship before making it legally binding.
- Around 40% saw cohabitation as an alternative to marriage – they saw advantages to living together rather than marrying.
- Some mentioned the absence of legal ties – this gave them more freedom to end the relationship (*Social Trends*, 2002).

Causes

Over the past 50 years, cohabitation has increased rapidly. What accounts for this increase?

Changing attitudes Attitudes towards sexual relationships and living arrangements outside marriage have changed. Cohabitation is no longer seen as 'living in sin' or described with negative phrases such as 'living over the brush'.

Evidence for change can be seen from the 1996 British Household Panel Survey. Asked whether they thought 'living together outside marriage was always wrong', a third of those aged 60 and over thought it was wrong compared with less than a tenth of those under 30 (*Social Trends*, 2002).

Effective contraception From 1967, reliable contraception was made readily available to unmarried women with the passing of the NHS (Family Planning) Act. For the first time, full sexual relations could be an expression of love for a partner rather than a means of reproduction. Effective contraception made it possible for couples to cohabit with little fear of pregnancy (Allan & Crow, 2001).

Changes in parental control, education and housing There is some evidence that parental control over children has decreased over the past 50 years. The 1960s are often seen as the decade when young people revolted against the authority of their parents and the 'older generation'.

The expansion of higher education means that increasing numbers of young people are leaving home at an earlier age for reasons other than marriage. For example, there were 173,000 female undergraduates in the UK in 1970/71 compared with 602,000 in 2000/01. As a result, many young people have more freedom from parental authority at an earlier age, and they are able to live in their own housing. This makes it easier for couples to cohabit. In

activity21 cohabitation

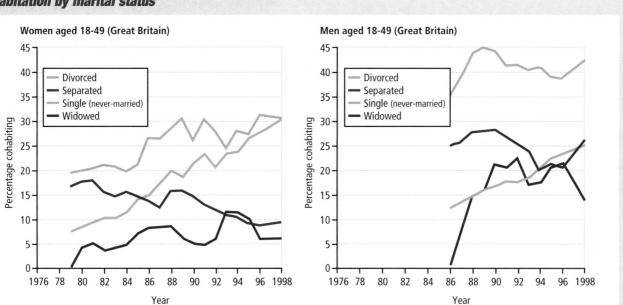

Cohabitation by marital status

Women aged 18-49 (Great Britain)
Men aged 18-49 (Great Britain)

Adapted from Haskey, 2001

questions

1 Describe the trends shown in the graphs.

2 Suggest a reason for the different percentages of divorced women and men cohabiting.

addition, building societies are now more likely to lend to unmarried couples – at one time they were very unlikely to lend to those 'living in sin' (Allan & Crow, 2001).

Changes in divorce The divorce rate has increased rapidly over the past 50 years. Couples in which one or both partners are divorced are the most likely to cohabit. Having already achieved independence from their parents, they are less likely to be affected by parental control. Also, if their divorce has not gone through, cohabitation is their only option if they want to live as a couple.

The rise in divorce means that the view of marriage as a 'union for life' has less power. This may lead many people to see cohabitation, without its binding legal ties, as an attractive alternative to marriage. Some people actually give 'fear of divorce' as a reason for cohabiting (McCrae, 1999; Allan & Crow, 2001).

4.3 Childbearing

Women are having fewer children. And fewer women are having any children. This section looks at the decline in *fertility*.

The fertility rate Fertility is measured by the fertility rate – the number of live births per 1,000 women aged 15 to 44. In 1900, the UK fertility rate was 115, in 1961 it was 91, and in 2000 it had fallen to 55. This is the lowest rate since records began.

Childless women Part of the decline in fertility in recent years is due to an increase in childless women. About 11% of women born in 1943 in England and Wales were childless by age 45, this rose to 16% for those born in 1953, and projections suggest that 23% of women born in 1973 will be childless at 45.

Probably all of the increase in childlessness since the 1950s is voluntary – it is chosen. Involuntary childlessness affects between 5% and 8% of couples – there is no reason to suppose this is increasing (Coleman & Chandola, 1999).

Age and fertility Women are having children later in life. In England and Wales, the average age at childbirth increased from 26.1 years in the early 1970s to 29.1 in 2000.

While the fertility rates of women under 30 have steadily fallen, the rates for those 30 years and older have risen since the mid-1970s (Ghee, 2001).

Births outside marriage An increasing proportion of births occur outside marriage. In 1900, the proportion was 4% compared with almost 10 times that a century later. The greatest increase has occurred in recent years – from 8% in England and Wales in 1971 to 39% in 2000.

Most of this increase in births outside marriage has been to cohabiting couples – to parents living at the same address. In 2000, about four-fifths of births outside marriage were jointly registered by both parents – three-quarters of these births were to parents living at the same address.

The proportion of births outside marriage registered by the mother alone has remained more or less the same at 7% to 8% since the late 1980s.

Explaining the trends

The following explanations have been suggested for the changes in childbearing outlined above.

Changing attitudes There is far greater tolerance of births outside marriage than in the past. In the early 1950s, unmarried mothers were sometimes seen as 'psychologically disturbed' (McCrae, 1999). Births outside marriage were defined as 'illegitimate' which literally means 'unlawful' and implies that such births were improper and immoral.

Attitudes to childlessness have also changed. The word 'childless' suggests a loss. Now many women who *choose* not to have children see themselves as 'childfree' – they emphasise liberation from children rather than loss of children.

Control of births As noted earlier, reliable contraception was made available on the NHS in 1967 to all women, both married and unmarried. It was now possible for women to control the number of births they wanted.

Changing opportunities Researchers often point to expanding educational opportunities and the increase in women's participation in the labour market as reasons for the decline in fertility. As noted earlier, the numbers of female undergraduates increased more than threefold between 1970/71 and 2000/01. And during those same years the numbers of women in paid employment in the UK increased from 10 to 14.1 million.

These changes provided alternatives to women's traditional role as mothers and child-raisers.

Changing values Some researchers claim that in recent years there has been increasing emphasis on individual freedom, on the individual's right to choose, and on personal fulfilment. As a result, people are increasingly concerned with constructing their own lifestyle. Some researchers see this concern reflected in *choosing* to cohabit rather than marry and in *choosing* to have fewer children or none at all.

key terms

Fertility rate The number of live births per 1000 women aged 15 to 44.
Childless women Women who, for whatever reason, do not produce children.
Childfree women Women who choose not to have children as a lifestyle option.

activity22 childbearing

Item A Fertility rates

United Kingdom			Live births per 1,000 women		
	1961	**1971**	**1981**	**1991**	**2000**
Under 20	37	50	28	33	29
20-24	173	154	107	89	69
25-29	178	155	130	120	95
30-34	106	79	70	87	88
35-39	51	34	22	32	40
40 and over	16	9	5	5	8
All ages	91	84	62	64	55

This table shows fertility rates by age of mother at childbirth.

Adapted from *Social Trends*, 2002

Item B Births outside marriage

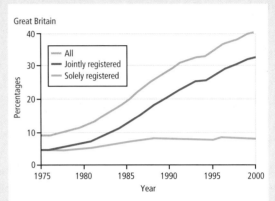

This graph shows births outside marriage as a percentage of all live births.

Adapted from *Social Trends*, 2002

Item C Childless women

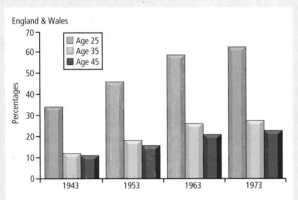

This chart shows the percentage of childless women at age 25, 35 and 45, by year of birth. Data for women age 35 and 45 in 1973, and those aged 45 in 1963 are projections.

Adapted from *Social Trends*, 2000

Item D Childfree couples

Famous childfree women – actress Helen Mirren and novelist Iris Murdoch.

Eighteen years ago, Barry Butler proposed to Lysette. They decided to have a childfree marriage. Now 42, Lysette Butler is a ward nurse in her local general hospital in Essex. She says, 'My life is about me and my husband; it's not about anybody else. I've been told so often that that makes me selfish but I don't understand why that is so. I just don't have any maternal feelings. I don't dislike children, they are just not a way of life for me.'

It was the freedom of not having children that led Catherine James, a 52-year-old writer in Edinburgh, to decide to be childfree. 'I can stay awake with my husband until the early hours, just talking. We can have sex at three in the afternoon without worrying that the children will walk in. We can go away for the weekend at the drop of a hat – and yes we do all of those things!'

Adapted from Hill, 2002

questions

1 Outline the trends shown in Items A, B and C.
2 Being childfree is a lifestyle choice. Discuss with reference to Item D.

4.4 Divorce and separation

This section looks at the breakup of partnerships. It is mainly concerned with divorce.

Trends in divorce

In the UK, as in other Western societies, there has been a dramatic rise in divorce during the 20th century. This can be seen from the actual number of divorces each year and from the increase in the *divorce rate* – the number of divorces per thousand married people.

Table 1 shows both these measures for *decrees absolute* (final divorces) in England and Wales from 1931 to 2000. Both the number and rate of divorce peaked in 1993. Since then, there has been a gradual decline. If the divorce rate continues at its present level, around 40% of marriages will end in divorce.

Table 1 Divorce: decrees absolute (England and Wales)

Year	Numbers	Rate per 1,000 married population
1931	3,668	0.4
1951	28,265	2.6
1964	34,868	2.9
1969	51,310	4.1
1972	119,025	9.5
1981	145,713	11.9
1991	158,745	13.4
1993	165,018	14.2
1996	157,107	13.9
1998	145,214	12.9
2000	141,135	12.7

From various issues of *Population Trends*

Interpreting divorce statistics

Divorce statistics provide an accurate measure of one type of marital breakdown – the legal termination of marriages. However, marriages can end in other ways.

Separation The married couple end their marriage by separating – living in separate residences. However, they remain legally married. Some couples obtain separation orders granted by magistrates' courts.

Empty-shell marriages The couple live together, remain legally married, but their marriage exists in name only. Love, sex and companionship are things of the past.

As the divorce rate increased, there may have been a decrease in separations and empty-shell marriages. From 1897-1906, around 8,000 separation orders were granted each year compared to 700 divorces. By 1971, only 94 separation orders were granted compared to over 74,000 divorces. There are no figures on informal ('unofficial') separations. Nor are there any figures on the extent of empty-shell marriages. Such marriages were often maintained in order to 'keep up appearances' and avoid the stigma (shame) of divorce. This stigma considerably reduced during the last half of the 20th century.

As the next section indicates, divorce has become easier and cheaper throughout the last century. In view of this,

people who previously separated or endured empty-shell marriages are probably more likely to choose divorce.

Cohabitation Marriage is only one form of partnership. As noted earlier, cohabitation is an increasingly popular form of partnership. Available evidence suggests that, in any given period, a significantly higher number of cohabitations are terminated than marriages (Allan & Crow, 2001).

Conclusion Are partnerships becoming more unstable, more likely to break up? In view of the evidence outlined above, it is not possible to answer this question. However, one sociologist, Robert Chester (1984), believes that the increase in divorce rates probably reflects an increase in marital breakdown – though he admits this cannot be proved.

---

key terms

Divorce The legal termination of a marriage.
Divorce rate The number of divorces per thousand married people.
Separation A married couple who end their relationship and live in separate residences but remain legally married.
Empty-shell marriage The couple share the same residence, remain legally married, but their marriage exists in name only.

Explaining changing divorce rates

Changes in the law Before 1857 a private Act of Parliament was required to obtain a divorce in Britain. This was an expensive and complicated procedure beyond the means of all but the most wealthy. In 1857 the Matrimonial Causes Act set up a new court for divorce. The grounds for divorce included adultery, cruelty and desertion. At least one partner had to be proven guilty of one of these 'matrimonial offences'. Although the costs of obtaining a divorce were now reduced, they were still beyond the reach of most people.

Throughout the first half of the 20th century a series of Acts simplified divorce proceedings, reduced the costs involved and widened the grounds for divorce. The financial burden of divorce was eased for the less well-off by the Legal Aid and Advice Act of 1949 which provided free legal advice and paid solicitors' fees for those who could not afford them.

The Divorce Reform Act of 1969 involved a major change in the grounds for divorce. Before this Act, a 'matrimonial offence' had to be proven, a 'guilty party' had to be found. However, many people who wanted a divorce had not committed adultery, been guilty of cruelty, and so on. The 1969 Act defined the grounds for divorce as 'the irretrievable breakdown of the marriage'. It was no longer necessary to prove guilt but simply to show that the marriage was beyond repair. The Act came into force in January 1971.

The Matrimonial Family Proceedings Act of 1984 came into effect in 1985. This Act reduced from three years to one the time a couple had to be married before they could petition for a divorce.

Changes in the law have made divorce a lot easier. The grounds for divorce have been widened, the procedure has been simplified and the expense reduced. Changes in the law have provided greater opportunities for divorce. However, this doesn't explain why more and more people are taking advantage of these opportunities.

activity23 divorce and the law

Divorce rates (England and Wales)

Year	Rate
1931	0.4
1951	2.6
1964	2.9
1972	9.5
1981	11.9
1991	13.4
2000	12.7

From various issues of *Population Trends*

question

How have changes in the law affected the divorce rate?

Changing expectations of love and marriage Since the 1950s, a number of sociologists have argued that changes in people's expectations of love and marriage have resulted in increasingly unstable relationships. Functionalists such as Ronald Fletcher and Talcott Parsons claim that people expect and demand more from marriage. Because of this, they are less likely to put up with an unhappy marriage and more likely to end it with divorce. Ronald Fletcher (1966) argues that a higher divorce rate reflects a higher value placed on marriage. In terms of this argument, the fact that a large proportion of divorcees remarry suggests that they are not rejecting the institution of marriage but simply expecting more from the relationship.

More recently, the British sociologist Anthony Giddens (1992) has seen a trend towards what he calls *confluent love*. This form of love focuses on intimacy, closeness and emotion. It forms the basis of relationships rather than the feelings of duty and obligation reflected in the traditional marriage vows of 'for better or worse, for richer or poorer, 'til death do us part'. Intimate relationships based on confluent love tend to last as long as partners find satisfaction and fulfilment.

The decision to marry is increasingly based on confluent love. When marriage ceases to provide the intimacy demanded by confluent love, individuals are likely to end it. If Giddens is correct, then marriage is an increasingly unstable and fragile institution, and divorce will become more frequent.

Changing social values Throughout the 20th century divorce became more socially acceptable. Couples were less likely to stay together in order to 'keep up appearances' and to avoid the stigma and shame formerly associated with divorce.

The rising divorce rate has led to the 'normalisation' of divorce. This, in itself, has made divorce more acceptable as a means of dealing with a failed marriage (Cockett & Tripp, 1994).

The economic position of women Women have often been 'trapped' in unhappy marriages because they cannot support themselves and their children without their husband's income. Unless they can become economically independent, their opportunities to divorce are severely restricted (Kurz, 1995).

Over the past 50 years, married women's chances of economic independence have improved significantly. Increasing numbers of women have entered the labour market, divorce settlements have taken more account of the financial needs of women, and welfare benefits for women with dependent children have improved (Allan & Crow, 2001). Although most women find themselves financially worse off after divorce, they are able to live independently from their former husband.

Women and marriage Feminists have seen rising divorce rates as symptomatic of all that is wrong with traditional patriarchal marriage – male dominance and the unequal division of domestic labour, with women still largely responsible for housework and childcare even when they are employed outside the home (see page 41). It is women rather than men who are increasingly dissatisfied with marriage.

There is some evidence for this view. Divorced men are more likely to remarry than divorced women. According to Diana Gittins (1993), this is because women are more disillusioned with marriage. In the 1940s, around two-thirds of divorce petitions were brought by husbands. By 2000, the situation was reversed with 70% of petitions brought by wives (*Population Trends, 109,* 2002). This may indicate that women are more dissatisfied with marriage than men. Or, it may reflect a greater need to settle financial and housing arrangements, particularly for women with dependent children (Allen & Crow, 2001).

activity24 *case studies*

Item A *Sarah*

Sarah, 39, runs a public relations consultancy. During her marriage she was largely responsible for caring for the children – two girls – and running the home – 'all the washing, the cleaning and the cooking' – as well as working full time. She found that, as the children grew older, 'I started to resent what I saw as the inequality in our lives'. Her husband Adam 'could not see what I thought was glaringly obvious'. She felt that she couldn't be herself because 'he used to put me down and was so controlling'.

She decided to divorce Adam. She notes, 'Economic independence played a big part. I knew I could afford to run my own life because I had a successful business, and it made it possible for me to initiate the breakup. I feel so much more myself, being in control of my life. I think it's hard for women to stay married today. We have high expectations, but men and women are still not equal and so many women are resentful about being expected to do it all.'

Adapted from Appleyard, 2002

Item B *Jan*

Jan, 43, is a writer. She has four children, three with her former husband and one with her new partner Mike. 'I met Mike four years ago, and happy as we are, I have no desire to marry. I want to be in control of my life – and the majority of women today feel the same.'

'The reason so many are initiating divorce is because we don't have to be dependent on – or controlled by – a man. We want to lead our lives in a way that makes us happy, without being answerable to men. When I was married, I was expected not only to bring money into the house, but to do all the domestic chores as well. The big issue between us was always money. He was earning £30,000 a year, which was a big salary, but I wasn't allowed to buy as much as a magazine without asking him first.'

Adapted from Appleyard, 2002

Item C *Domestic labour*

question

To what extent do Items A, B and C support the explanations given for divorce?

Who divorces?

So far, this section has been concerned with the rise in divorce rates. The focus now is on the social distribution of divorce – on the variation in divorce rates between different social groups. This variation is particularly apparent for age and social class groups.

Age In general, the earlier the age of marriage, the more likely it is to end in divorce. For women who were under 20 when they married in the late 1980s, 24% had separated within 5 years compared with 8% who married between the ages of 25 and 29. Reasons suggested for the high divorce rate of young marrieds include:

- The bride is more likely to be pregnant which places a strain on the marriage.
- Money problems – young people are more likely to be low paid or unemployed.
- Lack of experience in choosing a suitable partner.

- Lack of awareness of the demands of marriage.
- More likely to 'grow apart' as their attitudes and beliefs are still developing.

Social class In general, the lower the class position of the husband, the more likely the couple are to divorce. Financial problems appear to be the main cause. Unemployment, reliance on state benefits and low income are all associated with high divorce rates (Kiernan & Mueller, 1999).

Other factors A number of other factors are associated with high divorce rates. They include:

- Experience of parents' divorce – this may cause psychological problems which are carried forward to the child's marriage. Or, it may simply make divorce more acceptable.
- Remarriages are more likely to end in divorce than first marriages. Maybe the problems which caused the first divorce are carried through into the second marriage.
- Differences in class, ethnicity and religion between the couple are associated with higher divorce rates. They will have less in common, they may have different expectations about marriage, and these differences may result in conflict.

The consequences of divorce

Divorce has a variety of consequences – for the couple involved, for their children, their relatives and friends, and for the wider society. This section looks at the effects of divorce on children and on the wider society.

Divorce and children Opinions about the effects of divorce on children abound. Some see it as uniformly harmful and argue that parents should go to great lengths to stay together for the sake of the children. Others argue that if divorce frees children from a bitter and hostile family environment then, on balance, it is beneficial. In these circumstances parents should divorce for the sake of the children.

In a study entitled *Divorce and Separation: The Outcomes for Children*, Rodgers and Pryor (1998) reviewed some 200 studies. They attempted to find out whether claims about the harmful effects of divorce on children were supported by research evidence.

The review confirmed that children of divorced or separated parents have a higher probability of experiencing a range of problems such as poverty, poor housing, behavioural problems (eg, bedwetting and anti-social behaviour), teenage pregnancy and educational under-achievement. Although children of divorced and separated parents have around twice the chance of experiencing these sorts of problems, only a minority actually do so. A key question is why a minority of children appear to suffer from divorce while most do not.

Rodgers and Pryor suggest that it is not divorce alone which causes these problems, but the association of divorce with other factors. These include:

- Financial hardship – which may have an effect on educational achievement.
- Family conflict – which may create behavioural problems for children.
- Parental ability to cope with the changes that divorce brings – if parents cannot cope, then children are less likely to do so.
- Multiple changes in family structure – if divorce is accompanied by other changes, such as moving in with a step-family, children are more likely to experience problems.
- Quality and degree of contact with the parent who has left – children who have regular contact appear to cope better.

According to Rodgers and Pryor, these findings help to explain why some children experience problems with divorce, while the majority, at least in the long term, do not.

A large-scale research project conducted by Mavis Hetherington (2002) in the USA reached similar conclusions. Her findings are based on a longitudinal study over 25 years of 2500 people from childhood in 1400 families. Her evidence includes tens of thousands of hours of videotapes of families at dinner, at play, relaxing and having rows. Hetherington concludes that three out of four children experience little long-term damage from divorce. She admits that 25% have serious emotional or social problems which compares with 10% from families that stay together. In her view, the negative effects on children have been exaggerated and we must accept that 'divorce is a reasonable solution to an unhappy, acrimonious, destructive marital relationship' (Hetherington, 2002).

Divorce and society From a New Right perspective (see pages 38-40) high divorce rates, and the lone-parent families that often result from divorce, are a serious threat to society. Most lone-parent families are headed by women. They lack a father-figure – a male role model who can provide discipline and an example for the future. This can lead to inadequate socialisation, particularly for boys, which can result in anti-social behaviour. Some New Right thinkers see a direct relationship between rising divorce rates and rising crime rates. In Patricia Morgan's (1999) words, 'large numbers of fatherless youths represent a high risk factor for crime'. A return to 'traditional family values' is needed to strengthen marriage, and 'tougher' laws are required because divorce has become 'too easy'. These measures will lower the divorce rate and so reduce the threat to social stability.

In contrast, many feminists strongly object to any barriers to divorce. Compared to the past, the present divorce laws provide freedom and choice, particularly for women. Restrictions on divorce may force them to endure unhappy marriages, and in some cases, physical and sexual abuse of themselves and their children. Liberal divorce laws offer greater independence for women and represent a positive step towards gender equality.

activity25 the all-American family

Item A Eminem

Born Marshall Mathers III, deserted by his father and raised by his mother, Eminem has a step-brother Nathan, a daughter Haile and an ex-wife Kim. Judging by his songs he hates his mother and despises what he sees as his excuse for a family. Talking about his mother in *Cleanin' Out My Closet*, he says,

> You're getting older now
> And it's cold when you're lonely
> And Nathan's growing up so quick
> He gonna know you're a phoney
> And Haile's getting so big now
> Can't you see that she's beautiful
> But you'll never see her
> She won't even be at your funeral
> You selfish bitch
> I hope you burn in hell for this shit.

Excerpt from *Cleanin' Out My Closet* written by Marshall Mathers and Jeff Bass

Eminem

Item B Social critic

According to Paul Gilroy, professor of sociology at Yale University, 'Eminem is one of America's more acute social critics. He is one of the few voices that is telling the truth about the implosion of White family life in America. Everything he says runs contrary to the all-American mythology of Mom and Pop and the happy children that Bush still propagates. And he speaks directly to all those kids who are the product of broken homes, domestic violence and parental neglect. Those images are there in all his videos, in the anger of his lyrics. Eminem is the bard of the destruction of the all-American family.'
Quoted in O'Hagan, 2003

Item C 'Family Portrait'

Pink

You fight about money
About me and my brother
And this I come home to
This is my shelter
It ain't easy, growing up in WW3.

* * * * * * * * *

Can we be a family
I promise I'll be better
Daddy please don't leave.

Excerpts from *Family Portrait* recorded by Pink and written by Pink and Scott Storch

question

Judging from Items A, B and C, how seriously should we take family conflict and family breakup?

summary

1 There has been a significant decline in first marriages and in the overall total of marriages since the early 1970s. Within this total, there has been an increase in the numbers and proportion of remarriages.

2 There has been an increase in singlehood – living without a partner.

3 There has been a large increase in cohabitation from the 1970s onwards. Cohabitation before marriage is now the norm. While most people see it as a prelude to marriage, some see it as an alternative to marriage.

4 The following reasons have been suggested for the increase in cohabitation.
- Changing attitudes
- Availability of reliable contraception
- Reduction of parental control
- Expansion of higher education
- Increased availability of housing for non-married people
- Increase in divorce rate.

5 There has been a significant decline in fertility during the 20th century, particularly since the 1960s. This is due to increasing numbers of women deciding to have either fewer children or none at all.

6 An increasing proportion of births are occurring outside marriage.

7 There has been a dramatic rise in the divorce rate during the 20th century. In England and Wales the rate peaked in 1993.

8 Reasons for the rise in divorce include changes in:
- the law, leading to cheaper and easier divorce
- expectations of love and marriage
- attitudes towards divorce
- the economic position of women and their view of marriage.

9 Divorce is not spread evenly throughout the population – eg there are age and class variations in divorce rates.

10 Most children appear to experience no long-term harm from their parents' divorce.

11 While the New Right sees the rise in divorce as a threat to society, feminists tend to see it as an expression of women's right to choose.

Unit 5 Family diversity

keyissues

1 How diverse are families?

2 What are the main explanations for family diversity?

5.1 Introduction

Family diversity as a theme This unit is entitled *Family diversity*. Read any recent introductory textbook on the sociology of the family and one statement rings out loud and clear – families and households in today's society are more complex and diverse than ever before. Here is a typical statement by Susan McRae in the introduction to her edited book, *Changing Britain: Families and Households in the 1990s* (1999). 'Britain today is a much more complex society than in past times, with great diversity in the types of household within which people live: one-person; cohabiting; families with children and families without; stepfamilies; lone parents – whether divorced or never-married; gay and lesbian couples; pensioners.'

Family diversity as a cause for concern Alongside this recognition of family and household diversity is concern. For some, particularly the New Right, increasing diversity means increasing breakdown. A picture is presented of the family in crisis. Alternatives to the 'traditional family' are poor substitutes for the real thing. So, the families formed by cohabiting couples, the reconstituted families created by remarriage, and families headed by lone parents or by gay or lesbian couples are at best, second best. For some, they represent a disintegration of traditional family values, a breakdown of the traditional family.

The ideology of the nuclear family What is this wonderful family compared to which all others fall short? It is the nuclear family of mum, dad and the kids. For some, it was found in its ideal form in the 1950s with mum as a full-time mother and housewife and dad as the breadwinner. The couple are male and female rather than same-sex, they are married rather than cohabiting, and married for the first rather than the second or third time.

This image of the nuclear family is fostered by advertisers. Called the *cereal packet image of the family* by Edmund Leach (1967), it portrays happy, smiling nuclear families consuming family products from Corn Flakes to Oxo.

This picture can be seen as ideological. An ideology is a misleading view, based on value judgements, which obscures reality. Diana Gittins (1993) argues that the idealised picture of the nuclear family acts as a powerful ideology, defining what is normal and desirable and labelling alternative family forms as abnormal and undesirable.

It creates the impression that the nuclear family headed by a married, heterosexual couple is the only family unit that can effectively raise the next generation.

activity26 pictures of the family

Item A A TV ad

Item B Book covers

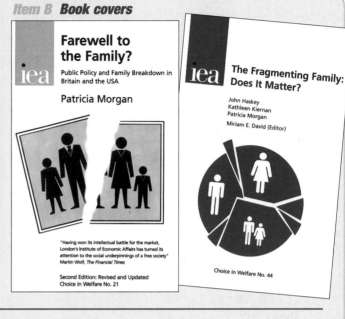

questions

1 How can ads portraying the nuclear family be seen as ideological?

2 How do the book covers in Item B picture the family today?

key term

Ideology A misleading view based on value judgements which obscures reality.

5.2 Changing households

This section looks at changes in household composition in Britain over the past 40 years. A *household* consists of people who occupy a dwelling unit, for example a house or a flat. Looking at household composition provides one way of assessing the extent of family diversity. And it gives an indication about what might be happening to the nuclear family.

Table 2 shows the changing proportions of each type of household from 1961 to 2001. During this period the proportion of households made up of a couple with dependent children has declined from 38% to 23%. During this same period, the proportion of lone-parent with dependent children households has risen from 2% to 6%. These figures have sometimes been used to indicate a decline in nuclear families. They have also been used to argue that the nuclear family is no longer the dominant family type.

Table 3 provides a somewhat different picture. It looks at the percentage of people living in each type of household. It shows that in 1961, 52% of people lived in households made up of a couple with dependent children. By 2001, this figure had dropped to 39%. Even so, this is still a lot of people living in nuclear family households.

Table 2 Households: by type of household and family

Great Britain   *Percentages*

	1961	1971	1981	1991	2001
One Person					
Under state pension age	4	6	8	11	14
Over state pension age	7	12	14	16	15
Two or more unrelated adults	5	4	5	3	3
One family households					
Couple					
No children	26	27	26	28	29
1-2 dependent children	30	26	25	20	19
3 or more dependent children	8	9	6	5	4
Non-dependent children only	10	8	8	8	6
Lone parent					
Dependent children	2	3	5	6	6
Non-dependent children only	4	4	4	4	3
Multi-family households	3	1	1	1	1
All households					
(=100%) (millions)	16.3	18.6	20.2	22.4	24.1

Adapted from *Social Trends*, 2002

Figures for one year are just a snapshot of one part of a family's life cycle. Many households contain people who have been, or will be, members of nuclear family households – for example, couples with no children and people living alone. And the majority of British children still live in couple-headed households – 70% in 2001. This suggests that living in a nuclear family is a phase that most people, as children and adults, go through in the course of their life (O'Brien, 2000).

Table 3 People in households: by type of household and family in which they live

Great Britain   *Percentages*

	1961	1971	1981	1991	2001
One family households					
Living alone	4	6	8	11	12
Couple					
No children	18	19	20	23	24
Dependent children	52	52	47	41	39
Non-dependent children only	12	10	10	11	9
Lone parent	3	4	6	10	10
Other households	12	9	9	4	5
Total population (millions)	51.4	54.4	54.8	56.2	57.2

Adapted from *Social Trends*, 2002

Family diversity assessed

The extent of family diversity should not be exaggerated. Most people, as children and adults, live parts of their lives in nuclear families. Even so, the trend is towards family diversity as the figures in Tables 2 and 3 indicate. There has been a significant decline in:

- the proportion of households made up of a couple with dependent children
- the proportion of people in such households and
- the proportion of dependent children living in couple families.

This decrease in nuclear families has been matched by an increase in lone-parent families. This indicates an increase in family diversity.

The terms nuclear family and couple family conceal further diversity. The couple may be:

- married for the first time
- remarried
- cohabiting
- opposite sex
- same sex.

Over the past 30 years there has been a significant increase in remarriage, cohabitation and same-sex couples. Again, this can be seen as indicating an increase in family diversity.

The rest of this unit looks at specific examples of family diversity, focusing on lone-parent families, reconstituted families, and gay and lesbian families.

5.3 Lone-parent families

Definition

The official definition of a lone-parent family goes as follows. A mother or father living without a partner, with their dependent child or children. The child must be never-married and aged either under 16 or 16 to under 19 and undertaking full-time education. Partner in this definition refers to either a marriage or cohabitation partner (Haskey, 2002).

The above definition is not as straightforward as it seems. What about a father who does not live with the mother and child but is in regular contact, takes part in 'family' decisions and provides for the family in various ways – from income support to helping the child with homework? Is he still a member of the family?

A number of separated and divorced couples attempt to share the responsibility for raising their children. This is known as *co-parenting* or *joint parenting*. It is difficult to see such arrangements as simply lone-parent families (Neale & Smart, 1997).

Faced with this kind of problem, some sociologists have argued that the term *lone-parent household* is more precise. It simply states that the 'absent parent' is not part of the household – ie, does not live under the same roof (Crow & Hardy, 1992).

Types of lone parents

Lone parents are a diverse group. This can be seen from the ways they became lone parents. The various routes into lone parenthood are summarised below.

- The ending of a marriage either by separation or divorce (separated and divorced lone parents)
- The ending of cohabitation where the partners separate (single lone parents)
- Birth to a never-married, non-cohabiting woman (single lone parents)
- Death of a partner – for example, a husband dies leaving his wife with dependent children (widowed lone parents).

Despite these diverse routes into lone parenthood, most lone-parent families have one thing in common, they are headed by women – over 90% in 2001.

Trends in lone-parenthood

In Britain, since the early 1970s, lone-parent families, as a proportion of all families with dependent children, have increased nearly threefold – from 8% in 1971 to 22% in 2001.

During the 1960s, divorce overtook death as the main source of lone-parent families. From then until the mid-

1980s, a large part of the increase was due to marital breakup – the separation or divorce of a married couple. After 1986, the number of single lone mothers grew at a faster rate. This group is made up of 1) never-married cohabiting women whose partnership ended after their child was born and 2) never-married women who were not cohabiting when their child was born. Each group accounts for around half of single lone mothers.

Table 4 illustrates these trends. It shows various types of lone parent families as a percentage of all families with dependent children.

The above statistics are snapshots at particular points in time. Families move in and out of lone parenthood. It is estimated that the average length of time spent as a lone parent is a little over 5 years (Allan & Crow, 2001). The routes in and out of lone parenthood are summarised in Activity 27.

Explaining the trends

Why has lone parenthood increased so rapidly over the past 30 years?

Divorce As Table 4 shows, a large part of the increase from

Table 4 *Lone-parent families*

Great Britain				*Percentages*
	1971	1981	1991	2001
Lone mothers				
Single	1	2	6	9
Widowed	2	2	1	1
Divorced	2	4	6	6
Separated	2	2	4	4
All lone mothers	7	11	18	20
Lone fathers	1	2	1	2
All lone parents	8	13	19	22

Adapted from *Social Trends*, 2002

key terms

Cereal packet image of the family Stereotypical view of the family common in advertising. The family is presented as nuclear with a traditional division of labour.
Lone-parent family A parent without a partner living with their dependent children.
Dependent children Children either under 16 or 16-19 and undertaking full-time education.
Co-parenting/joint parenting Parents who continue to share responsibility for raising their children after they have separated or divorced.

activity27 moving in and out of lone parenthood

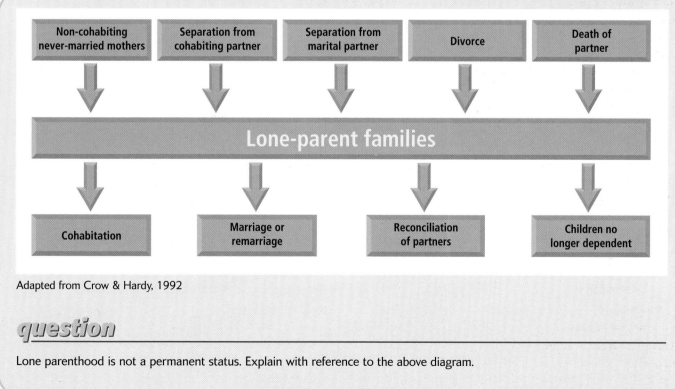

Adapted from Crow & Hardy, 1992

question

Lone parenthood is not a permanent status. Explain with reference to the above diagram.

1971 to 1991 was due to marital breakup. The divorce rate rose rapidly after the Divorce Reform Act came into force in 1971. Reasons for the rise in divorce are outlined on pages 61-62.

Cohabitation breakup Since the mid-1970s, the proportion of women under 50 who were cohabiting more than trebled – from 9% to over 27%. Nearly 40% of non-married women aged 25 to 29 were cohabiting in 1998 (Haskey, 2001). Over the same period, the number of marriages was steadily declining. Reasons for the increase in cohabitation are outlined on pages 58-59.

Since 1986 the number of single lone mothers has grown at a faster rate than any other category of lone parent. By 2001, they accounted for 45% of all lone mothers in Britain. Roughly half became lone mothers as a result of a breakup of their cohabitation. Cohabiting couples with children are twice as likely to end their relationship than married couples with children (Haskey, 2001).

Non-cohabiting never-married mothers This group form the other half of single lone mothers. Their children were born outside marriage and cohabitation. Their numbers have increased rapidly since the mid-1980s.

activity28 lone parents

Item A Divorced lone mother

Sarah Ferguson, formerly married to Prince Andrew, with her daughters at the première of Harry Potter and the Philosopher's Stone in London

Item B Single lone mother

Film star Michelle Pfeiffer with her baby. 'I really wanted a child but I didn't want some guy around to drive me nuts.'

Item C Household income

Families with dependent children					Great Britain: 2000
Family type		Usual gross weekly household income			
		Under £150	£150-£250	£250-£350	£350-£450	Over £450
Married couple	%	10	6	8	11	64
Cohabiting couple	%	15	11	12	12	51
Lone mother	%	46	21	12	8	12
Single	%	58	21	8	5	8
Divorced	%	35	20	20	7	18
Separated	%	39	23	10	16	12
Lone father	%	34	7	13	18	29
All lone parents	%	45	19	12	9	14

Adapted from *Living in Britain*, 2002 (General Household Survey, 2000)

questions

1 Why are the lone mothers in Items A and B untypical?

2 Outline the key points revealed by Item C.

Choice Very few women give lone parenthood as their first option. In other words, the vast majority would prefer to raise their children with a partner. For example, in one study only one out of 44 lone mothers had deliberately decided to become a lone mother from the outset (Berthoud et al., 1999).

However, this does not rule out choice. Many women choose to end a marriage or cohabitation. They see this decision as a solution to a problem. It ends a relationship which is unhappy, which may be violent and abusive, and destructive for themselves and their children (Bernardes, 1997). In this sense, they are choosing to become a lone parent.

Similarly, many non-cohabiting never-married mothers choose lone parenthood from the options available to them. These options are:

- An abortion
- Give the baby up for adoption
- In some cases, the opportunity to cohabit with or marry the father.

Many women decide against these options and choose lone parenthood. To some extent, this choice reflects changing attitudes.

Changing attitudes As outlined in the previous unit, there is greater tolerance of births outside marriage (see page 59). The stigma attached to children of unmarried mothers has reduced considerably. The term 'bastard' is rarely heard, and the less offensive 'illegitimate', which implies improper or immoral, is passing out of common usage.

There is far less pressure for single mothers to get married. The term 'shotgun wedding', frequently used in the 1950s and 60s, is not often heard today.

Lone-parent families are becoming increasingly acceptable. They are less likely to be described with negative phrases such as 'broken families' and 'incomplete families'.

Changing attitudes towards lone parenthood reflect a growing acceptance of the diversity of family life. This makes lone parenthood a more likely choice.

However, it is important not to exaggerate changing attitudes. As the following quotation shows, lone parents and their children are often still seen as second-class families. 'I think single parents have a lot to prove because we're constantly being told that we're not a correct family; that we can't look after our children the same as a two-parent family' (quoted in Beresford et al., 1999).

Economic independence Lone parenthood is only possible if individuals are able to support themselves and their children. However, for the majority, economic independence from a partner means barely making ends meet.

Most lone-mother families live in poverty – defined as living below 50% of average income after housing costs have been met. Often, the low pay levels of many 'women's jobs' plus the costs of childcare mean that lone mothers are better off on state benefit than in paid employment. However, there is some evidence that government New Deal schemes are helping some lone parents and their children out of poverty (see page 44).

Views of lone parenthood

The parents' views As noted earlier, becoming a lone parent was not usually the lone mother's or father's first choice option. The vast majority would rather raise their children with a partner in a happy relationship. Failing this, most choose to become lone parents. Many decide to separate from their partners, believing that it is better to become a lone parent rather than endure an unhappy and destructive relationship. Many decide to keep their child and raise it themselves, seeing this as preferable to abortion, to adoption, or to cohabiting with or marrying the child's other parent.

And, although being a lone parent is far from easy, many see benefits. In the words of one lone mother, 'I'm a bloody sight better off than many women who are married and have to run around after the husband as well as the kids' (Sharpe, 1984).

New Right views These views are outlined on pages 38-40. To recap, lone-parent families fail to provide adequate socialisation. In lone-mother families, there is no father present to discipline the children and provide a male role model. This can lead to underachievement at school, and anti-social behaviour ranging from rudeness to crime. Boys grow up with little awareness of the traditional responsibilities and duties of a father. Lone mothers become dependent on state benefits. Their children lack examples of the disciplines and responsibilities of paid employment.

As noted earlier, if the children of lone parents do have more problems, this may have little to do with lone parenthood as such. It may well result from the poverty that most lone parents experience (Allan & Crow, 2001).

Feminist views Lone parenthood usually means lone mothers. From a feminist viewpoint, this indicates that women have the freedom to choose. Rather than seeing the lone-parent family as a malfunctioning unit, some see it as an alternative family form in which women are free from male domination. And there is evidence that many single mothers welcome this independence and the opportunity it provides to take control of their own lives (Graham, 1987).

5.4 Reconstituted families

Many lone parents find new partners and form new families. These *reconstituted families* or *stepfamilies* are defined as a married or cohabiting couple with dependent children, at least one of whom is not the biological offspring of both partners (Haskey, 1994).

Compared to lone-parent families, there has been little research, public debate or government policy directed towards reconstituted families. This may be because such families tend to present themselves as 'normal' family groupings. And it may be because they are sometimes seen as a 'solution' to the so-called 'problem' of lone parenthood (Allan & Crow, 2001).

There has been a rapid increase in the number of reconstituted families. In 1998-99, they accounted for around 6% of all families with dependent children in Britain. According to one estimate, by 2010 they will outnumber families with two birth parents (Bedell, 2002).

Diversity and reconstituted families

Reconstituted families are a diverse group. Parentline Plus, formerly the National Stepfamily Association, has identified 72 different ways in which stepfamilies can be formed. For example, some are formed by first marriage, some by remarriage, some by cohabitation. And once formed, this diversity continues. For example, some children may have close and regular relationships with their absent biological parent, other children may hardly see them.

Children are likely to stay with their mother after the break-up of a partnership. This can be seen from Table 5 – nearly 9 out of 10 stepfamilies contain at least one child from the female partner's previous relationship.

Tensions within reconstituted families

Reconstituted families tend to present themselves as 'normal', 'ordinary' families. And, if estimates are correct,

Table 5 Stepfamilies

Type of stepfamily	Great Britain: 2000
	%
Couple with child(ren) from the woman's previous marriage/cohabitation	88
Couple with child(ren) from the man's previous marriage/cohabitation	9
Couple with child(ren) from both partners' previous marriage/cohabitation	3

Adapted from *Living in Britain*, 2002

they may well become 'the norm'. Many reject labels such as stepfamilies, step-parents and stepchildren. Despite this desire to present themselves simply as a family, reconstituted families experience particular problems.

Families are social groups with boundaries. These boundaries include some people (these are my family members) and exclude others (these are not). Clear boundaries give families a definite sense of identity and unity. Sometimes the boundaries of reconstituted families are not clearly drawn. They may become fuzzy when partners from the couple's previous relationships become involved in the new family, especially if the children

*activity*29 *the 'new extended families'*

questions

Reconstituted families have been described as the new extended families.

a) What does this mean?
b) What advantages does it suggest?

maintain a close relationship with the non-residential 'natural' parent. This may weaken the boundaries of the reconstituted family and threaten its unity (Allan & Crow, 2001).

Being a step-parent can be a difficult and delicate relationship. There are no clearly stated norms defining this role. For example, to what degree should a step-parent be involved in disciplining the child? Things are made more difficult if the child resents sharing their biological parent with a new partner and, in some cases, with other children. The role of the stepfather is often shifting and uncertain – a sort of uncle, father, big brother, friend or companion depending on the time and place (Bedell, 2002).

The additional strains of reconstituted families may help to explain their high level of breakup. A quarter of stepfamilies break up during their first year. And half of all remarriages which form a stepfamily end in divorce. But, as Peter Eldrid of Parentline Plus warns, 'It's important not to assume that every difficulty you face is to do with being a stepfamily. All families have upheavals' (quoted in Bedell, 2002). And, as reconstituted families become increasingly common, norms will probably develop to clarify the roles of those involved, so reducing the tension that lack of clarity brings.

New opportunities

Research has tended to focus on the problems of reconstituted families. There is another side to the coin. For the adults, they offer the chance of a successful partnership after an earlier one has failed. And, if the parents are happy and committed to making the new family work, then the children are likely to be happy too (Bedell, 2002).

Reconstituted families can provide new and rewarding relationships for all concerned. The family expands overnight with step-brothers and sisters, step-cousins, step-parents and uncles, and step-grandparents. An expanded family network can lead to arguments, jealousy and conflict. But, it can also lead to a wider support network and enriched relationships.

key term

Family of choice A family whose members have been chosen, rather than given by birth and marriage.

5.5 Gay and lesbian families

Until recently, there was little research on gay and lesbian families. This began to change in the 1990s.

Families of choice Judging from a series of in-depth interviews conducted in the mid-1990s, many gays and lesbians are developing new ways of understanding the idea of family (Weeks et al., 1999a). Many believe they are *choosing* their own family members and creating their own families.

These *families of choice* are based on partnerships, close friends and members of their family of origin. This network provides mutual support, loving relationships and a sense of identity. It feels like a family. As one interviewee put it, 'I think the friendships I have are family' (Weeks et al., 1999b).

Same-sex partnerships In recent years, increasing numbers of gays and lesbians have formed households based on same-sex partnerships. And many are demanding the same rights as heterosexual partnerships – for example, the right to marry and adopt children. This does not mean they wish to copy heterosexual relationships, they simply want the same rights as everybody else.

In practice, same-sex partnerships tend to be more democratic than heterosexual partnerships. Many gay and lesbian couples strive for a relationship based on negotiation and equality (Weeks et al., 1999a).

Same-sex parents A growing number of lesbians are choosing to have children and to raise them with a female partner. Many use artificial insemination with sperm donated by friends or anonymous donors. In the traditional sense of the word, they are choosing to have a 'family'.

Gay men have more limited options. Either they must find a surrogate mother to bear their children, or else adopt. In the UK, the adoption route was closed until 2002 when an Act of Parliament made it legal for gays and lesbians to adopt children.

Children Concerns about children's gender identity and sexual orientation have been the main focus of research on gay and lesbian parenting. Most studies show that children raised by gay and lesbian parents are no different from those raised by heterosexuals (Fitzgerald, 1999). The evidence suggests that what matters is the parent-child relationship rather than the sexual orientation of the parents.

5.6 Families and cultural diversity

This section looks at the effects of social class and ethnicity on family life.

Social class and family diversity

Many sociologists argue that social class has an important influence on family life. They make the following points.

Income inequality In general, the lower a person's class position, the lower their income. Income inequality leads to variations in living standards, housing quality and lifestyles. For example, low-income families are more likely to live in overcrowded and substandard housing, and less likely to own a car or afford a family holiday.

Life chances These refer to a person's chances of obtaining things defined as desirable – eg, good health – and avoiding things defined as undesirable – eg, unemployment. Often, there is a fairly close relationship between social class and life chances. For example, the higher the class position of a child's parents, the more likely the child is to attain high educational qualifications and a well paid, high status job.

activity30 families of choice

Item A A 'legal' family

Noah and Mackenlie pose with their parents, Hazel, left and Donna, right. Hazel is the biological parent of Noah, and Donna is the biological parent of Mackenlie. The two lesbians cross-adopted each other's child to legally form their family.

Item C A neighbour's response

We (a lesbian couple) live together in a stable unit with a child. It sometimes feels like a marriage. But I only have to walk out into the street to know that it's not. There's one neighbour next door that just won't speak to us. She spoke to us before we had the baby, and now she won't speak to us.

Adapted from Weeks et al., 1999b

Item B Our family

Amanda and her partner Ruth decided to have children – they each had a son. The father is a close friend. He is now seen as part of the family. Amanda writes:

'Our children love having two mummies. They know they are different. They are proud of being special. At this young age, mummies are still hot property, and to have two is twice as nice. They see their dad regularly, and ring him when they want. And having three parents, they get all the extra grandparents, aunties, uncles, and cousins too. All our families have been fantastic. Some of them had their doubts when we first told them that we were having children, but since our boys first came into the world they have been cherished by an extended family that goes beyond a basic biology.

I'm excited about our future. I know things will not always be easy. I know that as our children get older, and learn about sexuality and the pressures of conformity, they will have many questions. They may face prejudice themselves. I hate that thought, but I know that as a family we have the strength to help them deal with it.'

Adapted from The Independent, 4.2.02

question

There's no particular problem with gay or lesbian families – apart from some heterosexuals! Discuss.

Family breakup As noted earlier, the lower the class position of a married couple, the more likely they are to divorce. High divorce rates are related to poverty – to low income and reliance on state benefits (Kiernan & Mueller, 1999).

Ethnicity and family diversity

To some degree, ethnic groups have their own subcultures – norms and values which differ from those of mainstream culture. And to some degree, these subcultures influence family life. This section takes a brief look at ethnic minority groups and family diversity in the UK.

Diversity within ethnic groups There is a danger in talking about 'typical ethnic families'. Often there is as much family diversity within ethnic groups as there is within white society.

And there is a danger of ignoring cultural variation *within* ethnic groups. For example, within the South Asian community there are variations in religion – Sikhs, Muslims and Hindus – in countries of origin – India, Pakistan and Bangladesh – and in regions within those countries – for example, Goa and Bengal.

Finally, there is a danger of exaggerating differences

between ethnic and White families and of creating stereotypes in the process – for example, Asians live in extended families and their marriages are arranged.

Asian families Most Asian households are based on nuclear families. However, around 20% are extended families, a higher proportion than other groups. Although there is a trend towards nuclear families, wider kinship ties remain strong (Westwood & Bhachu, 1988).

Asians are more likely to marry and to marry earlier than their White counterparts. Cohabitation and divorce are rare (Berthoud & Beishon, 1997). Marriages are sometimes arranged, but there is little research on this subject. There is some evidence which suggests that the couple have more say in arranged marriages as Western ideas about love and romance become more influential (Allan & Crow, 2001).

African-Caribbean families In 2000, nearly 50% of African-Caribbean families with dependent children were lone-parent families compared to around 22% for Britain as a whole (Social Trends, 2002). African-Caribbeans have the lowest marriage rate, the highest proportion of single (never-married) lone mothers, and the highest divorce rate (Berthoud et al., 1999).

Statistics such as these have led some researchers to talk about the 'problem' of the 'African-Caribbean family'. However, this ignores the strength of wider kinship networks – in particular, the support provided for lone mothers by female relatives. This support can cross national boundaries with family members in the UK and West Indies providing support for each other (Goulborne, 1999).

Multicultural families Recent statistics suggest an increase in the number of partnerships between people from different ethnic groups. Elisabeth Beck-Gernsheim (2002) uses the term *multicultural families* for families in which the partners come from different ethnic backgrounds. She recognises that such couples may face prejudice from their ethnic groups of origin, and conflict because they bring differing expectations of family life to the relationship.

key terms

Life chances A person's chances of obtaining things defined as desirable and avoiding things defined as undesirable.
Multicultural families Families in which the partners are from different ethnic groups.

However, she is cautiously optimistic about the promise of multicultural families. They may help to break down barriers between ethnic groups. And they reflect a growing opportunity for individual choice – people are now choosing partners who fulfil their personal needs rather than being directed by the concerns of their parents or the norms of their ethnic group.

activity31 *class, ethnicity and family diversity*

Item A *Class differences*

Outside the family home

Outside the family home

Item B *A multicultural couple*

This couple have a business specialising in wedding accessories for multicultural couples

questions

1 With reference to Item A, suggest how class differences might affect family life.

2 Look at Item B.

   a) What problems might this couple experience?

   b) How can an increase in multicultural families be seen as a positive development?

5.7 Family diversity and society

This section examines family diversity in the context of the wider society. It looks at views which see increasing family diversity as a reflection of broader changes in society as a whole.

Giddens and late modernity

According to the British sociologist Anthony Giddens, we live in an era known as *late modernity*. This era is characterised by choice and change. Opportunities to choose an identity and select a lifestyle are increasingly available. In the pre-modern era, tradition defined who people were and what they should do. Today, people have far more freedom to try on different identities and to try out different lifestyles (Giddens, 1991; 1992).

Where does the family fit into late modernity? If Giddens is correct, family diversity is a reflection of the opportunities and priorities of late modernity. People have greater freedom to construct their own domestic arrangements. They are not bound by existing family forms and family roles. There are more choices available and more opportunities to experiment, create and change.

Within limits, people can tailor their partnerships and their families to meet their individual needs and to reflect their own identities. They can choose to cohabit or to marry, to end one partnership and to begin another. The emphasis is on building and constructing family units, on creating and defining family relationships. People build reconstituted families. They enter uncharted territory constructing gay and lesbian families with no clear patterns to work from. They choose to become lone parents rather than accept an unsatisfactory relationship.

According to Giddens (1992), relationships in late modernity are increasingly based on *confluent love* – deep emotional intimacy in which partners reveal their needs and concerns to each other. Commitment to the relationship lasts as long as the individual receives sufficient satisfaction and pleasure from it. Failure to experience this is justification, in itself, for ending the relationship. If Giddens is correct, this helps to explain the fragility of partnerships in late modernity, as seen in the high rates of separation and divorce.

Evaluation Giddens's views of late modernity help to explain the trend towards family diversity. However, he may have exaggerated people's freedom to choose. Take lone-parent families. In one sense they are *not* based on choice – at least not first choice. Most single (never-married) mothers did *not* choose to become pregnant. However, they did choose to have the baby and raise it themselves (Allen & Dowling, 1999). Similarly, divorced lone mothers did not set out to become lone parents. This was a second-best choice after the failure of their marriage.

Even so, there is evidence to support Giddens' claim of increased choice in late modernity. People can choose between marriage and cohabitation, they can choose to remain married or to divorce, they can choose to become a lone parent or to maintain a partnership, they can choose to remain a lone parent or to form a reconstituted family. There is far greater freedom to make these choices than there was 50 years ago.

Postmodernity

Some sociologists believe that the modern age has ended and that we now live in the *postmodern* era. They describe this era as a time of change, of flux, of fluidity and uncertainty. Gone is the consensus or agreement about norms and values which characterised most of the

summary

1. Many sociologists see families and households in today's society as more diverse than ever before.

2. In Britain, nuclear family households have declined as a proportion of all households. The proportion of people living in these households has also declined. Despite this, living in a nuclear family is a phase that most people go through.

3. There is diversity within nuclear families – eg, the couple may be married or cohabiting.

4. In Britain since the early 1970s, lone-parent families have increased from 8% to 22% of all families with dependent children.

5. Lone parents are a diverse group – eg, some were previously married, some cohabiting, some neither.

6. Although very few women choose lone parenthood as their first option, choices are involved – eg, whether to keep, abort, or give the baby up for adoption.

7. Lone parenthood has become increasingly acceptable.

8. There has been a rapid increase in reconstituted families. They are a diverse group – eg, some are formed by cohabitation, some by first marriage, others by remarriage.

9. There are particular tensions in reconstituted families, partly because the roles of family members often lack clear definition.

10. Reconstituted families offer new opportunities – they can lead to a wider support network and enriched relationships.

11. Gay and lesbian parents are adding further diversity to family life.

12. Most studies show that children raised by gay and lesbian parents are no different to those raised by heterosexuals.

13. Social class and ethnic differences add yet further diversity to family life.

14. According to Anthony Giddens, family diversity results from broader changes in late-modern society. In particular, family diversity reflects the growing freedom to choose identities and select lifestyles.

15. According to Judith Stacey, family diversity reflects the lack of consensus, the uncertainty and the fluidity of postmodern society.

modern age.

The American sociologist Judith Stacey (1996) sees family diversity as a reflection of postmodern society. There is no one family form to which everyone aspires. There are no generally agreed norms and values directing family life. In her words, 'Like postmodern culture, contemporary family arrangements are diverse, fluid and unresolved'.

Stacey welcomes this diversity, seeing it as an opportunity for people to develop family forms which suit their particular needs and situations. She looks forward to the possibility of more equal and democratic relationships which she sees in many gay and lesbian families.

Evaluation Stacey's research was conducted in Silicon Valley in California, home to many of the world's most advanced electronics companies. This is hardly typical of

American society in general. She also studied research findings on gay and lesbian families. Again, these groups are hardly typical. Despite this, Stacey may well have identified those at the forefront of a trend which is spreading to the wider society.

key terms

Late modernity The term used by Giddens to describe the contemporary period, which is characterised by choice and change.

Postmodernity The era after modernity which is characterised by fluidity, uncertainty and a lack of consensus.

Confluent love Deep emotional intimacy which individuals expect from their partnerships.

activity32 *choice and creativity*

Item A Lesbian families

'With no script to follow, we are making up our own story and hoping that we'll live happily ever after.'

Amanda Boulter referring to her lesbian partner and their two boys. Quoted in *The Independent*, 4.2.2002.

'I don't necessarily think we should be wanting to mimic everything, kind of anything that heterosexual couples or heterosexual relationships have. I don't see that we need to be mimicking them. I think it's about having choice and about being able to be creative and decide what we want for ourselves.'

From Weeks et al., 1999a

questions

1 How does Item A reflect Giddens' picture of late modernity?

2 Look at Item B. To what extent are reconstituted families based on choice?

Item B Reconstituted families

Unit 6 *Gender, power and domestic labour*

keyissues

1 To what extent is the division of domestic labour linked to gender?

2 To what extent is this division unequal?

3 What does this indicate about the distribution of power?

4 What changes have taken place in these areas?

6.1 Introduction

This unit looks at *domestic labour* – work conducted by people as members of a household. It looks, for example, at housework and childcare and asks who does what.

Most of the research in this area focuses on the contribution of husband and wife to domestic tasks. It asks four main questions.

● First, to what extent is the division of domestic labour

based on gender? For example, are certain household tasks done by men and others by women?

- Second, is the division of domestic labour equal – do partners pull their own weight, is the division of labour fair?
- Third, what does this indicate about the distribution of

power within the family? Is power shared equally between husband and wife or do men dominate the domestic scene?

- Fourth, what changes have taken place in these areas? For example, is there a move towards a more equal distribution of power?

activity33 gender and domestic labour

Item A Gender divisions

Great Britain	Allocation of tasks					
	1983			1991		
	Mainly man	Mainly woman	Shared equally	Mainly man	Mainly woman	Shared equally
Household shopping	5	51	44	8	45	47
Makes evening meal	5	77	17	9	70	20
Does evening dishes	17	40	40	28	33	37
Does household cleaning	3	72	24	4	68	27
Does washing and ironing	1	89	10	3	84	12
Repairs household equipment	82	6	10	82	6	10
Organises household money and bills	29	39	32	31	40	28
Looks after sick children	1	63	35	1	60	39
Teaches children discipline	10	12	77	9	17	73

Adapted from *Social Trends*, 1995

Item B Lagged adaptation

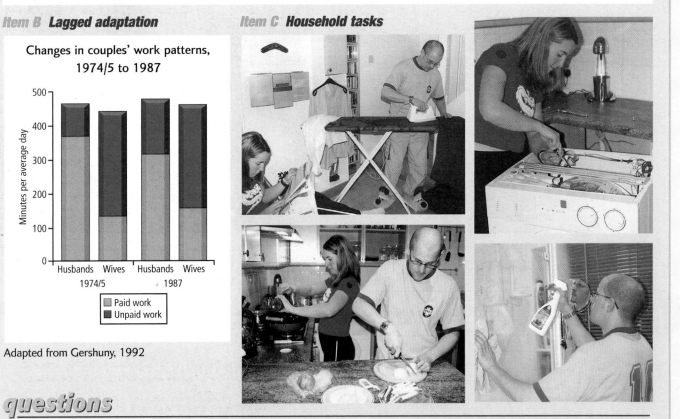

Changes in couples' work patterns, 1974/5 to 1987

Minutes per average day

- ☐ Paid work
- ■ Unpaid work

Adapted from Gershuny, 1992

Item C Household tasks

questions

1 Look at Item A.
   a) To what extent are tasks allocated on the basis of gender?
   b) To what extent has this changed from 1983 to 1991?

2 a) Summarise the changes shown in Item B.
   b) Suggest a reason for these changes.

3 Look at Item C. Judging from Item A, which of these pictures are untypical?

6.2 Gender and the domestic division of labour

In 1973, Michael Young and Peter Willmott announced the arrival of the *symmetrical family* (see page 51). They claimed that *conjugal roles*, the roles of husband and wife, were becoming increasingly similar. In the home, the couple 'shared their work; they shared their time'. Husbands increasingly helped with domestic chores such as washing up and cleaning. They also helped more with raising children, though this still remained the main responsibility of the wife. Decisions about family life were largely shared. It appeared that the division of labour based on gender was breaking down.

In 1974, Ann Oakley dismissed this view of the sharing caring husband. Young and Willmott had claimed that 72% of husbands 'help in the house'. To be included in this figure, husbands only had to perform one household chore a week. In Oakley's words, this is hardly convincing evidence of 'male domestication' (Oakley, 1974). Oakley's own research conducted in the early 1970s shows a clear division of labour along gender lines. Based on interviews with 40 women with one or more children under 5, it shows clearly that wives saw housework and childcare as their responsibility and received little help from their husbands.

Since these early studies, there has been considerable research on gender and the division of domestic labour. This research shows that most women:

- still become mothers and housewives
- experience a period of full-time housework, though this is becoming shorter
- return to work part time when their youngest child is at school.

This early period of full-time housework sets the pattern for the future, as the following findings indicate.

- Housework and childcare remain the primary responsibility of women.
- As women enter the labour market in increasing numbers, there is some evidence of men making a greater contribution to domestic tasks.
- However, this increased contribution is not significant. As a result, most working wives have a *dual burden* or a *dual shift* – paid employment and domestic labour (Allan & Crow, 2001).

The findings summarised above are taken from small-scale studies often based on interviews, and large-scale surveys usually based on questionnaires. For example, Fiona Devine's small-scale study of car workers' families in Luton indicated that men's contribution to domestic labour increased when their wives re-entered paid employment. But the man's role is secondary – 'Above all women remain responsible for childcare and housework and their husbands help them' (Devine, 1992). This picture is reflected in large-scale surveys such as the British Social Attitudes Survey and the British Household Panel Survey. These surveys show a clear gender division of labour in most household tasks. However, they do indicate a slight trend towards sharing tasks as shown in Activity 33.

Further evidence of a trend towards greater equality in the domestic division of labour is provided by Jonathan Gershuny's (1992) analysis of data from 1974/5 to 1987. It shows a gradual increase in the amount of domestic labour performed by men. This increase is greatest when wives are in full-time employment. From 1974/5 to 1987, husbands whose wives worked full time doubled the amount of time they spent cooking and cleaning.

Gershuny concludes that though women still bear the main burden of domestic labour, there is a gradual trend towards greater equality. He suggests there is a process of *lagged adaptation* – a time lag between women taking up paid employment and men making a greater contribution to domestic labour. At this rate, he reckons it may take a generation or more before men 'catch up' and make an equal contribution.

Gender and domestic tasks – evaluation

Much of the research into gender divisions of domestic labour is based on *time-use studies*. This research asks who does what and how long does it take them. There are problems with this method.

Time Women tend to underestimate time spent on domestic labour. This often happens when several tasks are performed at the same time. For example, women often combine childcare with tasks such as cleaning and preparing meals. As a result, they underestimate the amount of time spent on childcare (Leonard, 2000).

Men tend to overestimate time spent on domestic labour. For example, in one study, men estimated they spent an average of 11.3 hours a week on childcare. However, their diary entries showed only 1.7 hours a week (Pleck, 1985).

Urgency Time-use studies say little about the urgency of tasks. Women's domestic tasks, such as cooking and washing clothes, are more urgent than typical male tasks such as gardening and household maintenance (McMahon, 1999).

Responsibility vs help There is a big difference between being responsible for a task and helping with a task. For example, being responsible for cooking and cleaning is not the same as helping with those tasks. Being responsible

key terms

Conjugal roles Marital roles, the roles of husband and wife.
Symmetrical family A family in which the roles of husband and wife are similar.
Dual burden/dual shift The double burden/shift of paid employment and domestic labour.
Lagged adaptation A time lag between women taking up paid employment and men adapting to this by increasing their contribution to domestic labour.
Time-use studies Studies which examine how people use their time – how long they spend on various activities.

requires more thought and effort, it can be more tiring and more stressful (McMahon, 1999). Again, this aspect of gender divisions and domestic tasks is not revealed by time-use studies.

Job satisfaction Time-use studies tell us little about the amount of satisfaction women and men derive from domestic labour. Typical female tasks are often experienced as tedious, boring and monotonous. Typical male tasks are more likely to be experienced as interesting and creative. For example, some men regard DIY and gardening as hobbies rather than chores (Allan, 1985).

6.3 Gender and the division of emotion work

So far domestic labour has been defined as household tasks such as ironing and cooking, and time spent looking after children. Little has been said about the emotional side of domestic labour. Partnerships and families are kept together as much if not more by *emotion work* than by the more practical household tasks. Emotion work refers to the love, sympathy, understanding, praise, reassurance and attention which are involved in maintaining relationships.

According to many women, it is they rather than their male partners who are responsible for most of the emotion work. In other words, emotion work is gendered. A study conducted by Jean Duncombe and Dennis Marsden (1993, 1995) based on interviews with 40 couples found that most women complained of men's 'emotional distance'. They felt they were the ones who provided reassurance, tenderness and sympathy, while their partners had problems expressing intimate emotions. Men showed little awareness or understanding of their 'shortcomings', seeing their main role as a breadwinner – providing money rather than emotional support.

These findings are reflected in other studies. For example, research into family meals shows that women give priority to their partner's and children's tastes, often at the expense of their own. They do their best to make mealtime a happy family occasion (Charles & Kerr, 1988).

According to Duncombe and Marsden (1995), many women have to cope with a *triple shift* – 1) paid work 2) housework and childcare and 3) emotion work.

key terms

Emotion work The emotional support which members of a social group – in this case the family – provide for each other.
Triple shift The three areas of responsibility which many women have – 1) paid work, 2) housework and childcare, 3) emotion work.

6.4 Family finances

So far, this unit has outlined evidence which indicates that domestic tasks, childcare, and emotion work are divided

activity34 emotion work

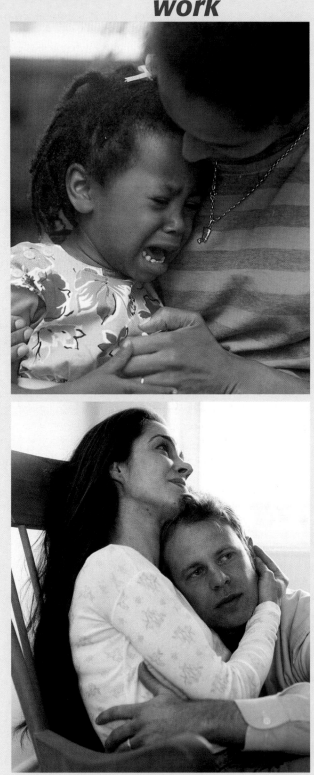

questions

1 How do the pictures illustrate emotion work?

2 Why do you think women are primarily responsible for emotion work in the family?

along gender lines. This section looks at money management within families. It reaches a similar conclusion – access to and control over money are gendered. And this division of labour along gender lines tends to favour men.

Systems of money management Jan Pahl's *Money and Marriage* (1989) identified various systems of money management used by the 102 couples in her study. They ranged from a *housekeeping allowance system* whereby the husbands give their wives a fixed sum of money for housekeeping expenses and control the remaining money, to a *pooling system* where both partners see themselves as equally responsible for and jointly controlling money management. A later study by Carolyn Vogler and Jan Pahl (1994), based on interviews with over 1200 British couples, showed that whatever money management system was used, men tended to come out on top.

Inequalities in money management Vogler and Pahl report the following results. When asked who gets most personal spending money, 58% of couples said it was equally distributed, 12% said the husband, 4% the wife, and the rest disagreed amongst themselves. When asked who suffers cutbacks when money is tight, it was wives who reported most hardship. They were more likely to cut back on their own food and clothing, and shield their children and husband from hard times. And when asked who has the final say in important financial decisions, 70% say both, 23% the husband and 7% the wife.

Trends Vogler and Pahl see a trend towards greater equality in access to and control of family finances. They argue that greater equality depends in part on women's full-time participation in the labour market. There is a large body of research which indicates that the partner with the largest income has the biggest say in family decision-making.

6.5 Domestic labour, power and gender

Are families *patriarchal* or male dominated? Are women exploited by their male partners? Do men get the best deal in the home? Do they get their own way in domestic situations?

Are these questions still relevant today? Aren't partnerships rapidly moving towards equality? Haven't many already reached the stage where the domestic division of labour is equal?

These questions are about *power*. This section looks at various ways of defining and measuring power and applies them to family life.

Decision making

The decision-making model measures power in terms of who makes the decisions. For example, if wives made most of the decisions concerning the home then, in this context, they would have most power. However, this fails to take account of the importance of the decisions. For example, the wife may make more decisions but those decisions are

minor and trivial. The really important decisions are made by her husband.

The following study uses the decision-making approach and takes the importance of decisions into account. Stephen Edgell (1980) interviewed 38 middle-class couples. He asked them who made the decisions and how important those decisions were. Wives dominated decision making in three areas – interior decoration, children's clothes, and spending on food and other household items. These decisions were frequent and seen as not very important. Men had the main say when it came to moving house, buying a car and other major financial decisions. These decisions were infrequent and seen as important. Other decisions, such as holidays and children's education were made by both husband and wife (see Item A, Activity 35).

Based on decision making and the importance of the areas of decision, it appears that husbands have more power then their wives.

Evaluation This study is over 20 years old and is based on a small, unrepresentative sample – 38 middle-class couples. It uses the decision-making approach. There are a number of problems with this approach. For example, it ignores agenda-setting – which issues should be placed on the agenda to be decided upon. The person who sets the agenda may use this power to their own advantage.

Non-decisions

The decision-making approach fails to take account of non-decisions. Many actions do not involve conscious decisions – as such, they can be seen as 'non-decisions'. They are based on taken-for-granted assumptions – for example, women should take primary responsibility for childcare. Often there is little or no discussion because those involved are simply following social norms which are largely unquestioned.

In terms of domestic labour, there are a number of non-decisions. The following are traditionally seen as women's work.

● Washing, cleaning, ironing
● Childcare
● Emotion work.

It is often taken for granted that the man's job is more important than his partner's, since she will probably give up paid employment when the couple have children.

Who benefits? Those who gain from non-decisions can be seen as more powerful than those who don't. Take the assumption that men's jobs are more important than their female partner's jobs. This assumption lies behind the following behaviour of newly-wed couples.

● Around 1/3 of men changed jobs at or near their wedding. Typically, this change advanced their careers.
● Over 2/3 of women changed jobs at or near their wedding. Typically, this resulted in lower pay and lower job status (Mansfield & Collard, 1988).

Judging by this study, men gain and women lose from the taken-for-granted assumption that men's jobs should take priority over women's jobs. In terms of the consequences of this non-decision, men have more power than women.

At some time in their lives, most women are full-time mothers and housewives. Who benefits from following these traditional social roles? According to many feminist writers, men are the beneficiaries. First, they gain from avoiding the negative aspects of these roles. Second, they directly benefit from much of their partner's domestic labour.

Full-time domestic labour means that the wife is economically dependent on the male breadwinner. This reduces her power in the household. There is a tendency to see housework as low status, as different from 'real' work (Oakley, 1974). Typical women's jobs – washing, ironing and cleaning – are often experienced as boring, monotonous and unfulfilling. And these are the very jobs which directly benefit their partner, providing him with clean clothes and a clean home. Similarly, women's responsibility for emotion work can be seen as an example of 'he gains, she loses'.

activity35 gender, power and domestic labour

Item A Making decisions

Decision area	Perceived importance	Frequency	Decision maker
Moving	Very important	Infrequent	Husband
Finance	Very important	Infrequent	Husband
Car	Important	Infrequent	Husband
House	Very important	Infrequent	Husband and wife
Children's education	Very important	Infrequent	Husband and wife
Holidays	Important	Infrequent	Husband and wife
Weekends	Not important	Frequent	Husband and wife
Other leisure activities	Not important	Frequent	Husband and wife
Furniture	Not important	Infrequent	Husband and wife
Interior decorations	Not important	Infrequent	Wife
Food and other domestic spending	Not important	Frequent	Wife
Children's clothes	Not important	Frequent	Wife

Adapted from Edgell, 1980

Item B Satisfaction

Many women appear to be satisfied with the domestic division of labour. They recognise that they do most of the work, but only 14% said they were dissatisfied with their partner's contribution.

Adapted from Baxter & Western, 1998

Item C Choice

In recent years, there has been a string of newspaper articles about successful and powerful career women who gave up highly-paid jobs in order to take care of their children. They include:

- Lisa Gordon, corporate affairs director of Chrysalis Records who earned £336,000 a year.
- Penny Hughes, formerly in charge of Coca-Cola UK, who gave up £250,000 a year.
- Tina Gaudoin, former editor of the glossy women's magazine Frank.

Adapted from Weale, 2002

Item D The triple shift

questions

1 Judging from Item A, who has most power – husbands or wives? Give reasons for your answer.

2 a) Use Items B, C and D to argue that men have more power than women.

   b) Using the same information, criticise this view.

Allocating housework and emotion work to women is often based on a non-decision – it is 'normal' and 'natural' for women to perform such tasks therefore there is no decision to make. In terms of this view of power, men gain at the expense of women therefore men have more power than women.

Evaluation Choosing winners and losers is based on judgements. What's wrong with being a housewife and a mother? Housework might be boring and monotonous but so are many jobs outside the home. Today, many women have the freedom to choose between a career and becoming a full-time mother and housewife. This is hardly a non-decision. And many women who give up paid employment feel they've gained from the decision (see Activity 33).

There is, however, plenty of evidence to support the view that in general men gain and women lose. Take the triple shift – women combining paid work, domestic labour and emotion work. The clear winner here is the man.

Shaping desires

Power can be seen as the ability to shape the wishes and desires of others in order to further one's own interests. In this way, a dominant group can persuade others to accept, or actually desire, their subordinate position. In terms of this argument, men have power over women because many women accept and even desire their traditional roles as mothers and housewives, and accept their subordinate status. For example, women often put their partners and children's preferences first when shopping for food. And they usually put 'the family' first when spending on clothes and entertainment (Charles, 1990).

Women get satisfaction from self-sacrifice. Her loved ones gain pleasure from her actions. This confirms her identity as a good mother and wife (Allan & Crow, 2001). The fact that she wants to serve and sacrifice can be seen as an indication of male power.

Evaluation This view of power is based on the assumption that it is not in women's interests to accept or desire their traditional roles as housewife and mother. Any pleasure they experience from their 'subordination' is 'false pleasure' because it disguises their exploitation and makes it more bearable.

But who is to say that women in the family are exploited and oppressed? As noted earlier, it's a matter of weighing the evidence and making a judgement.

Power and same-sex households

So far, this section has looked at the distribution of power in heterosexual families – families in which the partners are male and female. The focus now moves to power in same-sex families where both partners are either male or female.

Equality as an ideal Most studies of gay and lesbian partnerships are based on interviews. Bearing in mind that people don't always do what they say, this is what the interviews reveal. Same-sex couples emphasise equality

and strive to remove power differences from their relationship. They see issues like the division of domestic labour as a matter for discussion and negotiation. They feel that being lesbian or gay offers more opportunities for equality. As one woman put it, 'It's much easier to have equal relations if you're the same sex' (Weeks et al., 1999a).

Women focus on alternatives to the unequal division of domestic labour which they see in heterosexual relationships. Men focus on alternatives to the macho male and the passive female which they see in heterosexual relationships. In both cases the emphasis is on equality (Weeks et al., 1992a).

summary

1. The division of domestic labour is gendered – household tasks are divided along gender lines.

2. Housework and childcare remain the primary responsibility of women.

3. There is evidence of a gradual increase in men's contribution to domestic labour, especially where their partners are in full-time employment.

4. There are problems with time-use studies of domestic labour. For example, women tend to underestimate and men to overestimate time spent on household tasks.

5. Emotion work is mainly performed by women. As a result, many women have a triple shift – 1) paid work, 2) housework and childcare, 3) emotion work.

6. Research into money management within families indicates that control over money is gendered – men tend to have greater control.

7. There is evidence of a trend to greater equality in access to and control of family finances, especially where women are in full-time employment.

8. Research indicates that power is unequally distributed in families, with male partners having the largest share.

9. Decision-making studies indicate that in general husbands have more power than their wives.

10. Non-decisions – issues that do not reach the point of decision-making – tend to favour men. They are likely to gain at the expense of their partners.

11. There is a tendency for many women to accept their subordinate position. From this, it can be argued that men have power over women.

12. Studies of lesbian and gay households suggest that there is a more equal division of domestic labour between partners.

Lesbian households A study of 37 cohabiting lesbian couples by Gillian Dunne (1997) indicates how far these ideals are translated into reality. Some of the couples have children, and in most cases childcare was shared. Similarly, time spent on housework tended to be shared equally. However, when one partner was in full-time employment, she did less housework than her partner in part-time work.

Explanations Why are same-sex relationships more equal than heterosexual relationships? Gillian Dunne (1997) suggests the following reasons.

- Gender inequalities in the labour market shape gender inequalities in partnerships. Men generally have jobs with higher status and pay than their partners and this tends to shape their relationships at home.
- Gay and lesbian partnerships are free from the social norms and conventions which surround and direct heterosexual relationships. They are not weighed down by this cultural baggage. As a result, they have more freedom to construct 'families of choice' (see pages 73-74).

activity36 *same-sex relationships*

Item A *Talking about relationships*

'Everything has to be discussed, everything is negotiable.'

'There are no assumptions about how you will relate, what you will do, who does what.'

Lesbian women quoted in Weeks et al., 1999a

question

With some reference to Items A and B, suggest why the domestic division of labour in lesbian families may be more equal than in heterosexual families.

Item B *Partners and mothers*

Lesbian couple sharing childcare

Unit 7 *Childhood and children*

keyissues

1 How have views of childhood changed?
2 How have children been affected by these changes?

The social construction of childhood

Childhood can be seen as a *social construction*. From this point of view, it is not a natural state or a biological stage. Instead, it is shaped and given meaning by culture and society. As a result, the idea of childhood, the types of behaviour considered appropriate for children, the way children should be treated, and the length of time that childhood should last, are socially constructed.

Cross-cultural evidence Evidence from different cultures provides support for the view that childhood is a social construction. If childhood were simply a 'natural' state, then it would be similar across all cultures. This is not the case.

Anthropological studies show that other cultures treat children in ways which might seem unusual or even unnatural in contemporary Britain. Raymond Firth (1963), in his study of the Pacific island of Tikopia, found that children carried out dangerous tasks such as using sharp tools and fishing in the open sea. They were allowed to carry out these tasks when they themselves felt ready rather than when adults decided they were competent or safe to do so.

A brief history of childhood

In *Centuries of Childhood* (1962), the French historian Philippe Ariès argued that the concept of childhood did not exist in medieval Europe. He based his argument on contemporary letters, diaries and other documents, plus the way children were depicted in paintings of the time. Ariès claimed that soon after children were weaned, they were regarded as little adults and treated as such. From an early age, they worked alongside adults in the fields or in cottage industries, they dressed like adults and in many ways behaved like adults.

The emergence of modern childhood Ariès sees the modern concept of childhood developing from the separation of children from the world of adults. This process began in the 16th century when the upper classes sent their children to schools to be educated. In the early years of the industrial revolution, child labour was widespread – children and adults worked side by side. Throughout the 19th century, a series of factory acts banned the employment of children in mines and factories. By the end of the 19th century, elementary state education was compulsory in most European countries. Children were now physically separated from adult settings and had

a separate legal status.

This process was accompanied by the development of experts specialising in children – child psychologists, paediatricians (doctors who specialise in children), educationalists and parenting experts. According to Ariès, 'Our world is obsessed by the physical, moral and sexual problems of childhood'. Children are seen as different from adults. As a result, they have special needs. Because of this they require treatment, training and guidance from an army of specially trained adults. This is very different from the Middle Ages when 'the child became the natural companion of the adult'.

Evaluation Ariès has been criticised for overstating his case. In certain respects, children in medieval Europe were seen

activity37 childhood across cultures

Item A **Child soldier**

A member of a local militia in Zaire

Item B **Blackfoot boys**

The Blackfoot Indians lived on the Plains of Western Canada. Children were taught the skills of horse riding at an early age. One of Long Lance's earliest recollections was falling off a horse. He was picked up by his eldest brother and planted firmly on the horse's back. His brother said, 'Now, you stay there! You are four years old, and if you cannot ride a horse, we will put girls' clothing on you and let you grow up a woman.'

Fathers were responsible for the physical training of the Blackfoot boys. They wanted to harden their bodies and make them brave and strong. Fathers used to whip their sons each morning with fir branches. Far from disliking this treatment, the youngsters proudly displayed the welts produced by whipping. Sometimes they were whipped in public and they competed to see who could stand the most pain.

Adapted from Long Lance, 1956

question

How do Items A and B indicate that childhood is socially constructed?

activity38 little adults

Item A Medieval Europe

In medieval society the idea of childhood did not exist. This is not to suggest that children were neglected, forsaken or despised. The idea of childhood is not to be confused with affection for children: it corresponds to an awareness of the particular nature of childhood, that particular nature which distinguishes the child from the adult, even the young adult. In medieval society, this awareness was lacking. That is why, as soon as the child could live without the constant solicitude (care) of his mother, his nanny or his cradle-rocker, he belonged to adult society.

Adapted from Ariès, 1962

Item B Paintings

Family saying grace before a meal (1585)

question

What evidence do the paintings in Item B provide to support Ariès' statement in Item A?

Group of doctors (right) and men, women and children (left), 15th century

---

as different from adults. For example, there were laws prohibiting the marriage of children under 12 (Bukatko & Daehler, 2001). However, many historians agree with the broad outline of Ariès's history of childhood in Western Europe.

key term

Social construction Something that is created by society, constructed from social meanings and definitions.

Images of childhood

Wendy Stainton Rogers (2001) looks at the social construction of childhood in 20th century Europe. She identifies two 'images' of childhood – 'the innocent and wholesome child' and 'the wicked and sinful child'. Both images coexist – they exist together. Both have a long history and continue to the present day. They can be seen

in a variety of forms – for example, in novels such as Arthur Ransome's *Swallows and Amazons* with its charming and wholesome children and William Golding's *Lord of the Flies* where children descend to their 'natural' savage and barbaric selves.

Each image suggests a particular way of acting towards children. The image of the innocent and wholesome child suggests that children should be protected from everything that is nasty about the adult world, from violence and from the worries and concerns of adults. Childhood should be a happy, joyous and carefree time. By contrast, the idea of an essentially sinful child suggests that children should be restrained, regulated and disciplined.

Both these views of childhood imply that adults should be concerned about children and take responsibility for their upbringing.

The welfare view The first view suggests that children are vulnerable and need protection. This 'welfare view' forms the basis of social policy towards children in the UK today.

For example, the Children Act of 1989 states that 'When a court determines any question with respect to the upbringing of a child … the child's welfare shall be the court's paramount consideration'.

The control view The second view assumes that children are unable to control their anti-social tendencies. As a result, they need regulation and discipline. This 'control view' is reflected in education policy – children must submit to education and the form and content of their education must be strictly controlled from above.

According to Wendy Stainton Rogers, these images of childhood are social constructions. She argues that 'there is no *natural* distinction that marks off children as a certain category of person'. Seeing children as innocent and wholesome or wicked and sinful or a mixture of both is not right or wrong, it is simply a meaning given to childhood at a particular time and place (Stainton Rogers, 2001).

Childhood in an age of uncertainty

Nick Lee (2001) sees a change in the social construction of childhood towards the end of the 20th century. He claims that for most of the century adults and children were seen as 'fundamentally different kinds of humans'. Adults were stable and complete, children were unstable and incomplete. Adults had become, children were becoming. Adults were self-controlling, children were in need of control.

In the early 21st century, 'growing up' is no longer seen as a journey towards personal completion and stability. This is because adulthood is no longer complete and stable. Adult relationships are increasingly unstable as indicated by high divorce rates. The labour market is changing rapidly and 'jobs for life' are a thing of the past. With new partners and new jobs, adults are in a constant state of becoming. They are living in an 'age of uncertainty'.

Where does this leave children? For much of the 20th century, childhood was defined in relation to adulthood. Adults and children were very different. Children had yet to become full human beings. They were not fully rational, they were not seen as 'persons in their own right', they had to be guided along the path to adulthood by child experts and child trainers such as teachers and social workers.

By the 21st century, adults were becoming more like children. Both were in a continual state of becoming, both were defining and redefining their identities, both were unstable and incomplete.

This growing similarity between adults and children is leading to a new social construction of childhood. Children are seen increasingly as 'beings in their own right'. As such, they have their own concerns, their own interests, and should have their own rights, just like adult members of society. This is reflected in the UN Convention on the Rights of the Child (1989). Article 3 states:

'In all actions concerning children, whether undertaken by public or private social welfare institutions, courts of law, administrative authorities or legislative bodies, the best interests of the child shall be a primary consideration.'

Changes in the social construction of childhood result in changes in the way adults treat children. This can be seen from the 1989 Children Act which stated that in court proceedings, 'the child's welfare must be paramount'. In cases of divorce, the court used to decide which parent had custody of the children. Since 1989, the child's view is taken into account – children have a say in decisions about who they will live with. This is a long way from the traditional view that children should be seen and not heard.

The end of childhood?

Will the 21st century see the end of childhood? Will new social constructions end up abolishing the whole idea of childhood?

According to Neil Postman (1983) in *The Disappearance of Childhood*, this process is well underway. Postman argues that childhood is only possible if children can be separated, and therefore protected from, the adult world. In his words, 'Without secrets, of course, there can be no such thing as childhood'. The mass media, and television in particular, have brought the adult world into the lives of children. Secrecy has been wiped out by television. As a result, the boundaries between the worlds of children and adults are breaking down. Postman believes that in the long run, this means the end of childhood.

Dual status Postman has been criticised for overstating his case. Clearly television and the media in general have brought adult priorities and concerns into the lives of children. But childhood is a long way from disappearing. For example, children in late 20th century Western societies have become a major economic force. Their tastes and preferences, not just in toys and games, but also in information and communication technologies such as personal computers and mobile phones, have a major effect on what is produced and purchased (Buckingham, 2000).

According to Nick Lee (2001), childhood has not disappeared, it has become more complex and ambiguous. Children are dependent on their parents, but in another sense they are independent. There is a mass children's market which children influence – they make choices, they decide which products succeed and fail, though at the end of the day, they depend on their parents' purchasing power.

This is one of the ambiguities of childhood in the 21st century. Things are not clearcut. Children are both dependent and independent.

summary

1. Many sociologists see childhood as a social construction rather than a natural state. Ideas about childhood vary between different societies and different times.

2. According to Philippe Ariès,
   - The concept of childhood did not exist in medieval Europe. Children were seen as little adults.
   - Modern ideas of childhood as a separate state began with the onset of formal education and the gradual withdrawal of children from the workplace.

3. Wendy Stainton Rogers identifies two images of childhood in modern Western society – 'the innocent and wholesome child' and 'the wicked and sinful child'. The first image suggests that children are vulnerable and need protection – the welfare view. The second image suggests children need regulation and discipline – the control view.

4. According to Nick Lee, adulthood has become less stable and more uncertain. In these respects, it has become more like childhood. This similarity has led to a change in the social construction of childhood in the 21st century. Children are increasingly seen as having their own rights and interests.

5. Neil Postman argues that the media is breaking down the boundaries between the worlds of children and adults, leading to the 'disappearance of childhood'.

6. Postman has been criticised for overstating his case. Childhood is a long way from disappearing. For example, children remain a distinct group – they are a major force in the market place. And they remain dependent on their parents.

activity39 ambiguities of childhood

Item A 'Pester-power'

Children can influence what adults buy through 'pester-power'. In the UK, the take-up of satellite and cable television, video, camcorders and home computers is much higher in households with children: 35% of households with children now subscribe to cable or satellite television, for example, as compared with 25% overall; while 90% of households with children have access to a video cassette recorder as compared with 75% overall.

Adapted from Buckingham, 2000

Item B Young and sophisticated

Aged 11

question

Why is childhood in the 21st century seen as 'ambiguous'? Make some reference to Items A and B in your answer.

3 Education

Introduction

Why do we spend the best years of our life in school? Until recently, most people managed quite well without a formal education. They learned what they needed from family, friends, and neighbours.

This type of informal education continues to be an important part of the socialisation process. What's new is a state system of formal education. It consists of specialised institutions – schools, colleges and universities – and selected knowledge and skills transmitted by professionals – teachers and lecturers.

Education is important. It takes up a significant proportion of people's lives – at least eleven years. And it affects them for the rest of their lives. It's very expensive – in 2001 government expenditure on education in the UK was £47 billion, 11.8% of all public expenditure. And the cost rises year by year (*Social Trends*, 2003).

Starting out

chaptersummary

▶ **Unit 1** looks at the role of education in society.

▶ **Units 2, 3 and 4** outline explanations for the differences in educational attainment between different social classes, gender and ethnic groups.

▶ **Unit 5** focuses on the classroom. It examines the hidden

curriculum, pupil subcultures, teacher-pupil relationships and the organisation of teaching and learning.

▶ **Unit 6** looks at how government policy has shaped the education system from 1870 to the present day.

Unit 1 The role of the education system

keyissues

1 What are the main views of the role of the education system?

2 What are their strengths and weaknesses?

This unit looks at the role of education in society. In simple terms, this means what does education do? Does it benefit society and if so, how? Is it harmful to society, or to certain groups within society? Is it doing its job well or badly?

1.1 Functionalist perspectives

Functionalists usually begin with the following questions.

● How does education contribute to the maintenance and wellbeing of society?

● What are the relationships between education and other parts of the social system?

Here are some of the answers functionalists have given.

Emile Durkheim

Social solidarity Writing over 100 years ago, the French sociologist Emile Durkheim argued that *social solidarity* – social unity – is essential for the survival of society. Social solidarity is based on 'essential similarities' between members of society. According to Durkheim, one of the main functions of education is to develop these similarities and so bind members of society together.

The USA provides a vivid illustration of Durkheim's views. Its population is drawn from all over the world. A common educational system has helped to weld this diverse mass of human beings into a nation. It has provided common norms and values, a shared sense of

activity1 social solidarity

Item A Oath of allegiance

American schoolchildren pledging loyalty to their flag and country

question

How can Items A and B be used to illustrate the view that education helps to unite members of society?

Item B Teaching history

Davy Crockett's story has been retold on countless occasions in schools across the USA. Davy Crockett pulled himself up by his own bootstraps. He became a skilled hunter and marksman in the backwoods of Tennessee, before joining the US army as a scout. He was elected three times as a Congressman. Hearing of the Texans' fight for freedom against Mexico, he gathered a dozen volunteers to help them. He died fighting the Mexican army in 1836.

Adapted from Newark, 1980

Davy Crockett at the Alamo

history and a feeling of belonging to a wider society.

History and social solidarity Durkheim sees a common history as vital for uniting members of society. American schoolchildren grow up with stories about their country's founders, eg George Washington cutting down his father's cherry tree, and their country's heroes, eg Davy Crockett who grew up in the backwoods of Tennessee, was elected to Congress, and died a hero, fighting for freedom against the overwhelming force of the Mexican army at the Battle of the Alamo in Texas in 1836.

With a shared history, people feel part of a wider social group – it is their country, made up of people like themselves. In this way, education contributes to the development of social solidarity.

Specialised skills Industrial society has a *specialised division of labour* – people have specialised jobs with specific skill and knowledge requirements. For example, the skills and knowledge required by plumbers, electricians, teachers and doctors are very different. In preindustrial societies there were fewer specialised occupations. Occupational skills were often passed from parents to children. According to Durkheim, the specialised division of labour in industrial societies relies increasingly on the educational system to provide the skills and knowledge required by the workforce.

Talcott Parsons

Secondary socialisation Writing in the 1950s and 1960s, the American sociologist Talcott Parsons developed Durkheim's ideas. He saw the educational system as the main agency of *secondary socialisation*, acting as a bridge between the family and the wider society. Schools build on the primary socialisation provided by the family, developing *value consensus* – agreement about the values of society – and preparing young people for their adult roles (Parsons, 1951, 1961).

Individual achievement is a major value in modern industrial society. In schools, young people are encouraged to achieve as individuals. High achievement is rewarded with praise, high status, good grades and valuable qualifications. This prepares young people to achieve as individuals in the world of work.

Equality of opportunity – an equal chance for everybody – is another major value in modern society. Schools transmit this value by offering all their pupils an equal chance of success.

According to Parsons, schools are miniature versions of the wider society. They reflect the values of the wider society. Young people are required to act in terms of those values in the classroom. And, as a result, they are prepared for adult roles.

Role allocation Parsons sees role allocation as one of the main functions of the educational system. This involves sifting, sorting, assessing and evaluating young people in terms of their talents and abilities, then allocating them to appropriate roles in the wider society. For example, people with artistic talent are directed towards and trained for occupations such as photographer, graphic designer and fashion designer.

Role allocation involves testing students in order to discover their talents, developing those talents on appropriate courses, then matching those talents to the jobs for which they are best suited.

Functionalism and education – evaluation

The following criticisms have been made of functionalist views of education.

- Rather than transmitting society's values, the education system may be transmitting the values of a ruling class or ruling elite.

- History in schools may reflect a white, middle-class view. This may discourage social solidarity. Many ethnic minority groups are demanding that history teaching reflect *their* historical experience and *their* viewpoint. For example, in the USA, African-American history is now a major part of the history curriculum.

- There is evidence that certain groups underachieve in schools – for example, the working class and certain ethnic minority groups. This suggests that a) pupils do not have an equal opportunity b) their talents have not been effectively developed and assessed and c) the system of role allocation is not very efficient.

- Is the educational system providing the knowledge and skills required in the workplace? It is difficult to see a direct link between many school subjects and the world of work.

key terms

Social solidarity Social unity.
Specialised division of labour A labour force with a large number of specialised occupations.
Secondary socialisation The process of socialisation which builds on the primary socialisation usually conducted by the family.
Value consensus An agreement about the major values of society.
Individual achievement Achieving success as an individual rather than as a member of a group.
Equality of opportunity A system in which every person has an equal chance of success.
Role allocation The system of allocating people to roles which suit their aptitudes and capabilities.

1.2 Marxist perspectives

In Marx's words the ruling class 'rule also as thinkers, as producers of ideas'. These ideas justify their position, conceal the true source of their power and disguise their exploitation of the subject class. In Marx's view this *ruling class ideology* is a far more effective means of domination than more obvious forms of control such as physical force. It presents a false picture of society which keeps the subject class in its place.

activity2 examinations

questions

How can the type of formal examinations pictured here

a) encourage individual achievement

b) form part of the process of role allocation?

Education and ideology

Louis Althusser, a French Marxist philosopher, argues that no class can hold power for long simply by the use of force. Ideology provides a much more effective means of control – if people's hearts and minds are won over then force becomes unnecessary.

Althusser (1972) argues that in modern society the education system has largely replaced the church as the main agency for ideological control. In the past, people tended to accept their station in life because they saw it as God's will. Today, this acceptance comes in part from their experience of education.

First, schools transmit an ideology which states that capitalism is just and reasonable. Second, schools prepare pupils for their roles in the workforce. Most are trained as workers – they are taught to accept their future exploitation and provided with an education and qualifications to match their adult work roles. Some – the future managers, administrators and politicians – are trained to control the workforce. Their educational qualifications *legitimate* – justify and make right – their position of power. They become the 'agents of exploitation and repression'.

Althusser argues that ideology in capitalist society is fundamental to social control. He sees the main role of education as transmitting this ideology.

Correspondence theory

In *Schooling in Capitalist America* (1976) Samuel Bowles and Herbert Gintis claim that there is a close correspondence between the social relationships in the classroom and those in the workplace. This correspondence is essential for *social reproduction* – the reproduction of new generations of workers appropriately schooled to accept their roles in capitalist society.

School and workplace Schools, like the wider society, are based on hierarchies – layers of authority. Teachers give orders, pupils are expected to obey. Pupils have little control over their work, over the curriculum they follow. This corresponds to their later experience of lack of control in the workplace. Schools reward punctuality, obedience and hard work, they discourage creativity, independence and critical awareness. This is directly in line with the kind of worker required by employers in capitalist society.

Young people get little direct satisfaction from their education. They are motivated largely by external rewards

activity3 social reproduction

Item A *Role allocation and rewards*

Item B *Two views of role allocation*

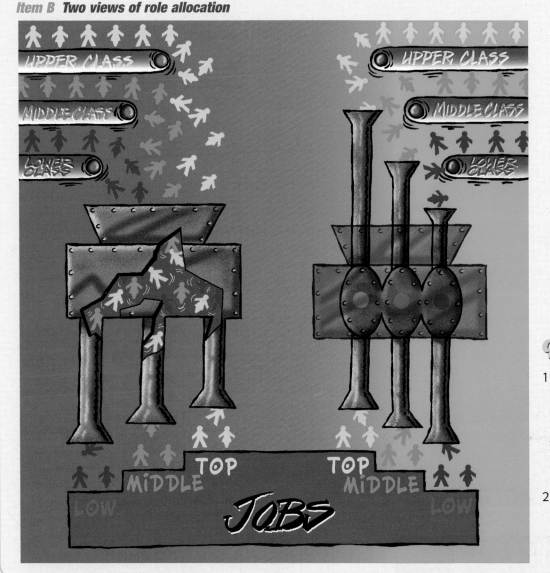

UPPER CLASS
MIDDLE CLASS
LOWER CLASS

UPPER CLASS
MIDDLE CLASS
LOWER CLASS

LOW MIDDLE TOP TOP MIDDLE LOW

Jobs

questions

1 How does the ideologically sound young woman in Item A illustrate Bowles and Gintis's theory of the role of education in society?

2 Using Item B, briefly compare functionalist and Marxist views of role allocation.

such as educational qualifications. This is reflected in the workplace – work itself provides little satisfaction, workers are motivated by external rewards such as pay. Bowles and Gintis argue that this correspondence between school and the workplace effectively reproduces workers from one generation to the next.

Social inequality Capitalist society is unequal. If this inequality were seriously questioned it might threaten social stability. One way of avoiding this is to promote the belief that inequality is justified. According to Bowles and Gintis, education legitimates social inequality by broadcasting the myth that it offers everybody an equal chance. It follows that those who achieve high qualifications deserve their success. And since high qualifications lead to top jobs, people who get those jobs have earned them. In this way social inequality appears just and legitimate.

However, Bowles and Gintis argue that rewards in education and occupation are based not on ability but on social background. The higher a person's class of origin – the class they began in – the more likely they are to attain high educational qualifications and a top job. The class system tends to reproduce itself from generation to generation and this process is legitimised by education. In Bowles and Gintis's words, 'Education reproduces inequality by justifying privilege and attributing poverty to personal failure'.

Role allocation Bowles and Gintis reject the functionalist view of role allocation. Those who get the highest qualifications and the top jobs do so because of their social background and because they work hard and do what they're told. Bowles and Gintis found that students with high grades tend to be hardworking, obedient, conforming and dependable rather than creative, original and independent. These characteristics are rewarded with high grades because they are the very qualities required for a subordinate, obedient and disciplined workforce.

Learning to labour

In a study entitled, *Learning to Labour: How working-class kids get working-class jobs* (1977), the British sociologist Paul Willis studied a group of 12 working-class boys (the 'lads') during their last year and a half at school and their first few months at work.

Counter-school culture Willis did not find a simple correspondence between school and work. Nor did he find that the lads were shaped by the educational system. Instead, the lads rejected school and created their own *counter-school culture*. But, it was this very rejection of school which prepared them for the low-skill, low-status jobs they were to end up in.

The lads rejected educational success as defined by the school. They saw the conformist behaviour of hardworking pupils – the ear 'oles – as a matter for amusement and mockery. School was good for a laugh and not much else. Boredom was relieved by mucking around and breaking rules. The lads actively created a counter-school culture based on opposition to authority. In some respects this behaviour made sense. They were destined for low-skill jobs so why bother to work hard.

School and work Willis found a number of similarities between the attitudes and behaviour developed by the lads in school and those of the shopfloor at work. Having a laugh was important in both situations as a means of dealing with monotony, boredom and authority. And at work, as at school, a bunch of mates to mess around with and support you in an 'us and them' situation remained important.

So, like Bowles and Gintis, Willis argues for a correspondence between school and work. But this is not produced by the school – the lads are not the docile, obedient pupils of Bowles and Gintis's study. The lads themselves have produced the correspondence by their rejection of the school. And in doing so they have prepared themselves for their place in the workforce. They have learned to have a laugh, to put up with boredom and monotony, and to accept the drudgery of low-skill jobs.

Twenty years on Willis's study was conducted in a secondary school in Birmingham in the 1970s. Twenty years later, a similar study was conducted in the West Midlands by Máirtín Mac an Ghaill (1994). Some of the working-class young men – the 'macho lads' – were similar to Willis's lads. They rejected the authority of the teachers and the values of the school. However, this was a time of high unemployment when many traditional low-skill working-class jobs were disappearing. Because of this, the macho lads' behaviour was 'outdated' – the jobs it prepared them for were fast becoming a thing of the past.

Marxism and education – evaluation

Marxists see education in a negative light. It transmits ruling class ideology and produces a passive and obedient workforce which fits the requirements of capitalism. And when young people actively reject schooling, this can prepare them for monotonous, low-skill jobs. This view of the role of education is based partly on the belief that capitalism is unjust and oppressive, and that it exploits the workforce.

activity4 learning to labour

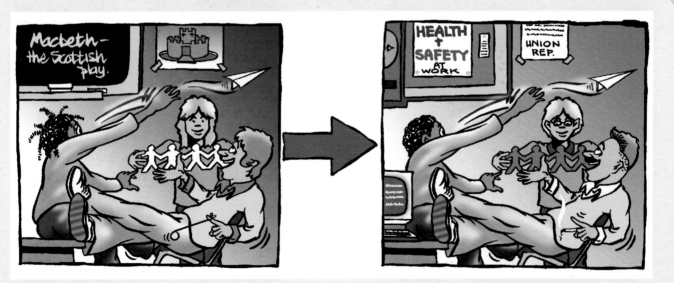

question

How does this cartoon illustrate Willis's view of how lads adapt to low-skill, boring jobs?

However, it is possible to accept some of the findings of Marxist sociologists without accepting their view of capitalism. Both Bowles and Gintis and Willis provide evidence to support their claims. Schools *do* reward hard work, conformity and obedience. And some students who learn to live with what they see as the boredom of school are prepared for the monotony of low-skill jobs.

key terms

Ruling class ideology A false picture of society which justifies the position of the ruling and subject classes.
Legitimate Justify, make right.
Correspondence theory A theory which shows a correspondence or similarity between two things and suggests that they are causally related – for example, the experience of school and work is similar, and the requirements of the workplace shape what goes on in the classroom.
Social reproduction The reproduction of new generations of workers with the skills and attitudes required for their roles in capitalist society.
Counter-school culture A rejection of the norms and values of the school and their replacement with anti-school norms and values.

1.3 Feminist perspectives

As outlined in Chapter 1, feminist perspectives focus on gender inequalities in society (see pp 24-25). Feminist research has revealed the extent of male domination and the ways in which male supremacy has been maintained. From a feminist viewpoint, one of the main roles of education has been to maintain gender inequality.

Gender and education

From the 1960s onwards, feminist sociologists highlighted the following gender inequalities in education.

Gendered language Reflecting the wider society, school textbooks (and teachers) tended to use *gendered language* – 'he', 'him', 'his', 'man' and 'men' when referring to a person or people. This tended to downgrade women and make them invisible.

Gendered roles School textbooks have tended to present males and females in traditional gender roles – for example, women as mothers and housewives. This is particularly evident in reading schemes from the 1960s and 1970s.

Gender stereotypes Reading schemes have also tended to present traditional gender *stereotypes*. For example, an analysis of six reading schemes from the 1960s and 70s found that:

- Boys are presented as more adventurous than girls
- As physically stronger
- As having more choices.
- Girls are presented as more caring than boys

- As more interested in domestic matters
- As followers rather than leaders (Lobban, 1974).

Women in the curriculum In terms of what's taught in schools – the *curriculum* – women tend to be missing, in the background, or in second place. Feminists often argue that women have been 'hidden from history' – history has been the history of men.

Subject choice Traditionally, female students have tended to avoid maths, science and technology. Certain subjects were seen as 'boys' subjects' and 'girls' subjects'. Often girl's subjects had lower status and lower market value.

Discrimination There is evidence of discrimination against girls in education simply because of their gender. For example, when the 11-plus exam was introduced in the 1940s, the pass mark for boys was set lower than the mark for girls in order to make sure there were roughly equal numbers of boys and girls in grammar schools. In other words girls were artificially 'failed' so boys could 'succeed'.

Further and higher education Traditionally, the number of female students going on to further and higher education has been lower than for boys. There is evidence that teachers often gave boys more encouragement than girls to go on to university (Stanworth, 1983).

Feminist perspectives – evaluation

Feminist perspectives have been valuable for exposing gender inequality in education. Partly as a result of sociological research, a lot has changed – for example, much of the *sexism* in reading schemes has now disappeared.

Today, women have overtaken men on most measures of educational attainment. Their grades at GCSE and A level are significantly higher than those of male students. And more women than men are going on to higher education. The concern now is the underachievement of boys rather than discrimination against girls.

key terms

Gendered language Language which uses one gender to refer to both genders.
Stereotype An exaggerated and distorted view of the characteristics of members of a social group.
Curriculum The subjects taught in school and their content.
Sexism Bias against a particular gender – usually females.

1.4 Social democratic perspectives

Social democratic perspectives on education developed in the 1960s. They have had an important influence on government educational policy.

Social democratic theorists start from the view that everybody should have an equal chance to succeed in the educational system. This is not only fair and just, it also

activity5 gender and education

Item A Learning to launder

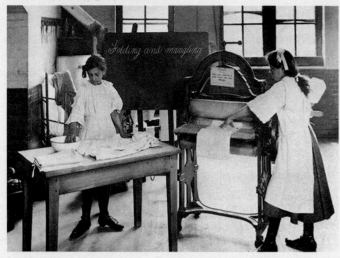

Girls at school learning to do the laundry, 1908. The girl on the right is using a mangle to get water out of the clothes.

Item B Peter and Jane

These pictures are taken from the Ladybird Key Words Reading Scheme published in 1964.

Item C In the classroom

Michelle Stanworth's research looked at gender relations in A level classes at a further education college.

Interviews with teachers and pupils revealed that both men and women teachers took more interest in their male pupils, asking them more questions in class and giving them more help. Asked which students they were most concerned about, women teachers named boys twice as often as girls. Male teachers named boys ten times as often as girls. When asked which pupils they were most 'attached' to, teachers named boys three times as often as girls.

Teachers underestimate girls' ambitions. Only one girl was mentioned as likely to get a management job and male teachers could not envisage any occupation other than marriage for two thirds of the girls. One girl, who was getting the top marks in her class in both her main A level subjects, and who wanted a career in the diplomatic service, was described by her woman teacher as likely to become 'the personal assistant to somebody rather important'.

Adapted from Stanworth, 1983

questions

1 How might a feminist sociologist analyse Items A and B?

2 Use Item C to support the view that there is discrimination against girls in the classroom.

---

brings practical benefits. A well-educated workforce will lead to economic growth.

Equal opportunity

The British sociologist A.H. Halsey is one of the leading social democratic theorists. He criticised functionalist views which claimed that the education system in Western industrial societies provided equality of opportunity. Halsey's work from the 1960s onwards showed clearly that social class has a significant effect on educational attainment. In general, the higher a person's social class of origin – the class into which they were born – the higher their educational qualifications. For example, middle-class students tend to achieve higher qualifications than working-class students. This suggests that schools are not providing equality of opportunity for all young people (Halsey et al., 1961; 1980).

According to social democratic theorists, this is both wrong and inefficient. It is wrong because in a democracy, everybody has a right to equal opportunity. It is inefficient because it wastes talent. If people don't have the opportunity to develop their aptitudes and abilities, then their contribution to society as a whole will be reduced. Inequality of educational opportunity means that everybody suffers.

Education and the economy

According to social democratic theorists, there is a close link between education and economic growth. Modern economies require an increasingly specialised and highly-trained workforce. The educational system reflects this requirement (Halsey et al., 1961).

Over the past 50 years there has been more education, and more specialised education. The school leaving age has steadily risen and growing numbers of young people are continuing into further and higher education. There has also been a rapid growth in vocational education – education which aims to provide specific workplace skills.

Social democratic perspectives – evaluation

It is difficult to unravel the relationships between education and the economy. Some researchers argue that the growth in education greatly exceeds the needs of the economy. For example, Randall Collins (1972) points to studies which suggest that once mass literacy has been achieved, education makes little difference to economic growth. He claims that when companies do require specific skills, they usually provide their own training courses.

Other researchers claim that the growth in vocational education with its focus on workplace skills is vital for economic development. And still others argue that the increased pace of technological and economic change calls for a flexible workforce with a good general education rather than specific *vocational training* (Brown et al., 1997). These points will be returned to in Unit 4 of this chapter.

key term

Vocational education Education which aims to provide specific workplace skills.

1.5 New Right perspectives

New Right ideas developed in the early 1980s. They took a very different view of the route to educational and economic success.

The problem

According to New Right thinkers, advanced industrial economies such as the USA and Britain were declining. Much of this decline was due to social democratic policies. These policies resulted in:

- Too much state control – the 'nanny state' got too involved in people's lives.
- This crushed people's initiative and stifled their enterprise. They relied on the state rather than taking responsibility for their own lives.
- This can be seen in welfare dependency – the poor had come to depend on state 'handouts' rather than pulling themselves up by their own bootstraps.
- State control and welfare benefits cost a lot of money which meant high taxation.
- Because of this there was less money to invest in private industry – the really productive sector of the economy.

The solution

The New Right offered the following solution to the decline of advanced industrial societies.

- Restore enterprise and initiative.
- Roll back the state and make people responsible for their own destiny rather than relying on state institutions, state guidance and state handouts.
- Increase competition not only in the private sector but

activity6 a social democratic view

question

How does this cartoon illustrate the social democratic view of education?

also the public sector – schools and hospitals should compete in much the same way as companies in the private sector.

- This will increase productivity and efficiency, and result in economic growth.

Education

Where does education fit into all this? The job of schools is to raise educational standards and instil enterprise, drive and competitive spirit.

The New Right's programme for raising educational standards runs as follows.

- Competition between schools and colleges – the best will attract more students, the worst won't get any and go out of business. This means that teachers and administrators will have real incentives to improve standards. And parents and their children will have real choice.
- Allowing schools and colleges to become self-managing. This means giving teachers and administrators control over finance, staffing and school policy. This encourages grassroot initiative and enterprise rather than relying on direction from above. And this will motivate teachers to improve standards.
- The above measures will lead to better school management and higher quality teaching. This is what's needed to raise educational standards for all (Chubb & Moe, 1997).
- Higher standards will mean higher qualifications, particularly for those at the bottom. And this will give them a better chance of escaping from welfare dependency.

New Right perspectives – evaluation

New Right views leave a number of unanswered questions (Halsey et al., 1997).

First, does competition between schools raise standards? Measured in terms of GCSE and A level results, standards are improving. However, this may have little or nothing to do with competition between schools.

Second, is a choice of schools and colleges available? In some areas, there is no alternative to the local comprehensive. In other areas, where choice exists, middle-class parents are in a better position to get their children into the best schools. For example, where there are limited places, they tend to be more successful at negotiating with teachers.

Third, can schools make up for inequalities in the wider society? For example, with good management and high quality teaching, can schools provide equality of opportunity for students from low-income backgrounds? Available evidence suggests that the answer is 'no' (Halsey et al., 1997).

summary

1. From a functionalist perspective, education performs the following functions:
   - Developing and reinforcing social solidarity
   - Providing the skills and knowledge required for a specialised division of labour
   - Developing value consensus and preparing young people for adult roles
   - Assessing young people in terms of their talents and abilities and allocating them to appropriate roles in the wider society.

2. From a Marxist perspective, education:
   - Transmits ruling class ideology
   - Prepares pupils for their role in the workplace
   - Legitimises inequality and disguises exploitation
   - Rewards conformity and obedience
   - Reproduces new generations of workers, schooled to accept their place in capitalist society.

3. From a feminist perspective, education has promoted, and to some extent still does promote, male dominance by:
   - The use of gendered language and gender stereotypes
   - Omitting women from the curriculum
   - Defining certain subjects as 'girls' subjects' and others as 'boys' subjects'
   - Discriminating against female students in terms of grammar school, further and higher education places.

4. From a social democratic perspective, education:
   - Should provide every young person with an equal chance to develop their talents and abilities
   - This will benefit society as a whole by producing economic growth.

5. According to the New Right, the role of education is to instil drive, initiative and enterprise. This will come from:
   - Competition between schools and colleges
   - Motivating teachers to improve standards
   - Providing parents and students with a choice of schools and colleges.

key term

Welfare dependency Depending on state benefits for support and accepting this as a way of life.

activity7 the educational market-place

question

How does this cartoon illustrate New Right views of education?

Unit 2 Social class and educational attainment

keyissues

1 What are the differences in educational attainment between social class groups?

2 What explanations are given for these differences?

Class, gender and ethnicity make a difference to *educational attainment* – the educational qualifications and grades students achieve. If you want the best possible start, you should be born at the top of the class system, as a female, and as a member of the Indian ethnic group. Statistics indicate that *in general* the higher your social class, the higher your attainment, that Indians are the most successful ethnic group, and that girls do better than boys.

How important are class, ethnicity and gender?

- **Class** is most important. Its effect on educational attainment is nearly three times greater than ethnicity.
- **Ethnicity** comes next. It has about twice the effect of gender.
- **Gender** Despite capturing public attention, gender is least important. Class has over five times the effect on educational attainment (Gillborn & Mirza, 2000).

This unit looks at class differences in educational

attainment. The next two units look at ethnic and gender differences.

2.1 Measuring class and educational attainment

In general, the higher a person's social class of origin – the class they were born into – the higher their educational qualifications. This has been shown time and time again over the past 50 years by sociological research and government statistics.

To what extent does social class affect educational attainment? How has the effect of class changed over time? This is where we run into problems. Is it possible to directly compare statistics over the years? The short answer is 'no'. Definitions of social class vary from study to study. The official definition of class used in government research changes – the last major change was in 2001. And educational qualifications change – from O levels to GCSEs, from GNVQs to vocational A levels, and so on.

But whatever the level or type of educational qualification, and whatever the definition of social class, there is no doubt that class has a significant effect on educational attainment. To appreciate this effect, work carefully through Activity 8.

activity8 educational attainment and social class

Item A GCSE and social class, 2002

Pupils achieving five or more GCSE grades A* to C

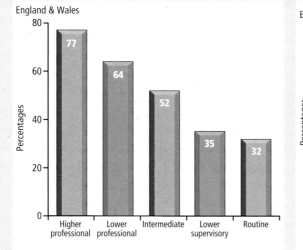

Adapted from *Youth Cohort Study*, 2002 (National Statistics Online, 20.02.03)

Item B GCSE and social class, 1989 and 2000

Pupils achieving five or more GCSE grades A* to C

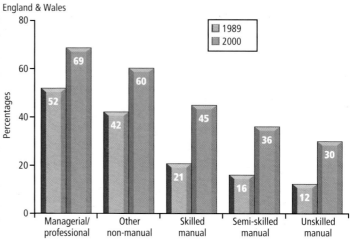

Adapted from *Social Trends*, 2001

Item C Higher education and social class

Participation rates in higher education

Great Britain   Percentages

Social class	1991	1992	1993	1994	1995	1996	1997	1998	1999	2000	Gain 1991-2000
Professional	55	71	73	78	79	82	79	82	73	76	+21
Intermediate	36	39	42	45	45	47	48	45	45	48	+12
Skilled non-manual	22	27	29	31	31	32	31	29	30	33	+11
Skilled manual	11	15	17	18	18	18	19	18	18	19	+8
Partly skilled	12	14	16	17	17	17	18	17	17	19	+7
Unskilled	6	9	11	11	12	13	14	13	13	14	+8
All social classes	23	28	30	32	32	33	33	31	32	33	+10

Adapted from *Age Participation Index*, Department of Education and Skills, 2003

The table shows the percentage of people under 21 from each social class who enter undergraduate courses in higher education. The figures on the right show the increase in percentage points for each class from 1991 to 2000.

questions

1 What does Item A suggest about the relationship between social class and educational attainment?

2 No matter what definition of social class is used, there are significant class differences in educational attainment. Comment on this statement using Items A and B which use different definitions of class.

3 What changes does Item B indicate between 1989 and 2000?

4 Summarise the trends shown in Item C.

2.2 Explaining class differences in attainment

During the 1960s and 70s, class differences in attainment were the main focus of the sociology of education. During the 1980s and 90s, class went out of fashion. Sociologists turned to ethnic and gender differences in attainment. And some claimed that class was not nearly as important as it used to be.

Only in the last ten years have a few sociologists returned to class and attainment. Because of this, the research in this section is either recent or drawn from the 1960s and 70s. Despite the earlier research being dated, it remains important. Class is still the most significant social factor accounting for differences in educational attainment.

Class, intelligence and attainment

At every level of education – from nursery to university – upper and middle-class children tend to do better than working-class children. This remains the case even when they have the same intelligence quotient (IQ).

Most researchers believe that the same range of ability is present in every social class. This means that class differences in educational attainment are *not* due to class differences in intelligence.

Material deprivation

During the 1960s, sociologists claimed that the low attainment of many working-class pupils resulted from a lack of something. They were *deprived*. This deprivation was *material* – a lack of money and the things that money could buy – and *cultural* – an absence of the attitudes and skills that were needed for educational success.

In general, the higher a child's class of origin, the higher their family income. High income can provide many educational advantages – a comfortable well-heated home, spacious rooms with a desk to work at, a home computer with internet access, reference and revision books, extra home tuition and the option of private education.

At the other end of the scale, children in poverty often live in cramped, cold and draughty conditions. Shortage of money means they are more likely to have part-time jobs in the evenings and at weekends, and to leave school at the minimum leaving age. Poverty often leads to ill health. And this can result in absence from school, tiredness and irritability.

activity9 material deprivation

Item A Growing up poor

question

How might growing up in poverty disadvantage children at school?

Item B Homelessness

A report on the effects of homelessness on schoolchildren by Her Majesty's Inspectorate for Schools makes the following points.

Their chances of doing well are slim. 'Sustainable achievement is often beyond their reach.' Cramped sleeping conditions leave the children tired, listless and unable to concentrate. In one London school, a four-year-old boy spent a whole day sleeping outside the headteacher's office.

The inspectors found evidence of ill health caused by poor diet, and stress from permanent insecurity. For some, the crises which led to homelessness produce social and emotional difficulties.

Weak reading, writing and verbal skills among primary school children are combined with a poor self-image. 'I can't read,' a seven-year-old girl told her teacher. 'Don't you know I'm simple?'

The report notes that many hostel rooms lack such basics as chairs and table. As a result, children often find it hard to do homework. A fourth year GCSE pupil had to work on her bed and could only start when the sisters she shared the room with were asleep.

Adapted from *The Times Educational Supplement*. 10.8.90

The costs of education Traditionally, many working-class students left school at the minimum leaving age because their parents could no longer afford to support them. However, since the introduction of the GCSE examination in 1988, a far higher proportion of 16-19 year olds have continued into further education.

More recently, the introduction of tuition fees and the abolition of student grants has meant that many young people with working-class backgrounds feel they cannot afford to go on to higher education. As Item C in Activity 8 shows, it is those at the top of the class system who have benefited most from the expansion of university places. Even though grants are available for students from low-income families, many are still put off by the costs of higher education (Machin, 2003).

Home and school

Many sociologists in the 1960s saw differences in primary socialisation as the main reason for class differences in attainment. In a large-scale study of British children entitled *The Home and the School*, J.W.B. Douglas (1964) claimed that middle-class children received more attention and encouragement from their parents during their early years. This provided a foundation for high attainment in their later years.

Based on questionnaires given to over 5000 parents, Douglas concluded that the degree of parents' interest in their children's education was the single, most important factor affecting attainment. His research suggested that, in general, middle-class parents showed more interest than working-class parents. They were more likely to visit the school and to encourage their children to stay on beyond the minimum school leaving age.

Class subcultures

Differences in *social class subcultures* – the norms, attitudes and values typical of each class – were often seen as part of the explanation for class differences in attainment.

The British sociologist Barry Sugarman (1970) described working-class subculture as:

- *Fatalistic* – accepting the situation rather than working to improve it
- *Present-time orientated* – living for the moment rather than planning for the future
- Concerned with *immediate gratification* – taking pleasures now rather than making sacrifices for the future.

By comparison, middle-class subculture was seen as non-fatalistic, future-time orientated and concerned with deferred gratification.

These differences in class subcultures were seen to place pupils from working-class backgrounds at a disadvantage. For example, fatalism will not encourage pupils to improve their grades. And present-time orientation and immediate gratification will discourage sustained effort for examination success.

Cultural deprivation theory

The views of sociologists such as Douglas and Sugarman have been used to provide support for what came to be known as *cultural deprivation theory*. This theory states that those at the bottom of the class system are deprived of important values, attitudes, experiences and skills which are essential for educational success. Their home life lacks the kind of stimulation needed for high attainment – for example, there is an absence of books and educational toys. They receive little encouragement from parents and, as a result, lack the motivation to succeed at school.

To make matters worse, what the 'culturally deprived child' has tends to be seen as 'substandard' – well below the high quality norms and values of middle-class subculture. Deprived of what's needed for success and saddled with low standard norms and values, it's no wonder, so the argument goes, that culturally deprived children fail in droves.

Evaluation Cultural deprivation theory has been strongly criticised. There is evidence that if class differences in culture exist, then they are slight and of little significance. Much so-called culturally deprived behaviour may be due to lack of money rather than lack of the norms and values needed for high attainment. For example, working-class students may leave school earlier because of low income rather than lack of motivation and parental encouragement.

Cultural deprivation theory blames the failings of the child on his or her background. This diverts attention from the failings of the educational system which may contribute to, or account for, class differences in attainment. This view will be considered shortly.

Speech patterns and class

Cultural deprivation theory Extreme versions of cultural deprivation theory see the speech patterns of those at the bottom of the class system as inferior. For example, the American psychologist Carl Bereiter argues that the speech patterns of many low-income children are inadequate to meet the demands of the education system. As a result, they directly contribute to educational failure.

This view has been rejected by the American linguist William Labov (1973). He examined the speech patterns of low-income African-American children from Harlem in New York. He claimed that their speech patterns were not inferior to standard English, they were just different. Those who saw them as inferior simply failed to understand low-income black dialect.

Restricted and elaborated codes The British sociologist Basil Bernstein identified two forms of speech pattern, the *restricted code* and the *elaborated code*. The restricted code is a kind of shorthand speech, usually found in conversations between people who have a lot in common, eg friends and family members. It is often tied to a context, eg it cannot be fully understood outside the family circle, and its meanings tend to be particularistic, that is, specific to the speaker and listener. Sentences are often short, simple and unfinished, detail is omitted, explanations not given and information taken for granted. This is because a considerable amount of shared knowledge between speaker and listener is assumed.

By comparison, the elaborated code spells out what the restricted code takes for granted. Meanings are made explicit, explanations provided, details spelt out. As such, the elaborated code tends to be context-free (not tied to a context such as a particular friendship group) and its meanings are universalistic (they can be understood by everybody).

Class and speech codes According to Bernstein, most middle-class children have been socialised in both the restricted and elaborated codes and are fluent in each, whereas many working-class children are limited to the restricted code. Since teachers use the elaborated code, working-class pupils are placed at a distinct disadvantage. They are less likely to understand what teachers say and are more likely to be misunderstood and criticised for what they themselves say.

Bernstein insists that working-class speech patterns are not substandard or inadequate. However, they do place working-class pupils at a disadvantage since the elaborated code is the language of education.

Evaluation Bernstein's research shows how schools can contribute to class differences in educational attainment. Because schools demand the use of the elaborated code, middle-class pupils have a built-in advantage.

Some researchers have questioned Bernstein's view that members of the working-class are limited to the restricted code. He provides little hard evidence to support his view. And much of this evidence comes from interviews given by middle-class adults to five-year-old working-class boys. Such interviews may reveal little about the linguistic ability of young people – see Activity 10, Item B.

activity 10 speech patterns

Item A *Speech codes*

Bernstein showed four pictures to five-year-old boys and asked them to describe what was going on. Here are two examples, the first by a working-class boy using the restricted code, the second by a middle-class boy using the elaborated code.

Restricted code 'They're playing football and he kicks it, and it goes through there. It breaks the window and they're looking at it and he comes out and shouts at them because they've broken it. So they run away and then she looks out and she tells them off.'

Elaborated code 'Two boys are playing football and one boy kicks the ball and it goes through the window. The ball breaks the window and the boys are looking at it, and a man comes out and shouts at them because they've broken the window. So they run away and then that lady looks out of her window, and she tells the boys off.'

Adapted from Bernstein, 1973

Item B *Three interviews*

The boys in the following interviews are African-Americans from low-income families in Harlem, New York.

Interview 1 An eight-year-old boy is interviewed by a 'friendly' White interviewer who presents him with a toy jet plane and asks him to describe it. The setting is formal. There are long silences followed by short two or three word answers, which hardly provide an adequate description of the plane.

Interview 2 Another Black boy from Harlem is interviewed. Again the setting is formal but this time the interviewer is Black and raised in Harlem. The boy responds in much the same way as the boy in the first interview.

Interview 3 The boy and the interviewer are the same as in the second interview. This time the interviewer sits on the floor, the boy is provided with a supply of potato crisps and his best friend is invited along. The change is dramatic. The boy's conversation is articulate and enthusiastic, and, in linguistic terms, rich and diverse. He provides a detailed description of the toy plane.

Adapted from Labov, 1973

Harlem, New York

questions

1   How do the examples in Item A illustrate some of the features of the restricted and elaborated codes?

2   How might Item B be used to criticise:

  a)   Those who see working-class speech patterns as inadequate?

  b)   Bernstein's claim that the working class are limited to the restricted code?

key terms

Restricted code Shorthand speech in which detail is omitted and information taken for granted.
Elaborated code A speech pattern in which details are spelt out, explanations provided and meanings made explicit.

Cultural capital

The French sociologist Pierre Bourdieu (1977) starts from the idea that there is a *dominant culture* in society. The higher people's position in the class system, the greater the amount of dominant culture they are likely to have. This culture is generally regarded as superior because those at the top have the power to define it as such. In reality, however, it is no better or worse than any other culture. But because it is highly valued and sought after, it forms the basis of the educational system.

Children born into the middle and upper classes have a built-in advantage. Their culture is closer to the culture of the school so they will be more likely to succeed. For example, their language is closer to that of teachers so they are more likely to understand what's being taught and to be rewarded for what they say and write.

According to Bourdieu, the dominant culture can be seen as *cultural capital* since it can be converted into material rewards – high qualifications, high status jobs, high salaries, high living standards.

Bourdieu concludes that the primary purpose of education is cultural and social reproduction. The education system reproduces the dominant culture and in doing so helps to reproduce the class system. And, by creating educational success and failure, it legitimates the positions of those at the top and those at the bottom.

Bourdieu's idea of cultural capital has been influential in the renewed interest in class and educational attainment in the 1990s and 2000s. This can be seen from the following two studies.

Class, mothers and cultural capital

In an important study entitled *Class Work: Mothers' involvement in their children's primary schooling*, Diane Reay (1998) states that, 'It is mothers who are making cultural capital work for their children'. Her research is based on interviews with the mothers of 33 children at two London primary schools.

All the mothers are actively involved in their children's education. The working-class mothers worked just as hard as the middle-class mothers. But it was not hard work that counted. Instead, it was the amount of cultural capital available. And the middle-class mothers had most.

Middle-class mothers had more educational qualifications and more information about how the educational system operated. They used this cultural capital to good effect – helping children with their homework, bolstering their confidence and sorting out problems with their teachers. Where the middle-class mothers had the confidence and self-assurance to make demands on teachers, the working-class mothers talked in terms of 'plucking up courage' and 'making myself go and see the teacher'. Where middle-class mothers knew what the school expected from their children and how to help them, working-class mothers felt they lacked the knowledge and ability to help their children.

Middle-class mothers not only have more cultural capital, they also have more material capital. Over half the middle-class mothers had cleaners, au pairs or both. This gave them more time to support their children. Working-class mothers could not afford help with domestic work. Nor could they afford private tuition which many middle-class mothers provided for their children.

According to Diane Reay, it is mothers who have the main influence on their children's education. Their effectiveness depends on the amount of cultural capital at their disposal. And this depends on their social class.

Education, class and choice

In recent years, government education policy has encouraged schools to compete, and offered parents and students choices between schools. Choosing the 'right' primary and secondary school is important. It can make a difference to students' examination results and their chances of climbing the educational ladder.

In Class Strategies and the Education Market: The middle classes and social advantage, Stephen J. Ball (2003) argues that government policies of choice and competition place the middle class at an advantage. They have the knowledge and skills to make the most of the opportunities on offer. Compared to the working class, they have more material capital, more cultural capital and more *social capital* – access to social networks and contacts which can provide information and support. In Ball's words, middle-class parents have 'enough capitals in the right currency to ensure a high probability of success for their children'.

Strategies The aim of parents is to give their children maximum advantage in the education system. The choice of school is vital. And this is where middle-class parents come into their own. Compared to working-class parents, they are more comfortable, more at home in dealing with public institutions like schools. They are more used to extracting and assessing information. For example, they use their social networks to talk to parents whose children are attending the schools on offer. They collect and analyse information – for example, the GCSE results of the various schools. And they are more used to dealing with and negotiating with teachers and administrators. As a result, when entry into a popular school is limited, they are more likely to gain a place for their child.

The school/parent alliance Middle-class parents want middle-class schools. In general, schools with mainly middle-class pupils have the best results and the highest status. And these schools want middle-class pupils. They are seen as easy to teach and likely to perform well. They will maintain or increase the school's position in the exam league table and its status in the education market.

Conclusion Many middle-class parents work extremely hard to get their children into the most successful schools. But, what they gain for their children can be at the expense of working-class children.

2.3 Social class in schools

This section looks at social class in the classroom. In particular, it looks at evidence which suggests that schools sometimes discriminate against working-class pupils and in favour of middle-class pupils.

Labelling theory

Pupils are constantly being assessed and classified. They are defined as able or less able, placed in particular sets or streams, entered for particular examinations and given or denied access to certain parts of the school curriculum.

activity11 cultural and social capital

Item A Supporting your child

Liz, a middle-class mother, spells out how she supports her son at primary school.

'One is the support I give him at home, hearing him read, making him read every night, doing homework with him, trying to get the books he needs for his project. I see that as a support role. The other side, in the particular case of Martin, is where he has had difficulties and finds reading very, very difficult. So a lot of my time has been spent fighting for extra support for him and I mean fighting.'

Later in the interview, she discusses the tuition Martin receives.

'Well he just wasn't making enough progress in school so we decided we'd have to get him a tutor.'

Josie, a working-class mother talks about her son's reading difficulties.

'I have tried, I really have. I knew I should be playing a role in getting Leigh to read but I wasn't qualified. Therefore it put extra pressure on me because I was no good at reading myself, it was too important for me to handle and I'd get very upset and angry at Leigh.'

'I always found if I went to the class teacher, she'd take it very personal and think I was attacking her. I wasn't. I was just bringing it to her attention in case she didn't know, you know, that in my opinion he's not progressing.'

Adapted from Reay, 1998

Item B Choosing a school

Here are some comments from middle-class mothers about choosing schools for their children.

'You talk to other people who've got children there who come from Riverway, how are they coping. You spend a lot of time talking outside the school gates to people you know in the same situation, that's how you discover things really.'

(Mrs Grafton)

'We spoke to teachers in the schools, spoke to other parents, and spoke to my friends who are scattered across the borough and where their children went and what they thought about it.'

(Mrs Gosling)

'There was definitely a feeling that this step into secondary education would have a very, very big influence on what they do in the rest of their life. So you had to put a lot of your attention into each school and approach each school as if your child was definitely going to go there, and size it up, assess your own reactions to it and all the rest of it.'

(Mrs Cornwell)

Adapted from Ball, 2003

Item C The school/parent alliance

questions

1 Using Item A, suggest how cultural capital might give middle-class children an advantage.

2 Using Item B, suggest how social capital might give middle-class children an advantage.

3 How does the cartoon in Item C illustrate the school/parent alliance?

Research indicates that teachers are more likely to define middle rather than working-class pupils as 'able', 'good students' and 'well behaved'. This may well disadvantage working-class pupils.

A *label* is a major identifying characteristic. If, for example, a pupil is labelled as 'bright', others will tend to respond to them and interpret their actions in terms of this label. There is a tendency for a *self-fulfilling prophecy* to result. The pupil will act in terms of the label and see themselves as bright (so fulfilling the prophecy others have made).

Setting and streaming

Most secondary schools have some system for placing pupils in teaching groups in terms of their perceived ability – ie, the way teachers see their ability. These groups include *sets* in which pupils are placed in subject groups (they may be in set 1 for maths, set 3 for art) or *streams* in which they are placed into class groups (class 1, 2, 3) and taught at that level for all subjects.

A number of studies (eg Hargreaves, 1967; Lacey, 1970; Ball, 1981) have looked at the effects of ability grouping in secondary schools. In general, they have found a tendency for middle-class pupils to be placed in the higher groups and for working-class pupils to be placed in the lower groups.

Most teachers prefer to teach higher ability groups. The conduct of pupils in higher groups is likely to be better than of those in lower groups. Those in lower groups tend to develop an *anti-school subculture* in which breaking school rules is highly regarded by some pupils. Teachers spend more time controlling behaviour in these groups at the expense of teaching. They expect less from these pupils, deny them access to higher level knowledge and skills, and place them in lower level examination tiers.

Evaluation To what extent does setting and streaming advantage the largely middle-class higher groups and disadvantage the largely working-class lower groups? The evidence is inconclusive – it is not possible to reach a firm conclusion. In general, research indicates that setting and streaming have little or no effect on pupils' achievement. However, there is some evidence that ability grouping may raise attainment in the top groups and lower it in the bottom groups (Ireson & Hallam, 2001). Where ability groups do have a major effect is in setting for examination entry.

Examination sets

GCSE examinations are tiered. Most are split into higher and foundation tiers. Pupils entered for the foundation tier cannot obtain Grades A* to B. In other words, the highest grade they can achieve is Grade C. Mathematics is divided into three tiers – higher, intermediate and foundation. Grades A* to B are only available to students entered for the higher level. Grade C is the highest grade possible in the intermediate exam, Grade D is the highest grade possible in the foundation exam.

Students are usually placed in sets for exam entry – for example, in the higher or lower History set for entry to the higher or foundation tier History exam. Middle-class students tend to be placed in the higher sets, working-class students in the lower sets. Set placement is based on teachers' assessment of students' ability. According to research by David Gillborn and Deborah Youdell (2001),

summary

1. Class, ethnicity and gender make a difference to educational attainment. Class makes the greatest difference.

2. The following explanations have been given to explain why pupils with working-class backgrounds are less successful.

   - Material deprivation – a lack of money and the things that money can buy.

   - A lack of encouragement, stimulation and interest from parents.

   - Working-class subculture with its emphasis on fatalism, present-time orientation and immediate gratification.

   - Cultural deprivation – an absence of the norms, values and skills needed for high attainment. This view has been strongly criticised.

   - The use of the elaborated code in schools which disadvantages many working-class pupils.

   - A lack of cultural capital. According to Diane Reay, it is

   mothers who have the main influence on their child's education. Their effectiveness depends on the amount of cultural capital at their disposal. Middle-class mothers have most.

   - A lack of social capital. Stephen Ball's research argues that social capital is vital when choosing schools. Middle-class mothers, with their wide social networks, have most.

   - Middle-class pupils are more likely to be placed in higher streams, working-class pupils in lower streams. In general, research indicates that streaming and setting have little or no effect on pupils' achievement. However, they may raise attainment in the top groups and lower it in the bottom groups.

   - What does have an effect is the tendency to enter more working-class pupils for lower level exams, so denying them the opportunity to obtain the top grades.

teachers are more likely to see middle-class students as having the ability to enter higher level exams. And this has more to do with teachers' perceptions of what counts as ability than students' actual ability. The result is discrimination against many working-class students. They are denied the opportunity of even attempting to obtain the higher grades.

Conclusion

This section has looked at social class and educational attainment in terms of what happens within the school. Some researchers argue that class differences in attainment result from the sifting, sorting and assessment of pupils in terms of teachers' perceptions of social class, ability and conduct.

Others argue that class differences in attainment are primarily due to what happens outside the school – to the social inequalities generated by the class structure. Schools from this point of view do little more than reflect and rubber stamp existing inequalities.

Other researchers see class differences in attainment resulting from a combination of what happens inside and outside the school. From this viewpoint the inequalities of the class system are reinforced in the classroom.

Unit 3 Gender and educational attainment

key issues

1 What are the gender differences in educational attainment?
2 What explanations are given for these differences?

In the 1960s and 70s, sociologists were concerned about the apparent underachievement of girls. Why weren't they more ambitious? Why did fewer girls than boys take high status subjects such as maths, physics and chemistry? Why were girls less likely to go to university?

By the 1990s, the concern had shifted to underachieving boys. The so-called *gender gap* in education now meant failing boys and successful girls. For Professor of Education, Ted Wragg, 'the underachievement of boys has become one of the biggest challenges facing society today'. For the former Chief Inspector of Schools, Chris Woodhead,

activity 12 gender and educational attainment

Item A GCSEs

Attainment of 5 or more GCSEs A*- C in Year 11

England and Wales   Percentages

Year	1989	1992	1994	1996	1998	2000	2002
Males	28	33	37	40	42	44	46
Females	31	40	46	49	51	54	56

Adapted from *Youth Cohort Study*, 2002

Item B A levels

Attainment at GCE A level or equivalent qualification

England and Wales   Percentages

	Males		Females	
	2 or more A levels	1 A level	2 or more A levels	1 A level
1995/96	27	7	33	9
1996/97	27	7	33	8
1997/98	30	6	37	7
1998/99	30	6	37	7
1999/2000	31	6	39	7
2000/01	33	4	42	5

Adapted from *Social Trends*, 2003

Item C Higher education

Students in higher education

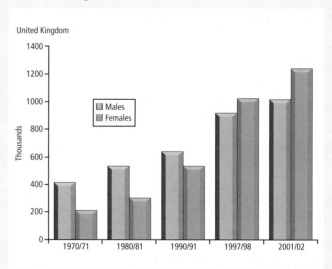

Adapted from various issues of *Social Trends*

question

Briefly summarise the trends shown in Items A, B and C.

underachieving boys are 'one of the most disturbing problems facing the education system'.

The impression sometimes given by the media is of boys failing in droves and of girls racing ahead. But is there really a gender crisis in education? Work carefully through Activity 12. It contains the kind of statistics on which claims of a gender crisis are often based. Then we'll look at various ways of interpreting this evidence.

3.1 Interpreting the statistics

The picture of failing boys and achieving girls is based on the kind of statistics presented in Activity 12. What's wrong with this picture?

Boys are doing better Over the past 50 years, the educational performance of boys and young men has steadily improved. The performance of girls has risen at a faster rate at some levels and in some subjects. However, this hardly justifies blanketing all boys as underachievers. Many boys are doing extremely well (Coffey, 2001).

Only some boys are failing Only certain groups of boys are underachieving. There is a close link between male underachievement and social class – compared to other groups, a high proportion of working-class boys are failing (Epstein et al., 1998).

What's new? In some respects, there's nothing new about girls outperforming boys. When the 11-plus exam was introduced in the 1940s, more girls passed than boys. The results had to be fiddled so that roughly equal numbers of boys and girls went to grammar schools. If the results hadn't been 'adjusted', then two-thirds of grammar school places would have gone to girls (Chitty, 2002).

Hiding girls' failure The preoccupation with so-called 'failing boys' diverts attention from underachieving girls. A high proportion of working-class girls are failing in the school system (Plummer, 2000).

What has changed? In general, the educational performance of girls has improved significantly since the 1980s. And, in general, their improvement has been greater than that of boys. But this does not mean that boys as a group are failing. As noted earlier, the educational performance of most boys is improving.

3.2 Explaining girls' improvement

Why are girls doing so well? Here are some of the explanations suggested by researchers.

Changing attitudes

Judging from a number of studies, girls and young women's attitudes towards education, work and marriage have changed in recent years. Sue Sharpe compared the attitudes of working-class girls in London schools in the early 1970s and 1990s (Sharpe, 1976 & 1994). She found that the 1990s girls were:

- more confident
- more assertive
- more ambitious
- more committed to gender equality.

The main priorities of the 70s girls were 'love, marriage, husbands and children'. By the 1990s, this had changed to 'job, career and being able to support themselves'. And education was seen as the main route to a good job and financial independence.

Changes in the adult world

Changes in the world of work, in the home and in adult relationships may have changed attitudes.

- There has been a steady rise in the numbers of women in the labour force. By 2002, the number of men and women in paid employment was virtually the same (*Social Trends*, 2003). Working mothers provided role models for their daughters. As a result, girls were more likely to see their future in the workplace and to value education as a means to a good job.
- According to Sue Sharpe (1994), girls were increasingly wary of marriage. They had seen adult relationships breaking up all around them. And they had seen women coping alone in what was once a 'man's world'. Girls were now concerned with standing on their own two feet rather than being dependent on a man. As a result, they were more likely to see education as a means to financial independence.

Changes in schools

The abolition of the 11-plus exam and the introduction of comprehensive schools by most local education authorities has removed some of the barriers to girls' achievement. No longer are girls artificially 'failed' in order to get equal numbers of boys and girls into grammar schools.

There has been a growing awareness of gender bias in schools and attempts to remove it. For example, there was a recognition that girls were put off by what were traditionally seen as 'boys' subjects' such as maths, technology, physics and chemistry. This led to the introduction of equal opportunity initiatives such as Girls into Science and Technology.

In 1988, the National Curriculum provided a compulsory core curriculum for all students up to the age of 16 – no matter what their gender. Although the compulsory core has now been slimmed down, all students still have to take maths and science.

activity 13 changing girls

Item A Girl power

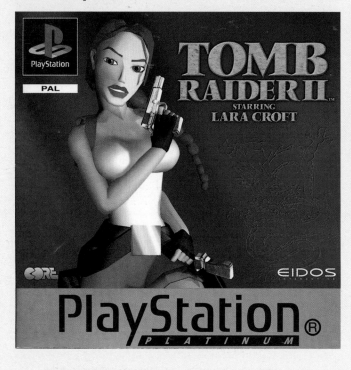

Item B Changing times

Celebrating straight As at A level at Colchester County High School for Girls.

Twenty years ago you watched bright girls leave before A levels, planning only a stop-gap job between marriage and motherhood. Between the extremes of university and supermarket checkout stretched an endless wasteland of dreary typing jobs with criminal rates of pay. If you were one of the tiny minority hoping for university, you worked hard; if not, why bother?

Item C Changing drinks

Early 1970s   Early 1990s

But now that middle ground has been filled with a shimmering improvement of choices – service industries, media jobs and information technology, providing a sexless workplace paradise with no barriers and no preference for men. Whether they get the message from the Spice Girls, Madonna, or their savvy mothers, girls now know that independence means power, and both start with a decent job. This translates into an ambition to get on, and never be financially dependent on a man if you can help it. About time too.

Adapted from White, 1998

question

How might Items A, B and C help to explain girls' rising educational attainment?

3.3 Why are some boys failing?

As noted earlier, most boys and young men are improving their performance in primary, secondary, further and higher education. However, their levels of attainment are rising more slowly than those of girls. And some boys are doing badly – in particular some working-class boys.

Working-class boys have always had problems with the educational system for the reasons outlined in Unit 2. Some researchers believe that these problems have grown in recent years for the following reasons.

Changes in the job market

Manual jobs With the decline in manufacturing and the increasing automation of production, there has been a rapid reduction in semi-skilled and unskilled jobs. The shrinking of this section of the job market has hit working-class males hard. In 2002, the highest unemployment rate – at 10% – was for men in semi-skilled and unskilled occupations which do not usually require formal qualifications (*Social Trends*, 2003).

Manual 'macho' jobs fitted traditional working-class masculine identities. The collapse of this sector of the job market has left these identities uncertain, threatened and confused (Jackson, 1998).

Service sector jobs The new jobs in the service sector tend to be desk jobs in offices and call centres, or jobs involving care for others which require sensitivity and interpersonal skills. These jobs do not sit happily with traditional working-class masculine identities. And even the more 'macho' jobs in the public services – eg, police, fire service and paramedics – now require higher levels of sensitivity and social skills (Mahony, 1998).

Changes in male roles

Traditionally the working man was a father, husband and breadwinner. With increasing numbers of lone-parent families, over 90% of which are headed by women, these roles are closed to many men (see pages 68-71). And boys growing up in these families lack the role models of father, husband and breadwinner.

Lone-parent, mother-headed families are concentrated in the lower working class. Growing up in such families can threaten traditional working-class masculine identities (Jackson, 1998).

Work, home and school

In recent years, working-class boys have become increasingly vulnerable and insecure. They have seen jobless men in the neighbourhood, dependent on welfare with little hope for the future. They have seen traditional working-class jobs drying up. They have seen more and more men fail as breadwinners and fathers.

The result is a 'crisis' in working-class masculinity. How do boys deal with this crisis at school?

School and working-class identity Some working-class boys attempt to deal with the identity problem by adopting an aggressive, macho 'laddishness'. They reject what they see as the middle-class values of the school. Schoolwork is defined as 'sissy' work. As one boy put it, 'The work you do here is girls' work. It's not real work' (Mac an Ghaill, 1994). In other words, it's not the kind of work that 'real' men do. Those who work hard are put down as 'swots' and 'keenos'.

As a result, the anti-school subculture described by Paul Willis in his study of working-class 'lads', develops and directs the boys' behaviour (see page 94). Rejecting the values of the school, some boys look for acceptance, recognition and respect by acting out the norms and values of the anti-school subculture. Reinforced by their peers, they make a considerable contribution to their own educational failure.

summary

1. The educational performance of females has improved significantly since the 1980s. They have overtaken males at every level from primary to higher education.

2. Overall, the performance of males has also improved, but at a slower rate.

3. The following reasons have been suggested for the improvement in female performance:
   - Changing attitudes, eg more ambitious
   - Changes in the adult world, eg growing numbers of women in the labour force
   - Changes in schools, eg reduction in gender bias.

4. In recent years, the attainment levels of some working-class boys have been particularly low. Suggested reasons for this include:
   - Changes in the job market, eg rapid reduction in semi-skilled and unskilled jobs
   - Changes in male roles, eg growing number of female-headed, lone-parent families
   - An adoption of aggressive masculinity along with an increasing rejection of the school and its values.

activity 14 a changing world

Item A The decline of manufacturing

Derelict engineering works, Willenhall, West Midlands

Item B Aggressive masculinity

For many working-class boys, the traditional route to status, pride and security is closed. What some boys are left with is a bitter sense that trying to get work is pointless, and an aggressive culture of masculinity to fill in the despairing gaps.

Adapted from Jackson, 1998

Item C New opportunities

Working in a call centre

If the sort of work available to young working-class people is largely in the service industries, they will need qualities such as warmth, empathy, sensitivity to unspoken needs, and high levels of interpersonal skills to build an effective relationship with customers.

Adapted from Mahoney, 1998

question

Use Items A to C to provide an explanation for the educational failure of some working-class boys.

Unit 4 Ethnicity and educational attainment

key issues

1 How does ethnicity affect educational attainment?
2 What explanations have been given for ethnic differences in attainment?

In 2000, the Office for Standards in Education (OFSTED) published a report entitled *Educational Inequality*. Based in part on information from 118 local education authorities, the report showed that:

- All groups – Whites and ethnic minorities – have improved their educational attainment.
- There are significant differences in the attainment of ethnic groups (Gillborn & Mirza, 2000).

The following section looks at some of the evidence on which these statements are based.

4.1 Ethnicity and attainment – evidence

Activity 15 looks at ethnicity and educational attainment at GCSE level.

activity 15 ethnicity and attainment

Attainment of 5 or more GCSEs A*- C in Year 11
England and Wales   (percentages)

Ethnic group	1988	1995	1997	2000	2002	Improvement (1988-2002)
White	26	42	44	50	52	+26
Black	17	21	28	39	36	+19
Indian	23	44	49	60	60	+37
Pakistani	20	22	28	29	40	+20
Bangladeshi	13	23	32	29	41	+28

Note: Black includes people of African-Caribbean and Black African origin.

Adapted from various *Youth Cohort Studies*

question

Summarise the relationship between ethnicity and educational attainment indicated by the table.

Change over time Activity 15 presents a snapshot of educational attainment at Year 11. It tells us nothing about educational attainment before or after Year 11. It is important to recognise this. For example, the attainment of Pakistani and Bangladeshi pupils is low in the early years of schooling but shows significant improvement once their English improves in secondary school. By comparison, African-Caribbean students make a good start in primary school but their performance shows a marked decline as they move through secondary school (Gillborn & Mirza, 2000).

Gains and losses The table in Activity 15 indicates that, in general, all groups have improved their performance since the introduction of GCSEs. Some have made greater gains than others – for example, the Indian group with an increase of 37 percentage points. However, the Black group have caused concern with a decline in their performance between 2000 and 2002.

Ethnicity, gender and class Just how much are the differences in attainment at GCSE due to ethnicity? We already know that social class and gender affect attainment. Before going further, it is important to look at their effects in order to assess the effect of ethnicity.

Work through Activity 16 now in order to assess the effect of gender.

activity 16 ethnicity, gender and attainment at GCSE

Attainment of 5 or more GCSEs A*- C in Year 11, 2000

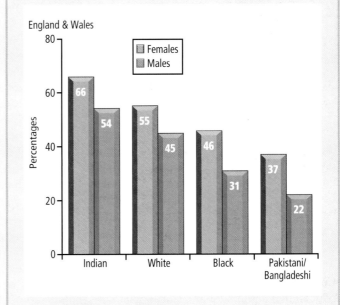

Adapted from *Social Trends*, 2002

question

What relationships between ethnicity, gender and educational attainment are indicated by the bar chart?

The bar chart in Activity 16 shows that in each of the ethnic groups, girls do better than boys. Clearly, there is a gender gap in attainment. But, even taking this into account, there are still important ethnic differences. For example, Indian girls do better than Indian boys, but they also do better than girls from other ethnic groups.

Now work through Activity 17 in order to assess the effect of class.

activity18 ethnicity and setting

Item A Allocation to exam sets

Ethnicity	Pupil	Third year exam results (marks out of 100)				Set placement (O = GCE O level)			
		English	Maths	French	Physics	English	Maths	French	Physics
African-Caribbean	A	73	44	58	---	CSE	CSE	CSE	---
	B	62	63	60	59	CSE	CSE	CSE	CSE
	C	64	45	56	72	CSE	CSE	---	CSE
	D	68	37	82	---	CSE	CSE	CSE	---
Asian	E	51	77	---	55	O	O	---	O
	F	60	56	58	---	O	O	O	---
	G	61	62	55.5	---	O	O	O	---
	H	54	55	---	40	O	O	---	O
White	I	61	62	---	62	O	O	---	O
	J	52	57	55	---	O	O	O	---
	K	75	82	77.5	72	O	O	O	O
	L	54	75	64	72	O	O	O	O

A CSE grade 1 is equivalent to an O level grade C.

Adapted from Wright, 1986

Item B Setting and perceived behaviour

The deputy head admitted that setting was not based solely on exam results – 'It is the case that the school tends to put the dutiful children in O level groups'. Some teachers saw African-Caribbean students as 'less cooperative'. One English teacher described all her African-Caribbean students as 'a disruptive influence'. It appeared that at least some students were placed in lower sets on the basis of teachers' views of their behaviour rather than ability.

Adapted from Wright, 1986

question

In view of Items A and B, do you think that racial discrimination played a part in the setting of students? Explain your answer.

Asian children, especially the younger ones, were often seen as a problem, but as a problem that could be largely ignored. They received least attention, were often excluded from classroom discussions and rarely asked to answer questions. Teachers tended to assume that their command of English was insufficient for full classroom participation. Yet they also saw Asian pupils as well disciplined and highly motivated.

African-Caribbean children – especially boys – were expected to behave badly. They received considerable attention – nearly all of it negative. Their behaviour was usually seen as aggressive, disobedient and disruptive. They were often singled out for criticism, even for actions which were ignored in other pupils. As a result, they often felt picked on and treated unfairly.

Secondary schools Research by David Gillborn (1990) largely reflects Wright's findings. He spent two years studying an inner-city comprehensive school gathering data

from classroom observation and interviews with teachers and students. He found that the vast majority of teachers tried to treat all students fairly. However, they perceived students differently and on this basis treated them differently. In particular, they often saw the actions of African-Caribbean students as a threat where no threat was intended. And they reacted accordingly by disciplining them.

African-Caribbean students were more likely to be criticised and punished, even when members of other ethnic groups committed the same offence. As a result, there was considerable tension and conflict between White teachers and Caribbean students.

Máirtín Mac an Ghaill (1988) studied a boys' comprehensive in the early 1980s. The school was streamed with boys being demoted to lower streams for what was seen as bad behaviour. In the words of one teacher 'There are boys of relatively higher ability in the lower sets,

activity 19 different treatment

The following is taken from observation of a nursery class of four-year-olds.

Teacher:	Let's do one song before home time.
Peter:	(*White boy*) Humpty Dumpty
Teacher:	No, I'm choosing today. Let's do something we have not done for a while. I know, we'll do the Autumn song. What about the Autumn song we sing. Don't shout out, put your hand up nicely.
Mandy:	(*shouting out*) Two little leaves on a tree.
Teacher:	She's nearly right.
Marcus:	(*African-Caribbean boy with his hand up*) I know.
Teacher:	(*talking to the group*) Is she right when she says 'two little leaves on a tree'?
Whole group:	No.
Teacher:	What is it Peter?
Peter:	Four.
Teacher:	Nearly right.
Marcus:	(*waving his hand for attention*) Five.
Teacher:	Don't shout out Marcus, do you know Susan?
Susan:	(*White girl*) Five.
Teacher:	(*holding up one hand*) Good because we have got how many fingers on this hand?
Whole group:	Five.
Teacher:	OK, let's only have one hand because we've only got five leaves. How many would we have if we had too many. Don't shout out, hands up.
Mandy:	(*shouting out*) One, two, three, four, five, six, seven, eight, nine, ten.
Teacher:	Good, OK how many fingers have we got?
Marcus:	Five.
Teacher:	Don't shout out Marcus, put your hand up. Deane, how many?
Deane:	Five.
Teacher:	That's right, we're going to use five today, what makes them dance about, these leaves?
Peter:	(*shouting out*) The wind.
Teacher:	That's right.

Adapted from Wright, 1992

question

Make out a case that the teacher's treatment of Marcus is

a) racist

b) non-racist.

especially among the West Indians. I've told you before Johnson and Brian were marvellous at Maths, especially problem-solving. But it's their, it's the West Indians' attitude and that must decide it in the end. You can't promote a boy who is known to be a troublemaker, who's a dodger. It will look like a reward for bad behaviour.'

Many African-Caribbean pupils responded with resistance. They formed an anti-school peer group, the Rasta Heads, which rejected many of the school's norms and values.

Racism in schools – evaluation

Methodology Wright, Gillborn and Mac an Ghaill's studies use a research method known as *ethnography*. This involves direct observation of relatively small groups, often over fairly long periods of time. Because the samples are small, it is not possible to make generalisations – ie, to say that the findings apply to all multi-ethnic schools.

However, the insights ethnography provides are unlikely to come from research methods such as questionnaires. For example, in *The School Effect*, Smith and Tomlinson's questionnaire to parents revealed little evidence of racism in schools. Ethnographic methods often give a very different picture. But not always.

An alternative view Peter Foster (1990) conducted an ethnographic study of a multi-ethnic comprehensive between 1985 and 1987. He found no evidence of racism. Students from ethnic minorities were not treated differently from White students. In fact, minority students, especially African-Caribbean girls – achieved better results than White pupils.

Foster admitted that the school he studied was distinctive. It was situated in a community with a long history of ethnic cooperation. And, at the time of his study, the staff were involved in an anti-racist programme. Whatever the differences between this school and others, Foster's study warns against the dangers of generalising from a few examples.

Despite this warning, there is evidence of racism in schools. Ethnic minority pupils tend to be over-represented in the lower sets and in the lower tiers for GCSE exam entry. And African-Caribbean boys in particular tend to be regarded as badly behaved and troublesome by many teachers, even when their behaviour is similar to that of White boys. This can only disadvantage ethnic minority pupils (Pilkington, 2003).

key terms

Prejudice Prejudging members of groups in terms of stereotypes – sweeping generalisations which are applied to all members of the group. Prejudice can be positive or negative.
Discrimination Acting in a certain way towards people because they are seen to be members of a particular group. Discrimination can be positive or negative.
Racism Prejudice and discrimination against groups seen as racially different.
Ethnography A research method based on direct observation of relatively small groups, often over fairly long periods of time.

summary

1. There are significant differences in the educational attainment of ethnic groups.

2. The following factors outside the school have been seen to affect ethnic differences in attainment.
    - Social class – ethnic groups with the lowest attainment have the highest proportion of people in the working class.
    - Economic factors – low attainment is linked to low income. The lower a person's social class, the lower their income.
    - Cultural factors – available evidence suggests that ethnic subcultures have little effect on educational attainment.

3. The following factors within schools have been seen to affect ethnic differences in attainment.
    - Racism – particularly directed against African Caribbeans
    - Discrimination in setting
    - Discrimination in everyday classroom interaction.

Unit 5 Relationships and processes within schools

keyissues

1 What is the hidden curriculum and how does it operate?

2 What are pupil subcultures and how do they develop?

3 What factors shape teacher-pupil relationships?

4 How are teaching and learning organised?

5.1 The hidden curriculum

Look back to Activity 19 on page 117, which shows how Marcus, a four-year-old African-Caribbean boy, is given a hard time by his teacher. Let's assume that Marcus has a tendency to over-enthusiasm, but apart from this is a well-behaved and likeable boy. What message is the teacher sending to Marcus and the other children?

If she consistently puts all African-Caribbean children

down, then her unspoken message states that African-Caribbean children are different, that they should not be shown the same kindness and consideration as other children, and that they are troublesome and need keeping in check. If other teachers treat African-Caribbean pupils in the same way, then they are all transmitting similar messages. And these messages will form part of the *hidden curriculum* of the school.

Defining the hidden curriculum

The *formal school curriculum* consists of the knowledge and skills which pupils are expected to acquire. In state schools, part of this curriculum – the National Curriculum – is laid down by the government. It is spelt out in detail in official publications.

The hidden curriculum is the messages schools transmit to pupils without directly teaching them or spelling them out. It consists of ideas, beliefs, norms and values which are often taken for granted and transmitted as part of the normal routines and procedures of school life. It includes the unwritten and often unstated rules and regulations which guide and direct everyday school behaviour (Ballantine & Spade, 2001).

How is the hidden curriculum transmitted?

The hidden curriculum is transmitted in many different ways. Think about the following.

School organisation

- Is there a hierarchy of power, status and authority?
- Who holds the top posts (eg, headteacher, senior staff), who occupies the lowest (eg, cleaners)? What is their class, gender, ethnicity and age group?
- Are there mixed-ability classes, or are pupils divided into streams or sets? Are certain groups – eg, working-class boys – usually found in certain sets?
- Are lots of pupils excluded? If so, which pupils?

The behaviour and attitudes of those in authority

- How do the head, senior staff, other teachers and support staff (eg cooks and caretakers) relate to each other and to pupils?
- Are pupils allowed to have a say in school life?
- How do those in authority relate to pupils in general and to the class, gender and ethnicity of pupils?

Transmitting messages Messages are transmitted in all these areas. For example, if the top posts are filled by males, this says something about gender relationships. If pupils have little or no say in the running of the school, this says something about power in organisations. If disproportionate numbers of working-class boys are found in the lower sets, this says something about inequality in the wider society.

The hidden curriculum – functionalist and Marxist views

Functionalist and Marxist perspectives on education were outlined in Unit 1. Each contains a particular view of the hidden curriculum – what it is, how it is transmitted and how it relates to the wider society.

Functionalist views As outlined earlier, functionalists see the transmission of society's core values as one of the main functions of the education system. This can be seen as part of the hidden curriculum. It is hidden in the sense that teachers and pupils are often unaware of the process. It is part of the curriculum because it's found in every school.

Talcott Parsons (1951, 1961) provides an example using the value of individual achievement, one of the major values in Western industrial society. In schools young people are required to achieve as individuals. They take exams on their own, not as a member of a team. Their individual achievements are carefully graded and assessed. High achievement is rewarded with praise, high status,

activity20 hidden messages

Item A Power and gender

In Britain's secondary schools, women tend to remain in the lower teaching ranks and in particular subject areas. Those who are promoted often end up as head of year, responsible for pastoral care – dealing with students' problems.

Adapted from Langham, 2000

Item C School assembly

Assembly started when teachers marched their tutorial groups to the hall, where they were expected to stand in straight lines. Here, senior house staff were much in evidence as they were concerned that pupils should stand up straight and stand quietly until the headmaster arrived. Meanwhile, other teachers stood around the edge of the hall, talking to each other, making jokes, and exchanging stories until the headmaster entered.

Adapted from Burgess, 1983

Item B Social control and ethnicity

Exclusion is one of the methods of social control which schools can use to deal with students they regard as troublesome. Black pupils are more likely to be excluded than White pupils. In 2000/01, 38 in every 10 thousand African-Caribbean pupils were permanently excluded compared to 13 in every 10 thousand White pupils.

Adapted from National Statistics Online, 2003

question

What messages are being transmitted by Items A, B and C?

good grades and valuable qualifications. In this way, young people are encouraged to value individual achievement. And this prepares them to achieve as individuals in the wider society.

Marxist views As outlined earlier, Marxists argue that the main job of schools is social reproduction – producing the next generation of workers *schooled* to accept their roles in capitalist society.

For Bowles and Gintis (1976), this is done primarily through the hidden curriculum. They claim that schools produce subordinate, well-disciplined workers who will submit to control from above and take orders rather than question them. Schools do this by rewarding conformity, obedience, hard work and punctuality, and by penalising creativity, originality and independence.

Conclusion

The idea of a hidden curriculum is useful. Clearly, there's a lot more being taught and learned in schools than the formal curriculum of English, maths, science, and so on. And clearly much of this is 'hidden' – teachers and learners are often unaware of what's going on.

The content of the hidden curriculum is open to interpretation. Have the functionalists got it right? Have the Marxists got it right? This partly depends on how you see capitalist society.

5.2 Pupil subcultures

Pupil subcultures are the distinctive norms and values developed by groups of young people in schools. The anti-school subculture identified by Paul Willis in his study of working-class boys in a secondary school is an example of a pupil subculture (see page 94).

This section asks what subcultures exist in schools and where do they come from. Are they a reflection of life outside the school – do pupils bring their subculture from the neighbourhood into the school? Or, do subcultures develop in response to pupils' experiences within schools – for example, their placement in particular sets? Or, do they develop from young people's experiences both inside and outside the school?

A white, male, middle-class subculture

One of the earliest studies of pupil subcultures was conducted in the late 1950s/early 60s by Colin Lacey (1970). The pupils were mainly middle class and attended Hightown Grammar School (not its real name). Many had been high achievers at their local primary school – they were the 'top scholars, team leaders, head boys and teachers' favourites'.

In their first year, all new boys showed high levels of commitment to the school, proudly wearing their school caps and jackets, and enthusiastically attending school functions and clubs. In class, they were eager, straining to answer questions, cooperating with their teachers and competing among themselves. Six months into the second year, one class was seen by their teachers as difficult to teach. In the words of one teacher, 'They're unacademic, they can't cope with the work'. What had happened to transform a group of high-achieving, academically-able first year pupils into 'unacademic' second year pupils? To help explain this, Lacey introduced two concepts – *differentiation* and *polarisation*.

activity21 views of the hidden curriculum

Item A　*Prize day*

Awards for academic excellence in an American school

Item B　*Learning to submit*

In a study of 237 students in their final year at a New York high school, the researchers claimed that high grades were linked with perseverance, obedience, consistency, dependability and punctuality. Students with high grades were often below average when measured in terms of creativity, originality and independence of judgement.

Adapted from Bowles & Gintis, 1976

questions

1　How can Item A be used to support a functionalist view of the hidden curriculum?

2　How can Item B be used to support a Marxist view of the hidden curriculum?

Differentiation This is the process by which teachers judge and rank pupils in terms of their academic ability (as perceived by the teacher) and their behaviour. On this basis, they are differentiated into streams. As time goes on, pupils get a sense of how both teachers and fellow pupils rate and rank them.

Polarisation Gradually, a gap opened up – and kept growing – between the pupils who were defined as successful and those defined as unsuccessful – the two groups became polarised.

The subculture of success Pupils in the top stream accepted the value system of the school – they worked hard and were well-behaved. The system rewarded them with prestige – they were praised and respected by teachers. And the boys reinforced each other's behaviour – they were members of a successful peer group sharing the same values.

The subculture of failure Pupils in the bottom stream developed an anti-school subculture which became more extreme as the years went by. The school's values were turned upside down – boys gained prestige for giving cheek to a teacher, truanting, refusing to do homework, and for smoking and drinking.

This was a group thing – boys gained respect from other members of the group for anti-school behaviour. In this way, they reinforced each other's behaviour. And in the process, their school work steadily deteriorated.

Conclusion Lacey's study suggests that pupil subcultures develop within the school. They are a response to the way pupils are perceived by teachers, by other pupils, and by themselves. And they are a reaction to the way school classes are organised – in this case, streamed – and all that this 'says' about pupils in different streams.

---

key terms

Pupil subcultures The distinctive norms and values developed by groups of young people in schools.
Differentiation Separating pupils into groups on the basis of their perceived ability and behaviour.
Polarisation The widening gap in terms of measured ability and behaviour between top and bottom classes.

White, male, working-class subcultures

The lads As outlined earlier, Paul Willis studied a small group of working-class boys – the 'lads' – during their last year and a half at school (see page 94). In many ways the anti-school subculture developed by the lads was similar to the behaviour of the boys in the bottom stream in Lacey's study of Hightown Grammar. However, Willis's explanation of the subculture's development is very different.

According to Willis, the lads' behaviour reflected a) their expectations of future employment and b) the working-class subculture they brought to school with them. The lads were keen to leave school as soon as possible and looked forward to 'real' work – adult, male, manual jobs. School

was a waste of time.

- The lads didn't need academic qualifications for the jobs they wanted.
- They despised those who conformed to the school's values – who they called the 'ear 'oles' – seeing them as cissies.
- They wanted a context – manual work – where they could be real men.

The lads' anti-school subculture reflected the working-class culture they'd learned from their fathers, elder brothers and other men in the neighbourhood. Having a 'laff', a lack of respect for authority and messing around are aspects of manual working-class male subculture. The lads are attracted to this kind of behaviour and reproduce it in the classroom.

For Willis, the lads' anti-school subculture is shaped mainly by their expectations about the jobs they hope to get and by the working-class subculture they bring with them to school.

Working-class peer groups Willis has been criticised for basing his conclusion on a very small sample – 12 boys – and for ignoring other pupil subcultures in the school. Máirtín Mac an Ghaill (1994) studied Year 11 students in the early 1990s, in Parnell School (not its real name), a comprehensive in the West Midlands. He identified three working-class male peer groups, each with a distinctive subculture.

Mac an Ghaill argues that to some extent these subcultures are shaped by:

- the way students are organised into sets
- the type of curriculum they follow
- the teacher-student social relations which result from the above.

Macho Lads The Macho Lads were relegated to the bottom two sets for all their subjects. They were academic failures and treated as such by their teachers. Like Willis's lads, they rejected the school's values and the teachers' authority. Their concerns were acting tough, having a laugh, looking after their mates and looking smart. The teachers viewed them with suspicion and policed their behaviour, banning certain clothes and hairstyles, and making constant demands – 'Sit up straight', 'Look at me when I'm talking to you' and 'Walk properly down the corridor'.

Academic Achievers Apart from the Macho Lads, Mac an Ghaill identified two other working-class pupil subcultures. The Academic Achievers saw hard work and educational qualifications as the route to success. They were in the top sets, and received preferential treatment in terms of timetabling, books and experienced teachers. The Academic Achievers tended to come from the upper levels of the working class.

New Enterprisers The New Enterprisers saw a different route to success. They focused on vocational subjects such as business studies and technology and looked forward to a future in high-skilled areas of the labour market.

activity22 the Macho Lads

Darren:	It's the teachers that make the rules. It's them that decide that it's either them or us. So you are often put into a situation with teachers where you have to defend yourself. Sometimes it's direct in the classroom. But it's mainly the headcases that would hit a teacher. Most of the time it's all the little things.
Interviewer:	Like what?
Gilroy:	Acting tough by truanting, coming late to lessons, not doing homework, acting cool by not answering teachers, pretending you didn't hear them; that gets them mad. Lots of different things.
Noel:	Teachers are always suspicious of us (the Macho Lads). Just like the cops, trying to set you up.

Adapted from Mac an Ghaill, 1994

Messing around

question

Provide a brief explanation for the attitudes expressed above.

White, female subcultures

Most of the research has focused on male subcultures. However, the following studies suggest some interesting contrasts between male and female pupil subcultures.

Exaggerated femininity Research by Scott Davies (1995) in Canada indicates that girls' resistance to schooling is less aggressive and confrontational than male anti-school behaviour. Where the 'lads' display an 'exaggerated masculinity', the Canadian girls adopt an 'exaggerated femininity'.

They expressed their opposition to school by focusing on traditional gender roles. In Davies's words, 'Girls accentuate their femininity in exaggerated displays of physical maturity and hyper-concerns with "romance" on the one hand, and prioritise domestic roles such as marriage, child-rearing and household duties over schooling on the other hand'. So they wrote school off and invested their hopes in romance and future domestic roles.

You're wasting my time John Abraham's study of an English comprehensive indicates a different strategy of resistance. The girls pushed the school rules to the limit and responded to discipline by suggesting that it prevented them from getting on with their work. Teachers' objections to their behaviour were rejected as a waste of their valuable time (Abraham, 1995).

African-Caribbean male subcultures

Anti-school subcultures A number of studies have identified African-Caribbean anti-school subcultures. These

subcultures are seen to develop from factors both inside and outside the school (Gaine & George, 1999).

Within schools, teachers tend to see African-Caribbean males as aggressive, challenging and disruptive. Often this is a misreading of African-Caribbean youth subculture – ways of walking, talking and dressing are sometimes interpreted by teachers as a challenge to their authority when none is intended. As a result of these misconceptions, African-Caribbean students tend to be singled out for punishment when White and Asian students are just as guilty. This leads some pupils to suspect teachers of racism. And this can lead to anti-school subcultures (Connolly, 1998).

As a result of both their class and ethnicity, a disproportionate number of African-Caribbean students are labelled as less able and placed in lower sets. Again, this can lead to anti-school subcultures.

As noted earlier, African-Caribbean students sometimes bring Black street culture into the classroom. And this can be seen by some teachers as disruptive with its emphasis on aggressive masculinity.

A variety of subcultures Sociologists tend to focus on anti-school subcultures. In some ways, they are more interesting and colourful than conformist subcultures. Particularly in the case of African-Caribbeans, this tends to overlook the variety of responses to schooling.

In a study of African-Caribbean students in a boys-only, 11-16 comprehensive school, Tony Sewell (1997) identifies four main responses.

- **Conformists** These pupils (41%) accepted the value of education and the means to achieve educational success – behaving well and working hard. Conformists felt they couldn't succeed educationally *and* embrace the values and norms of their own Black peer group. This is a gamble, because if they don't succeed, they may lose the security which comes from being seen as a part of the Black community.

- **Innovators** These students (35%) accepted the value of education and wanted academic success but rejected the schooling process. Although anti-school, they tried to keep out of trouble. They attempted to distance themselves from the conformists and from teachers.

- **Retreatists** A small group (6%) of loners who made themselves as inconspicuous as possible. Many had special educational needs.

- **Rebels** These students (18%) rejected the school and projected an image of aggressive masculinity. Some modelled themselves on the Jamaican Yard Man, noted for his supposed physical and sexual prowess. They treated the Conformists with contempt, they were challenging and confrontational, and sometimes violent. Many saw academic qualifications as worthless – White racism would prevent them from achieving high status occupations.

Conclusion The above study is important because it shows the variety of African-Caribbean pupil subcultures rather than simply focusing on anti-school subcultures.

This study also shows how pupil subcultures are influenced by what goes on inside and outside the school. For example, the Rebels drew on Black street culture, arriving at school with patterns in their hair. This was

activity23 African-Caribbean students

Item A *Working for himself*

Calvin has set up in business as a 'mobile barber'. Although still at school, he says he can make up to £300 a week.

Interviewer:	How important is it for you to own your own business?
Calvin:	It is important for Black people to make money because White people don't take us seriously because we're poor.
Interviewer:	Is education important to you?
Calvin:	Not really. I know what I need to know from the street. I'll give it three years and I bet no-one will bother with school. There ain't no jobs for no-one and they don't want to give jobs to Black people.

Adapted from Sewell, 1997

Item B *Setting a good example*

Interviewer:	Do you belong to a gang?
Kelvin:	No, because my mum says I shouldn't hang around students who get into trouble. I must take my opportunity while I can.
Interviewer:	What students in this school do you avoid?
Kelvin:	They are fourth years, you can easily spot the way they walk around in groups, they are mostly Black with one or two Whites. They're wearing baseball hats and bopping (*Black stylised walk*).
Interviewer:	Don't you ever bop?
Kelvin:	Sometimes for a laugh, but it's really a kind of walk for bad people. I wouldn't walk like this in school in front of the teachers. It sets a bad example.

Adapted from Sewell, 1997

Item C *Celebrating*

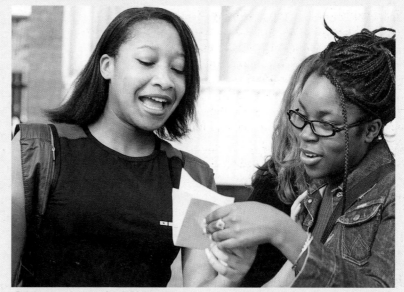

Celebrating successful GCSE results

questions

1. It is important not to see the anti-school subculture as the typical response of African-Caribbean young men. Discuss with some reference to Items A and B.

2. Briefly explain why African-Caribbean girls often do well at school and college.

banned, despite White boys being allowed to wear ponytails. This is seen as a lack of respect and pupils responded aggressively. Teachers punished them and so an anti-school subculture developed, shaped by factors from both inside and outside the school (Sewell, 1997).

African-Caribbean female subcultures

A number of studies of African-Caribbean female pupil subcultures have produced the following picture (Mac an Ghaill, 1988, 1992; Gillborn, 1990; Mirza, 1992). These findings apply to many, though by no means all, students.

Generally, African-Caribbean girls are pro-education – they are ambitious, determined to succeed, and are aiming for high-status, well-paid occupations. However, they tend not to identify with their teachers and school. This is partly in response to the open racism of a small number of teachers and the clumsy, well-meaning but often unhelpful 'help' offered by many teachers in response to the girls' ethnicity (Mirza, 1992) – see page 126.

African-Caribbean girls usually keep a low profile, keep their distance and avoid confrontation. In this way, they maintain their self-respect and don't have to compromise.

5.3 Teacher-pupil relationships

This section looks at the relationships between teachers and pupils. It focuses on the way teachers define, classify and evaluate pupils and how these processes affect pupils' behaviour.

Teacher expectations

A famous study conducted in 1964 by Robert Rosenthal and Leonora Jacobson, looked at the effects of teachers' expectations on pupils' behaviour. The researchers told teachers in a primary school in California that they had identified a number of pupils – the 'spurters' – as likely to make rapid progress. Unknown to the teachers, these pupils were selected at random. Yet, judging from the results of intelligence tests, the spurters made greater progress than their classmates over the next year.

Rosenthal and Jacobson concluded that their progress was due to the way they were defined. Their teachers expected more from them, conveyed this expectation to them, and the pupils acted accordingly. Yet, in Rosenthal and Jacobson's (1968) words, the only difference between the 'spurters' and their classmates was 'entirely in the minds of teachers'.

Rosenthal and Jacobson used the idea of a *self-fulfilling prophecy* to explain their results. If people are defined in a certain way, this definition includes a prediction or prophecy of their future behaviour. If others act as if the prophecy is true, then there is a tendency for it to come to pass – to fulfil itself.

The definition acts as a *label*. According to *labelling theory*, if someone is labelled as a certain kind of person,

others will respond to them in terms of the label. And there is a tendency for the person to adopt that identity and act in terms of it.

Evaluation Rosenthal and Jacobson's research has been extremely influential. However, attempts to replicate (repeat) their study have produced mixed results with some suggesting that labelling was of little or no significance. However, many researchers argue that labelling is important, that the self-fulfilling prophecy is real, and that it can help to explain differences in educational attainment.

Teachers' perceptions and social class

How do teachers assess pupils' ability? To some extent by their exam results and the reports of other teachers on pupils' progress and potential. But, as Units 2, 3 and 4 indicate, teachers' assessments can be affected by pupils' social class, ethnicity and gender. And this in turn, can affect teachers' relationships with pupils.

Class and the 'ideal pupil' An early study looking at the influence of pupils' class on teachers' perceptions was conducted in the early 1950s by the American sociologist Howard Becker. He interviewed 60 teachers from Chicago high schools and found they tended to share an image of the 'ideal pupil'.

Teachers perceived middle-class pupils as closest to this ideal, and pupils from the lower working class as furthest from it. Those in the lowest class grouping were seen as less able, lacking motivation and difficult to control. As a result, teachers felt the best they could do was 'just try to get some basic things over to them' (Becker, 1971).

Teachers were unaware that the social class background of pupils influenced their assessments. Nor did they realise that perceptions of class also influenced the level of work they felt appropriate for pupils.

Class in a nursery school An American study of children starting nursery school shows how early and how quickly the link between class and ability can be made. By the eighth day, children had been allocated to one of three tables depending on the teacher's perception of their ability. And this perception, unknown to the teacher, was based on the child's class background, with working-class children being placed on the 'lower-ability' table (Rist, 1970).

Class and 'ability' Research in Britain presents a similar picture. David Gillborn and Deborah Youdell (2001) conducted research in two London secondary schools from 1995 to 1997. They discovered that teachers had a 'common sense understanding of ability'. Using this as a yardstick, they allocated pupils to different examination sets.

Working-class pupils were more likely to be seen as disruptive, as lacking in motivation and lacking in parental support. As a result, they 'face a particular problem in convincing teachers that they have "ability" '. And because of this, they are more likely to be placed in lower level sets and entered for foundation tier examinations.

As a result of making a link between so-called 'ability' and social class, teachers systematically discriminated against working-class pupils (Gillborn & Youdell, 2001).

Class and teacher-pupil relationships As the section on pupil subcultures indicated, teachers' perceptions of students can have an important effect on day-to-day relationships. Generally, teachers prefer to teach pupils they see as able and highly motivated. They place these students in higher sets and respond more favourably towards them. As a result, teacher-pupil relationships tend to be positive.

Conversely, teachers' views of students who have been defined as less able and placed in lower sets tend to be less favourable. These students may respond with resentment and hostility. And this can result in discipline problems and negative relationships between teachers and pupils.

Teachers' perceptions and ethnicity

African-Caribbeans Gillborn and Youdell's (2001) findings about working-class pupils outlined above apply equally to African-Caribbean pupils, no matter what their social class. Thus, there was a tendency to see African-Caribbean pupils as less able and more disruptive. This reflects the findings of a number of studies, particularly of African-Caribbean boys (see pages 116-118 and 122-124).

Primary schools As noted earlier, Cecile Wright's research in inner-city primary schools indicated that teachers tended to see African-Caribbean children, especially boys, as aggressive and disobedient. They were singled out for criticism and punishment, for which they felt picked on and unfairly treated. As a result, teacher-pupil relationships tended to be negative – abrasive and sometimes hostile (Wright, 1992).

Secondary schools Wright's findings from primary schools are mirrored in studies of secondary schools. For example, Tony Sewell's (1997) study of a boys' 11-16 comprehensive school suggested that African-Caribbean boys' were singled out for punishment. For example, they made up 32% of the student population but comprised 85% of those excluded.

Relationships with teachers were often strained and difficult. According to Sewell, teachers were sometimes frightened by the physical size and aggression of some of the more assertive pupils. There was a tendency to lump all African-Caribbean boys together. Those who conformed to the school's values and those who rebelled against them were often judged and treated in terms of the same negative stereotypes.

Sewell divided the teachers into three groups in terms of their relationships with African-Caribbean pupils.

1 **Supportive teachers** About 10% of staff. They did their best to support and guide pupils and usually established good relationships.

2 **Irritated teachers** About 60% of staff. Although they could be supportive, they felt firmer discipline was needed. They blamed the boys' street culture for many of the school's problems.

3 **Antagonistic teachers** Around 30% who were either openly racist or objected to African-Caribbean street culture – for example, hairstyles and 'bopping' (a stylised walk). As the term 'antagonistic teachers' suggests, their relationships with African-Caribbean pupils were strained and sometimes hostile.

African-Caribbean girls A study by Heidi Mirza (1992) of two south London comprehensives focused on 62 young Black women, aged 15-19. Mirza identifies five types of teacher in terms of their relationships with and attitudes towards Black students.

activity24 an ideal pupil

questions

How does this cartoon illustrate:

a) the ideas of labelling and the self-fulfilling prophecy

b) teachers' expectations of and relationships with pupils?

1 **Overt racists** A small minority who the girls avoided where possible.

2 **The Christians** Tried to be 'colour blind', claiming to see no difference between ethnic groups and the White majority, and refusing to see racism as a problem. They sometimes expected too little of the girls and gave them glowing reports for average achievement.

3 **The crusaders** Anti-racists who tried to make their lessons relevant to Black students. Because they knew little about their students, lessons tended to be confusing and irrelevant.

4 **Liberal chauvinists** Like the crusaders, they were well-meaning, but tended to underestimate their students' ability.

5 **Black teachers** A small group who showed no favouritism and were liked and respected. The girls found their help and advice extremely valuable.

In general, the young women in Mirza's research were ambitious, hard-working and determined to succeed. They rejected the negative views of their blackness, the low expectations of their potential, and the patronising and unhelpful 'help'. They tended to keep their distance and maintain a cool relationship with their teachers.

South Asian pupils Cecile Wright's study of four inner-city primary schools gives the following picture of the relationship between teachers and Asian children in the nursery units.

Asian children, especially the younger ones, were often seen as a problem, but as a problem that could be largely ignored. They received least attention, were often excluded from classroom discussions and rarely asked to answer questions. Teachers tended to assume that their command of English was insufficient for full classroom participation. Yet they also saw Asian pupils as well disciplined and highly motivated (Wright, 1992).

Paul Connolly's (1998) study of a multi-ethnic, inner-city primary school gives the following picture of the relationship between South Asian 5 and 6-year-olds and their teachers. The children were seen as obedient, hard working and conformist. Teachers expected them to produce high quality work.

Girls were seen as models of good behaviour. When the boys did misbehave, this was seen as 'silly' rather than a challenge to the teacher's authority. As a result, they were not punished as much as African-Caribbean boys. Boys were often praised for good work, while girls tended to be left alone – teachers felt they didn't need the same help and encouragement (Connolly, 1998).

Teachers' perceptions and gender

'Girls get much less attention than boys 'cos boys make a fuss and make themselves noticed – they wanna be noticed so they make a racket' (quoted in Lees, 1986). This complaint finds support from a number of studies.

Typical boys and girls In his study of a comprehensive school, conducted in 1986, John Abraham (1995) asked teachers to describe a typical boy and a typical girl. The typical boy is not particularly bright, likes a laugh, sometimes deliberately misbehaves and always wants to be noticed. The typical girl is bright, well-behaved and hardworking, doesn't say much, can be timid, silly and gigglish.

Boys tend to be seen as behaviour problems. They were told off for misbehaviour much more often than girls. However, not all this attention was negative. Boys were asked many more questions than girls in maths and in some English classes. Maybe as a result of this imbalance, girls asked teachers far more questions than boys.

Attending to boys In *Invisible Women: The schooling scandal*, Dale Spender (1983) tape-recorded lessons given by herself and other teachers. Boys received over 60% of teachers' time – 62% in her case even though she tried to divide her time equally between boys and girls. Compared to boys, girls were 'invisible'. They tended to blend into the background, a strategy encouraged by the fact that boys often poked fun at their contributions to lessons. And teachers usually allowed boys to get away with insulting and abusive comments to girls.

Michelle Stanworth's (1983) study of A-level students and teachers in a college of further education reflects this focus on boys. Stanworth found that teachers gave more time and attention to boys, were more likely to know boys' names, and expressed more concern and interest in them (for further details, see page 96).

Gender and society Some studies suggest that if only teachers got rid of their sexist attitudes then everything would be alright. Boys and girls would then be treated equally. But classroom interaction is a two-way process. It is not simply teacher led.

Jane French (1986) argues that pupils bring their own behaviour patterns to the classroom, patterns which differ for boys and girls. Basing her research on video recordings of children in infant schools, French found that boys were more mobile and active, they were more disruptive and demanded more attention. Although girls were eager and interested, they were more likely to obey rules, for example, raising their hands and waiting for permission to speak. Simply because their behaviour was more problematic, boys got more attention.

Gender behaviour is shaped by the wider society and brought into the classroom. In French's view, 'the most determined action taken within the school cannot effectively counter the influence of peer group, magazines, television and family'.

5.4 The organisation of teaching and learning

This section looks at how pupils are allocated to teaching groups, and how this shapes what they are taught and the examinations they take. It draws together and develops

activity25 teachers and pupils

Item A Social class

Teacher A: Some of the class have written to Oldham Town Council for material for the New Town project.

Teacher B: They're really bright, are they?

Teacher A: Mostly from middle-class families, well motivated.

Adapted from Keddie, 1973

A Head of Faculty in a secondary school explains the school's poor showing in the 'league tables'. 'We are weighted down the lower end, unfortunately, because we are a working-class school.'

Adapted from Gillborn & Youdell, 2001

Item C Gender

Alison: All the teachers I didn't like, they always favoured the boys and never taught us – the girls.

Researcher: How did they favour the boys in their teaching?

Alison: It was usually the boys who were noisy in the class and if a girl put her hand up they always keep her waiting and just never get round to it. And if a boy and a girl put up their hand at the same time they'd always talk to the boy. They'd never have time for the girls.

Adapted from Abraham, 1995

Item B Ethnicity

Samuel, a seven-year-old African-Caribbean pupil, talks to a researcher.

Samuel: I always get done and always get picked on. I want to go to a Black school with all Black teachers, it's better. I want to go to a school with just Black people.

Researcher: Why?

Samuel: Because when you go to a school with White people they give you horrible food and you're always picked on when you don't do nothing. When it's White people, they just say stop that and stop doing this.

Researcher: How does this make you feel?

Samuel: (*Long thoughtful pause*) Sad.

Adapted from Wright, 1992

YES, JANET, WE'LL COME TO YOU LATER ...NOW, JOHN...

questions

1 What does Item A suggest about teachers' perceptions of middle and working-class pupils?

2 Read Item B. Samuel may deserve everything he gets *or* he may not. Briefly discuss.

3 In what ways do Alison's comments in Item C reflect the findings of research?

---

material from various parts of the chapter.

There are two main types of teaching groups – *ability groups* and *mixed-ability groups*.

Ability groups These are groups of pupils who are seen to have similar abilities. *Setting* and *streaming* are two ways of dividing students into ability groups. Setting allocates pupils to subject groups – a pupil could be in set 1 for English and set 3 for maths. Streaming places pupils in the same ability group for all subjects – for example, a pupil is placed in class 3 and taught at that level for all subjects.

Mixed-ability groups In these groups, pupils are randomly or intentionally mixed in terms of their perceived ability.

Setting is the most common form of ability grouping in schools in England and Wales. It becomes increasingly common as pupils approach GCSE. Streaming was typical of primary schools in the 1940s and 50s. It began to die out with the decline of the 11-plus exam. Mixed-ability teaching throughout pupils' school careers is found in only a small number of schools.

Ability groups

Supporters of ability groups make the following points.

Different abilities – different teaching Young people have different abilities. This means they need to be taught:

- At different speeds
- In different ways
- At different levels.

The most efficient way of doing this is to create teaching groups of pupils with similar abilities.

Item C Teachers' comments

Teacher A: You don't find any behaviour problems with the top set – they've got the intelligence.

Teacher B: When you get your next year's timetable and you see that it is a top or bottom set then you get certain images. If you get a top set you tend to think that their behaviour will be better. You tend to think with a bottom set you will get more discipline problems. I look forward to teaching my top-set third year but dread my bottom-set third year. With the bottom group I go in with a stony face but I know that with the top set if I say fun's over they will stop. But if I give a bottom set rope they'll take advantage of you.

Adapted from Abraham, 1995

questions

1 Write a letter of no more than 100 words to Tony Blair about his views in Item A.

2 Using the information in Item B, state why setting for examinations can make a real difference to pupils' attainment.

3 How might the teachers' views in Item C affect pupils' attainment?

Unit 6 State policy and education

keyissues

1 What have been the main state policies on education from 1870 onwards?

2 What effect have they had on the role of education and students' experience of education?

6.1 The 1870 Education Act

Before 1870, public schools educated the children of upper classes, and grammar schools taught the children of the middle classes. Both types of school were fee-paying. Working-class children were limited to elementary schools run by churches and charities. Standards were often appallingly low and around one third of children received no schooling at all (Royle, 1997).

The 1870 Education Act aimed to 'fill the gaps' left by church and charity schools. It provided state-run elementary schools for five to eleven-year-olds. They charged a maximum fee of nine pence a week.

In 1880, elementary education was made compulsory up to the age of 10. It aimed to teach basic literacy and numeracy, 'morality' and Biblical knowledge. In 1891, elementary education was made free. The school leaving age was raised to 12 in 1889 and to 14 in 1918.

The 1902 Education Act This Act made local authorities responsible for secondary education. It encouraged the building of fee-paying grammar schools, many of which offered free places to children from low-income backgrounds who passed a scholarship exam.

In broad terms, up to the Second World War (1939-1945), there were three types of school for children from different class backgrounds:

- elementary schools for the working classes
- grammar schools for the middle classes
- public schools for the upper classes.

6.2 The 1944 Education Act

During and after the Second World War, there was widespread debate over the kind of society that should follow the war. Education was a central issue in this debate. It was felt that the nation was not making full use of the talents of its people, particularly those in the lower classes. Changes in the education system were seen as a way to remedy this.

The 1944 Education Act aimed to give every pupil an equal chance to develop their abilities to the full within a free system of state education. The Act reorganised the structure of education in England and Wales into three stages.

- Primary for 5 to 11-year-olds
- Secondary for 11 to 15-year-olds
- Further/higher education.

The tripartite system

The major changes were in the secondary sector. The question was, what sort of secondary education would provide equality of educational opportunity for all children from the age of 11?

Types of pupil The response owed much to the theories of psychologists and educationalists of the 1920s and 1930s. These theories were based on the idea that there were different types of pupils, with differing aptitudes and abilities, and that a child's type could be identified by intelligence testing. On the basis of this, the 1944 Act introduced a national test for 11-year-olds – the 11-plus test – as a means of allocating children to one of three types of secondary school.

Types of school The three types of secondary school were grammar schools, technical schools and secondary modern schools. This became known as the *tripartite system* of secondary education.

Grammar schools were intended for pupils defined as bright and academic – those whose abilities lay in reasoning and solving logical problems. They were to study classics, mathematics, science and other 'difficult' subjects in preparation for GCE O and A-level exams. Around 20% of the school population went to grammar schools. Technical schools were intended for children with an aptitude for technical subjects. These schools emphasised vocational training and technical skills and were attended by around 5% of the school population. Most children went to secondary modern schools. These children were

activity27 intelligence tests

- Underline the odd one out:

  House   Igloo   Bungalow   Office   Hut

- Underline which of these is not a famous composer:

  ZOTRAM   SATSURS   REVID   MALESO

- Insert the word missing from the brackets:

  Fee (Tip) End
  Dance (....) Sphere

- Underline the odd one out:

- Draw the next one in the sequence:

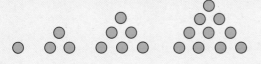

questions

1 Answer the test questions.
2 What are the problems of forecasting children's academic ability on the basis of intelligence tests?

seen as less academic and more practical. They were given a basic education with little opportunity to take external examinations until CSEs – a lower level exam – were introduced in the 1960s.

The tripartite system was intended to provide separate but equal types of schooling geared to the particular talents of the child. The Act stated that each type of school should have equal status, or 'parity of esteem', with buildings, equipment and staffing being of similar quality. However, these ideals did not work in practice.

Criticisms of the tripartite system

The 11-plus was unreliable It became increasingly clear that a young person's educational future could not be predicted by an IQ test at 11. When secondary modern pupils were finally allowed to take GCE O levels, some were getting better results than many grammar school pupils.

The selection process was unfair and wasteful Selecting pupils at 11 was unfair – it denied many the opportunity of continuing their education beyond 15. It was also a waste of ability, both for the student and for the nation.

No parity of esteem Secondary modern schools were seen as second-rate by parents, pupils and employers. Grammar schools always had higher status because they specialised in academic subjects which led to well-paid, high-status occupations. As a result, there was no parity of esteem – no equality of status – between the schools in the tripartite system.

Three-quarters of students 'failed' For most pupils, the alternatives at age 11 were a grammar or secondary modern school. There were relatively few technical schools. The 11-plus was intended as a selection device for allocating pupils to appropriate schools. It was soon seen as a pass/fail exam. Three-quarters of the school population 'failed' and went to secondary modern schools. And with this 'failure' came the danger of labelling and the self-fulfilling prophecy.

Social class divisions One of the main aims of the 1944 Act was to widen educational opportunities for working-class pupils. But the class divide in education remained. Research indicates that two-thirds of boys from middle-class backgrounds went to grammar schools compared to only a quarter of boys from working-class backgrounds (Halsey et al., 1980).

6.3 The comprehensive system

Educational policy in the 1960s was directed by social democratic ideas (see pages 95-97). From a social democratic perspective, everybody should have an equal chance to succeed. Clearly, the tripartite system was not providing equality of educational opportunity.

This was seen as both wrong and inefficient. A well-educated workforce leads to economic growth. The tripartite system wasted talent. This reduced people's

activity28 successes and failures

Item A *Failing*

As a youngster, I was a product of the 11-plus examination. In 1955, I failed the exam and still today remember the trauma, grief and unhappiness it caused. I can remember how, as 11-year-olds, we were called into the school hall and a list was read out of who had passed the exam. When my name was not read out, I was devastated. I can remember running out of the school gates, home. Because I had failed the 11-plus, my mother was distraught and I can recall the feeling of failure. It took many years to get over the trauma. I was fortunate to go to a secondary modern school that took GCEs and it was not until I had successfully passed those exams that the feeling of failure partially disappeared.

Labour MP Gerald Steinberg quoted in *The Guardian*, 22.1.1996

Item B *Pigeon-holed*

questions

1 Why did Gerald Steinberg feel a failure?
2 What does the cartoon suggest about the tripartite system?

---

contribution to the economy, which meant that everybody suffers.

Three into one The tripartite system had provided three schools of unequal quality and unequal status. Why not replace them with a single school for everyone? This simple solution would end inequality between schools. It promised equal opportunities for all young people to develop their talents and abilities in schools of equal status – in *comprehensive schools*.

In a comprehensive system, young people of all abilities and from all social backgrounds attend the same type of school (except for those in private education). They are provided with the same opportunities to obtain qualifications and training. There is no entrance exam, no selection at age 11.

The development of comprehensives

In 1965, the newly elected Labour government sent a circular to local authorities requesting them to submit plans to reorganise secondary education along comprehensive

lines. In 1970, when the Labour government was defeated, around one-third of young people in secondary education were attending comprehensive schools.

The Labour Party returned to power in 1974 and passed legislation requiring local authorities to go comprehensive. By the end of its period in office (May, 1979), over 80% of secondary school pupils attended comprehensives.

The limitations of comprehensives

There was a lot of hope riding on comprehensives. To some extent, this hope was justified. But it was too much to expect comprehensives to compensate for the inequalities in the wider society and provide equal opportunities for all.

Examination results Critics of the comprehensive system claimed it would lower educational standards. They believed that the 'high academic standards' of the grammar schools would be diluted in the comprehensives. Table 2 suggests that they were wrong. Educational standards were higher in 1983, when less than 4% of secondary school

Table 2 Highest qualifications of school leavers

	1969 (%)	1983 (%)
One or more A-levels	12	14
5 or more O-levels (A-C grades)	7	10
1 to 4 O-levels (A-C grades)	18	28
1 or more O levels (D-E grades)	37	52
No qualifications	50	10

Adapted from *Social Trends*, 1972 and 1986

pupils went to grammar schools, than in 1969, when 21% went to grammar schools.

Social class divisions Supporters of comprehensive education hoped that class differences in educational attainment would be reduced by the comprehensive system. In particular, they hoped that the examination results of working-class pupils would improve compared to those of middle-class pupils. Although the educational qualifications of *all* school leavers improved, class differences remained largely unchanged. In other words, examination results in general got better but the gap between top and bottom stayed more or less the same (Ferri et al., 2003).

Breaking down class barriers Many of those who supported the comprehensive system looked forward to schools attended by pupils from across the entire social class spectrum. They hoped that this social mix would help to break down class barriers. However, most comprehensives recruit from a local catchment area. Often, these areas are largely middle class or working class. As a result, many comprehensives are primarily 'single class', so tending to reinforce rather than break down existing class divisions.

Streaming and setting Many comprehensives divide pupils into ability groups. A disproportionate number of middle-class pupils are placed in the top streams and sets and a disproportionate number of working-class pupils in the bottom streams and sets. Some see this as another form of selection, not unlike the tripartite system.

6.4 Conservative educational policy, 1979-1997

In May 1979, the Conservative Party, led by former

activity29 class in the comprehensive

question

What problems of comprehensive schools are illustrated by this cartoon?

Education Minister Margaret Thatcher, were elected. Their aims were to:

- Develop an educational system which met the needs of industry
- Raise standards throughout Britain's schools and colleges.

The new vocationalism

Until the 1970s, vocational training – training for work – was seen as the responsibility of employers. They would teach new recruits the skills needed in the workplace. This view began to change with the rise in youth unemployment in the 1970s. Schools, it was argued, were producing young people who lacked the skills required by industry. And industry in turn was suffering from a skills shortage. This line of argument led to the *new vocationalism* – direct government involvement in youth training.

Training schemes Conservative governments introduced a number of training schemes for young people. For example, the Youth Training Scheme (YTS), started in 1983, was a one-year, work-based training scheme for school leavers. It was replaced by Youth Training (YT) in 1990. In addition to workplace training, YT offered young people the chance to take vocational qualifications.

Vocational qualifications The development of training schemes was accompanied by new vocational qualifications. The National Council for Vocational Qualifications, set up in 1986, established National Vocational Qualifications (NVQs) for a range of specific occupations.

More general vocational qualifications were also introduced. General National Vocational Qualifications (GNVQs) allowed young people to keep their options open rather than specialise in a particular occupation. GNVQs assessed skills, knowledge and understanding in broad occupational areas such as Art and Design, Business, Health and Social Care, Manufacturing, and Leisure and Tourism. They have now been replaced by Vocational GCSEs and Vocational A levels.

The new vocationalism – evaluation

Jobs not training are needed A number of critics argued that youth unemployment was due to a lack of jobs, not to a lack of skills. In other words, the problem was with the economy, not with young people and their education (Finn, 1987).

activity30 youth training

Item A *Training at the bank*

Each year about 20 young people, many with no qualifications, are recruited from the inner-city area to train under the Bank of England's clerical youth training scheme.

18-year-old Elton Thomas is in his second year, and came in without any qualifications. However, he's working towards achieving an NVQ this summer.

'I use computers a lot at the moment. I spend a lot of time on the phone chasing statements and invoices. I've worked in four different offices and gained a variety of experience. It's great working here. I really like wearing a suit to work and looking sharp. I'm in the bank's football team. We play other banks and companies and win a few and lose a few!'

Adapted from Employment Department Group and BBC Radio One, 1991

Item B *Cheap labour*

Well, the thing is, my son's education was all right until he left school and he'd got no job to go to. So he went to these job creation schemes, which is the biggest con there ever was. All it was was cheap labour, I mean, I saw all this because the firm I worked for actually got kids in and they were working as hard, if not harder, than the men that earned the money, but they never got paid for it. He was a damn good worker, keen to learn, but as soon as the training period was over, they got rid of him and started a new one, because it was cheap labour.

Adapted from McKenzie, 2001

Trainees at the Bank of England

question

The quality of youth training depends on who's providing the training. Briefly discuss with reference to Items A and B.

Quality and relevance of training According to Phil Cohen (1984), many trainees spent most of their time 'running errands' and 'being useful'. Few received any real occupational training, most were a source of cheap labour.

Not all youth training fitted this description. The better schemes and employers offered effective training in skills that were in demand in the labour market

A second-best option Middle-class students usually avoided Youth Training, seeing it as a second-best option to staying on at school or college. In practice, YT students tended to be young people from working-class backgrounds who couldn't get a job. It has been argued that YT was training for the less able which channelled them into low status, low paid occupations (Lee et al., 1990).

Status of vocational qualifications Traditionally, vocational qualifications have been seen as inferior to GCSEs and A levels. The introduction of NVQs and GNVQs may have improved their status. Vocational GCSEs and Vocational A levels may continue this improvement.

Raising standards

The first major aim of Margaret Thatcher's Conservative government was to make education more responsive to the needs of industry. The second major aim was to raise standards throughout Britain's schools and colleges.

Where Labour had been influenced by social democratic ideas, Conservative governments were influenced by the New Right (see pages 97-98). In line with New Right ideas, the aim was to create an education market-place in which the providers – schools and colleges – competed, and the consumers – parents and students – made choices. This would drive up standards since the consumers would choose successful schools and colleges, leaving unsuccessful institutions to go out of business.

To put these ideas into practice, the Conservatives gave schools more freedom and self-government in some areas and increased government control in other areas. This can be seen clearly from the Education Reform Act.

The Education Reform Act

The 1988 Education Reform Act is the most important and far reaching educational legislation since the 1944 Education Act. It established a national curriculum for all state schools in England and Wales and a national system of testing and assessment. It reduced the role of local education authorities by giving greater control to individual schools and their governing bodies. It established city technology colleges and grant maintained schools, both independent of local authority control.

Competition and choice Part of the thinking behind the Education Reform Act can be seen from a government circular entitled *Our Children's Education: The Updated Parent's Charter* (Department of Education, 1994). It tells parents that, 'Your choice of school directly affects that school's budget; every extra pupil means extra money for the school'. And 'the right to choose will encourage schools to aim for the highest possible standards'. From this point of view, parental choice means that schools will compete in order to attract pupils (and money) and in the process standards of education will rise.

Diversity and choice Will parents have a real choice? Aren't all comprehensives much of a muchness? In an attempt to offer real choice, the Education Reform Act encouraged diversity. It introduced two new types of school.

- **Grant maintained schools** are created when sufficient parents vote to withdraw the school from local authority control. They are financed directly by central government. They are self-governing with governors and headteachers taking decisions about the employment of staff, the curriculum, the provision of goods and services and the way pupils are selected for entry. The idea was to free schools to specialise – for example, in particular subjects or particular types of pupils such as the 'more academically able'. In this way, the choice for parents was seen to be widened.

- **City technology colleges** for 11 to 18-year-olds are financed by central government and private sector sponsorship. Located mainly in inner-city areas, they teach the National Curriculum while concentrating on maths, science and technology.

In the 1990s, the Conservatives introduced two further types of schools – schools specialising in either languages or technology. They were called colleges to indicate their prestige and importance.

By 1996, there were 1,100 grant maintained schools, including 660 secondary schools, accounting for one in five of all secondary students. There were 15 city technology colleges, 30 language colleges and 151 new technology colleges (Chitty, 2002).

The National Curriculum The Education Reform Act introduced the National Curriculum. For the first time in the history of state education, the government told teachers in England and Wales exactly what to teach. From the age of 5 to 16, all pupils in state schools must study three *core subjects* – English, maths and science – and seven foundation subjects. Pupils were tested in the core subjects by Standard Assessment Tasks (SATs – now renamed National Tests) at the ages of 7, 11 and 14. SATs results provided parents with information on which to judge the performance of schools.

League tables In 1992, all state secondary schools were required to publish the results of their SATs, GCSEs and A levels. In 1997, primary schools had to publish their SATs results. Local and national 'league tables' of schools were based on these results. They provided parents with information on which to base their choice of school. They were also intended to encourage competition between schools by spurring headteachers and staff to improve their position in the league.

Evaluation of Conservative policy

Choice Do parents have a real choice of schools? Popular schools are likely to be full, or to have only limited places. Where places are available, it is the articulate middle-class parents with their social and cultural capital who tend to obtain them. And in this situation, schools have more choice than parents – they are likely to choose middle-class pupils to maintain their position in the league tables. As a result, what choice exists is not equal – it operates on class lines and favours the middle class (Ball, 2003; Smith & Noble, 1995).

League tables Parents often look closely at examination results when assessing and choosing schools. But a simple league table which ranks schools in terms of results can be very misleading. There is evidence that some of the best schools in Britain do poorly on this kind of league table. These schools, often in run down inner-city areas, are achieving extremely good results given the social background of their pupils. They may be doing a far better job than schools well above them in the league table (see Activity 32).

Selection There is some evidence of selection on academic and/or social grounds in popular schools. They may be reluctant to accept pupils with special needs, low academic ability or so-called behaviour problems, seeing them as a threat to their standing in the league tables. In the early 1990s, around one-third of grant maintained schools selected pupils on the basis of interviews with parents and/or pupils and reports from previous schools (Bush et al., 1993).

Critics have seen this as a means of 'back door selection'. They see a return of the grammar school in the guise of the grant maintained secondary school. And there will be no need for a selection process like the 11-plus. The government will have provided the evidence with SATs at age 11.

Marketing schools Increased competition has led to schools using a variety of marketing strategies to present themselves in an attractive and positive light. These include glossy brochures, mission statements, open evenings and adverts in the local press. The resources devoted to marketing mean that less money is available to spend on things which directly benefit pupils – for example, teachers and textbooks (Gewirtz et al., 1995).

However, this emphasis on marketing has its benefits. Schools now give more attention to academic standards, to pastoral care, to discipline, and the state of their buildings. In the words of one researcher, schools have had to 'address their academic weaknesses and capitalise on their strengths' (Coffey, 2001).

*activity*31 *the education market-place*

question

How does this cartoon illustrate the aims of the Education Reform Act?

6.5 Labour educational policy, 1997-2003

During the election campaign of 1997, Tony Blair proclaimed that Labour's top three priorities were 'education, education, education'. New Labour was elected in May 1997 with surprisingly little in the way of new policies for education.

Diversity and choice

In many ways the Labour government continued the Conservatives' policies of diversity and choice.

Modernisation and comprehensives Tony Blair rejected what he called the 'one-size-fits-all' idea of comprehensive education. He saw the existing comprehensive system as providing the same type of school for everyone. Past Labour governments had seen this uniformity and standardisation as a way of providing equal opportunities for all. New Labour rejected this view, arguing that schools should reflect the diversity of young people – their particular aptitudes and talents, and their varying abilities.

Comprehensives should be 'modernised'. And part of this process involved more specialist schools.

Specialist schools In May 1997, Labour inherited 196 specialist schools from the Conservatives. By late 2002, they had almost 1000 in place. The plan is to have at least 2000 by 2006 and eventually to transform all comprehensives into specialist schools. By 2003, sports, arts, business and enterprise, engineering, maths and computing, music, and humanities colleges had been added to the Conservatives' specialist schools.

The idea of specialist schools is to provide centres of excellence and expertise in particular subject areas. They are intended to raise local standards of teaching and learning in these subjects and to open their doors to pupils from other schools and to community groups. They can select up to 10% of their pupils, choosing those who have an aptitude for their specialist subject.

Diversity within schools The diversity of aptitude and ability must also be reflected *within* schools. Tony Blair rejected mixed-ability groups, arguing that ability grouping is the best way of making sure that *all* pupils progress as far and fast as they can. In his view, this was essential for the modernisation of comprehensive schools.

Evaluation Many of the criticisms of Conservative policy also apply to Labour's policy of diversity and choice – see page 136 and 137. Choice usually means limited places and selection at the more popular schools. In this situation, the middle class with their cultural and social capital have the advantage.

Underachievement in deprived areas

Within three months of their election, the new Labour government published a policy document entitled *Excellence in Schools* (DfEE, 1997). It stated that they intended 'to overcome economic and social disadvantage and to make equality of opportunity a reality'. This involved finding new ways of motivating young people in deprived inner-city areas and doing something about 'underachieving schools'. New types of schools and new programmes were developed for this purpose.

Beacon schools These schools were 'centres of excellence'. Their job was to share their expertise with other schools, particularly those in inner-city areas.

*activity*32 *an alternative league table*

This league table refers to the top 20 local education authorities in England. The figures in brackets are taken from the 'official' league table based on exam results from secondary schools. The 'unofficial' placings from 1 to 20 are based on 'value-added scores'. These scores look at pupils' attainment levels when they first arrive at secondary school then see how much schools improve on these levels – that is, how much value is added.

The results show that schools can – and do – make an enormous difference. There are local authorities with a high proportion of very poor children who do badly in both tables. But the most significant finding is the number of inner-city authorities, languishing in the lower regions of the Department for Education table, who do exceedingly well in the new table.

Adapted from *The Observer*, 20.3.1994

1	Wirral	(31)	11	Bolton	(42)
2	Camden	(57)	12	Hackney	(102)
3	Barnet	(3)	13	W. Sussex	(2)
4	Kingston	(1)	14	E. Sussex	(17)
5	Sutton	(9)	15	Dorset	(12)
6	Bromley	(4)	16	Wigan	(30)
7	Liverpool	(98)	17	Harrow	(7)
8	Tower Hamlets	(105)	18	Cheshire	(18)
9	Lambeth	(100)	19	Redbridge	(23)
10	Bucks	(5)	20	Herts	(10)

question

Why is a league table based on value-added scores important?

activity33 diversity and choice

Item A Specialist schools

Specialist schools and colleges will have a key contribution to make in raising standards and delivering excellence in schools. They will help thousands of young people to learn new skills and progress into employment, further training and higher education, according to their individual abilities, aptitudes and ambitions.

Former Education Minister Estelle Morris quoted in Chitty, 2002

Item B Diversity and inequality

In a class-divided and competitive society, specialisms are not equal: they rapidly become ranked in a hierarchy of status.

A divided secondary system, with its hierarchy of schools firmly established, will continue to work to the advantage of the powerful, the influential and the articulate; while large numbers of children find themselves in less favoured institutions which attract the sort of criticisms once levelled at the secondary modern schools.

Adapted from Chitty, 1997

questions

1 How does the cartoon illustrate Labour's policy of diversity and choice?

2 With some reference to Item B, discuss how diversity can lead to inequality of educational opportunity.

Academies These were failed schools which were taken over by central government in partnership with businesses, churches, or voluntary organisations. They could offer special bonuses to teachers to attract and keep the best.

Education Action Zones (EAZs) These zones were located in deprived urban areas with low levels of educational attainment. By April 2003 there were 72 EAZs, each run by an Action Forum made up of parents, representatives from local schools and businesses and from local and national government. Each zone was given £1 million to spend. Teachers and schools were encouraged to be flexible and innovative – for example, running Saturday classes and a variety of work-related courses.

Evaluation Action Zones ploughed money and energy into disadvantaged areas, they encouraged innovation, and brought together expertise from local and national government. However, like similar experiments in the 1960s, such as Educational Priority Areas, they may fail to make up for the economic and social disadvantages of pupils from low-income, inner-city areas (Kirton, 1998).

Vocational education and training

Aims Labour's policies for vocational education have focused on two main areas.

- First, to provide the training needed for a high wage/high skill economy, so that the UK can compete successfully in world markets.
- Second, to reduce unemployment, particularly for young people (Strathdee, 2003).

New qualifications GNVQs were replaced by Vocational GCSEs and Vocational A levels. Part of the reason for this change was to raise the status of vocational qualifications to the level of academic qualifications.

National Vocational Qualifications (NVQs) were extended. They now ranged from an Initial Award – gained after a 26 week introductory training period – to a Level 5 award which is equivalent to a degree.

Evaluation NVQs have yet to prove themselves. Surveys suggest that about two-thirds of employers see little value in these qualifications. The government may have overestimated the demand for highly-skilled workers. In the

activity34 *grants not fees*

National Union of Students demonstrate against tuition fees and the student loans scheme.

question

Would you support this demonstration? Refer to the conclusion on page 140 in your answer.

1990s, the fastest growing job was care assistant in hospitals and nursing homes (Strathdee, 2003).

The New Deal Labour introduced the New Deal in 1998. It offered education and training for young people between the ages of 18 and 24 who had been out of work for more than six months. It was later extended to older people.

The New Deal provided personal advisors who offered direction and support to the unemployed, guiding them through the various options – academic courses, vocational training, self-employment, or voluntary work.

Evaluation The New Deal got off to a good start. Two years into the scheme, Tony Blair was able to claim that it had helped more than 250,000 young people find jobs. And it helped others move into higher education.

Conclusion

Government policies come and go, but one thing stays the same – the middle class gains! Whether it's the tripartite system, the comprehensive system or specialist schools, the attainment gap between the middle and working classes grows.

Recent research has followed the lives of two groups of children, one born in 1958 and the other in 1970 (Ferri et al., 2003). It shows that the chances of a young middle-class person gaining a degree have grown at a higher rate than those of a young working-class person. And this is despite the rapid expansion in university places from the 1980s onwards.

In 2003, the Labour government expressed concern about the relatively low numbers of working-class students going to university. This may have something to do with tuition fees and the replacement of grants with student loans. There is evidence that worries about debt are deterring some students, particularly those from low-income backgrounds, from going to university (Universities UK Online, 2003).

summary

1. The 1870 Education Act provided the first state-run schools.

2. The 1944 Education Act set up the tripartite system of secondary education – grammar, technical and secondary modern schools.

3. The tripartite system provided schools of unequal status and unequal quality. Middle-class pupils tended to go to high-status grammar schools, working-class pupils to low-status secondary modern schools.

4. The comprehensive system was designed to provide equality of opportunity by replacing the tripartite system with a single type of school for all young people.

5. Class differences in attainment remained, partly because pupils were placed in streams or sets with a disproportionate number of middle-class pupils in higher ability groups and working-class pupils in lower ability groups.

6. Conservative governments from 1979 to 1997 introduced work-related training schemes and vocational qualifications.

7. The Education Reform Act of 1988 aimed to provide competition between schools, a variety of schools, and choice for parents. In theory, standards would rise as parents chose successful schools, while failing schools would go out of business.

8. Choice usually meant limited places and selection at the more popular schools. In this situation, the middle class with their cultural and social capital have the advantage.

9. The National Curriculum, introduced in 1988, was assessed by SATs in its core subjects. The results of these tests provided parents with information to judge the performance of schools.

10. Labour continued the Conservatives' policy of diversity and choice. The idea of a single type of secondary school for all was rejected in favour of a range of specialist schools.

11. Labour introduced new types of schools and new programmes which aimed to raise standards in deprived inner-city areas.

12. The New Deal offered education and training for young people who had been out of work for over six months.

13. Whatever reforms governments make to the educational system, one thing remains – the middle class gains.

4 Sociological methods

Introduction

Are the following statements true or false?

- There has been a steady increase in lone-parent families.
- The higher the class position of a child's parents, the more likely the child is to achieve high grades in school examinations.
- More and more women are taking up paid employment.

According to the 2002 edition of *Social Trends*, published by the Office of National Statistics, all the statements are true.

- In Britain in 1981, 13% of families with dependent children were headed by lone parents. By 2000, this had doubled to 26%.
- In 2000, two-thirds of young people in England and Wales with parents in non-manual occupations achieved 5 or more A* to C grades at GCSE compared to one-third of those with parents in manual occupations.
- In the UK in 1981, 10.9 million women age 16 and over were members of the labour force. By 2001, this number had grown to 13.2 million.

The statements at the beginning of this introduction are not based on opinion or prejudice, they are not based on guesses or gossip. They are based on research.

Research involves systematically collecting and analysing information. The term *data* is often used for information gathered as part of a research project. This chapter looks at sociological research methods – the methods used by sociologists to collect and analyse data.

national STATISTICS — 2002 edition United Kingdom No 32 ISSN 0306-7742 — Social Trends

chaptersummary

- ▶ **Unit 1** looks at the kinds of data used in research.
- ▶ **Unit 2** takes an overview of the research process.
- ▶ **Units 3 and 4** look at two types of research – experiments and social surveys.

- ▶ **Unit 5, 6 and 7** examine three methods of data collection – questionnaires, interviews and observation.
- ▶ **Unit 8** looks at secondary sources of data.
- ▶ **Unit 9** examines further types of research, including life histories, longitudinal studies and comparative studies.

Unit 1 Types of data

keyissues

1 What types of data do sociologists use?
2 How good is that data?

1.1 Primary and secondary data

One of the first questions sociologists ask when starting a research project is 'What kind of data will I use?' There are two main types of data – *primary data* and *secondary data*. Often researchers use both types.

Primary data refers to information which was not present before the research began. It is generated by the researcher during the actual process of research. It includes data produced by questionnaires, interviews and observations.

Secondary data refers to data which already exists. It includes data from historical records, official statistics, government reports, diaries, autobiographies, novels, newspapers, films and recorded music.

1.2 Quantitative and qualitative data

A second question sociologists ask when starting research is 'What form do I want the data in?' There are two forms of data – *quantitative data* and *qualitative data*. Researchers often use both forms.

Quantitative data This is data in the form of numbers. Examples of quantitative data are given in the introduction to this chapter. Here are some more examples from the year 2000. Twenty-six per cent of 16 to 24 year olds in England and Wales had taken cannabis in the past year.

In Britain, nine per cent of people with managerial/ professional occupations went to the opera in the past year compared to one per cent of people with unskilled manual jobs (*Social Trends*, 2002).

Quantitative data is particularly useful for measuring the strength of relationships between various factors. The above examples would be useful data for measuring relationships between 1) age and illegal drug use and 2) social class and leisure activities.

Qualitative data This refers to all types of data that are not in the form of numbers. It includes:

- Descriptive data from observations, eg a description of behaviour in a pub
- Quotes from interviews, eg a woman discussing her marriage
- Written sources, eg diaries, novels and autobiographies
- Pictures, eg photographs, paintings and posters
- Films and recorded music.

Qualitative data can often provide a richer and more in-depth picture of social life than the numbers provided by quantitative data. Many sociologists combine quantitative and qualitative data in their research.

1.3 Validity and reliability

A third question sociologists often ask when starting research is 'How good will my data be?' Ideally, they want data which is valid and reliable.

Validity Data is valid if it presents a true and accurate description or measurement. For example, official statistics on crime are valid if they provide an accurate measurement of the extent of crime.

Reliability Data is reliable when different researchers using the same methods obtain the same results. For example, if a number of researchers observed the same crowd at the same sporting event and produced the same description of crowd behaviour, then their account would be reliable. The method – in this case observation – produces reliable results.

However, reliable data may not be valid. Say the crowd was at a baseball match in the USA, and the sociologists were English and knew nothing about baseball. They may well fail to understand the crowd's responses to the game. As a result, their description of the crowd's behaviour may be reliable – they all produce the same descriptions – but invalid – their descriptions are inaccurate.

activity1 types of data

Item A *World War 1 recruiting poster from USA*

These Men Have COME ACROSS They Are at the Front NOW JOIN THEM ENLIST in the NAVY

Item B *A Hamar woman*

Item C *Social class and leisure*

Great Britain
Percentages

	Managerial/ professional	Other non-manual	Skilled manual	Semi-skilled manual	Unskilled manual
Sporting events	24	20	18	15	7
Plays	29	17	8	6	5
Opera	9	3	2	1	1
Ballet	7	3	1	1	1
Contemporary dance	4	2	1	1	1
Classical music	17	8	4	2	2
Concerts	19	17	13	9	5
Art galleries/Exhibitions	30	18	8	6	7

Adapted from *Social Trends*, 2002

questions

1 What types of data are Items A, B and C, quantitative or qualitative? Give reasons for your answer.

2 How might a sociologist studying images of gender use Item A?

3 How might a sociologist use the data in Item C?

4 Ask 10 people what the rings round the neck of the woman in Item B indicate. Are their observations a) valid, b) reliable?

These rings or torques made of iron wrapped in leather are engagement presents. They indicate her future husband's wealth and are worn for life.

key terms

Data Information collected as part of a research project.

Primary data New data produced by the researcher during the research process.

Secondary data Data which already exists, which can then be used by the researcher.

Quantitative data Numerical data – data in the form of numbers.

Qualitative data All types of data that are not in the form of numbers.

Validity Data is valid if it presents a true and accurate description or measurement.

Reliability Data is reliable when different researchers using the same methods obtain the same results, ie the same description or measurement.

summary

1. Sociologists often use both primary and secondary data in their research.

2. Quantitative data is useful for measuring the strength of relationships between various factors.

3. Qualitative data can provide a rich and in-depth picture of social life.

4. Ideally, research data should be both valid and reliable.

Unit 2 *The research process*

keyissues

1 What practical and theoretical considerations influence the research process?

2 What ethical issues are raised by sociological research?

Designing a research project, conducting the research, and analysing the results involve a number of decisions. These include choosing a topic, selecting appropriate research methods, and deciding whether the research is morally right.

2.1 Choosing a topic

Choosing a topic for research is influenced by a range of factors. Some of these will now be briefly examined.

Values of the researcher Researchers are likely to study something they consider to be important. And what they see as important is influenced by their values. For example, a sociologist who believes strongly in equality of opportunity may study the relationship between social class and educational attainment, since there is evidence that class inequality prevents equality of educational

opportunity. Similarly, a sociologist who believes in gender equality may study the position of women at work and in the home, comparing their workloads and rewards with those of men.

Values of society The values of researchers often reflect the values of society. Feminists have criticised mainstream (or 'malestream') society as male-dominated and based on male values. They have made similar criticisms about sociology. For example, sociological research has traditionally focused on male concerns and male interests. As a result, female issues have been seen as unimportant and, until fairly recently, as unworthy of research. For example, Ann Oakley (1974) broke new ground when she chose to research housework, a topic then considered by many male sociologists to be of little significance.

Values in society change and with them the priorities and concerns of researchers. Today, gender inequality is seen as a major issue. And in sociology, it forms the focus of a large number of research projects.

Funding Choosing a research project is also influenced by a number of practical issues. For example, is it affordable? Most research projects conducted by professional sociologists require outside funding. Research funds are

activity2 choosing a research topic

Vegetable gardening

Women's jobs

questions

1 Choose one of these topics for research.
2 Explain why you have chosen this topic.

Asian and White rioters in Bradford, 2001

available from various sources – charitable foundations such as the Joseph Rowntree Foundation and the Runnymede Trust, government organisations such as the Economic and Social Research Council (ESRC), and industry. Each funding body has its own priorities. For example, industrial organisations will tend to fund projects dealing with their own particular concerns, such as solutions to stress in the workplace. The choice of research project is often shaped by the priorities of the funding body.

Availability of data It makes little sense to choose a research topic where there is little or no data available and little chance of producing it in the future. For example, there is probably insufficient data to conduct a study of child abuse in Anglo Saxon England. And there is little chance of conducting a systematic study of secret service organisations such as MI5 and MI6.

Theoretical position Choosing a research topic is also influenced by the theoretical position of the sociologist. As noted earlier, feminist sociologists will tend to select topics

which reflect feminist issues – in particular gender inequalities.

Every theoretical position sees certain aspects of society as particularly important. For example, Marxism sees the class system as the foundation of capitalist society. As a result, Marxists tend to focus on topics such as class inequality, class conflict and class identity.

2.2 Choosing research methods

Having selected a topic, the researcher must then choose appropriate methods to collect and analyse data. The choice of methods depends on a number of factors. Some of these factors will be introduced briefly in this section and examined in more detail in later sections.

Practical considerations

Some methods are more suitable than others for conducting particular types of research. Think about the problem of studying a teenage gang whose members sometimes commit illegal acts. They are often hostile to outsiders, particularly those they see as representing authority. Asking gang members for interviews or presenting them with questionnaires is unlikely to produce the required data. However, joining in their activities and gaining their trust can allow the researcher to obtain information by observing their behaviour. This method has been used successfully by a number of sociologists studying gang behaviour.

A researcher can only observe and record the behaviour of a small number of people. What if the research involved making general statements about the relationship between social class and criminal behaviour? Some sociologists have claimed that members of the working class are more likely to commit crime than members of other social classes. It would take a lifetime of observation to assess this claim. For purely practical reasons, some sociologists have turned to official statistics on crime to investigate the relationship between social class and criminal behaviour. (However, there are problems with the use of official statistics as Section 8.1 shows.)

activity3 *choosing methods*

Item A **Casual sex**

Laud Humphreys studied casual sex between gay men in public toilets in the USA. His main method of research was observation. He pretended to be a 'voyeur-lookout'. A voyeur doesn't join in but gets pleasure from watching the activities of others. A lookout warns of approaching police.

Adapted from Humphreys, 1970

Item B **Sex for money**

Don Kulick used observation to study transsexual prostitutes in Brazil during 1996. He rented a small room in a house with 13 transsexual prostitutes. The prostitutes are referred to as 'travestis'.

'I associated with travestis pretty much continually during those eight months, eating breakfasts of sweetened coffee and buttered rolls with them when they woke up about midday, chatting with them as they sat in doorsteps, plucking whiskers from their chins in the late afternoon sun, crowding onto mattresses with them as they lay pressed together smoking cigar-sized joints and watching late-night action movies on television. Every night, from about 8pm until 1 or 2am, I walked the streets with them at their various points of prostitution.'

Adapted from Kulick, 1998

question

Why do you think Humphreys and Kulick chose observation as their main research method?

A transsexual prostitute

Theoretical considerations

A number of sociologists suggest there are two main research traditions, or approaches to research, within sociology (Halfpenny, 1984). These 'approaches' are often called *interpretivism* and *positivism*. They are based on different views of human behaviour. They sometimes lead to the use of different research methods.

Interpretivism Some sociologists argue that understanding human behaviour involves seeing the world through the eyes of those being studied. People give meaning to their own behaviour and to the behaviour of others, they define situations in certain ways and act accordingly. To understand their behaviour, it is essential to discover and interpret the meanings and definitions which guide their actions.

This view of human activity is sometimes called interpretivism. Sociologists who support this view tend to favour particular research methods. For example, many see *participant observation* – observing the people being studied by joining their activities – as a suitable method for discovering the meanings which guide their actions. Interpretivists also tend to favour in-depth, unstructured interviews since this method gives people the opportunity to talk about their behaviour as they see it. Asking them to fill in a questionnaire is unlikely to provide such freedom of expression.

Interpretivist sociology attempts to discover and understand the meanings and definitions that direct social life. It assumes that some research methods are better than others for this purpose.

Positivism By contrast, positivist sociology tends to model itself on the natural sciences such as physics and chemistry. It favours 'hard', quantitative data, rather than the 'soft' qualitative data often used by interpretivist sociology. It is less concerned with the meanings people attach to their behaviour and more with the behaviour itself.

activity4 researching suicide

Item A *Explaining suicide*

In a famous study entitled *Suicide*, first published in 1895, the French sociologist Emile Durkheim examined the suicide rates of different groups in society. He compared the following groups and, using official statistics, found that in each case, the group on the left had a higher suicide rate than the group on the right.

> City dwellers : Rural dwellers
> Older adults : Younger adults
> Unmarried : Married
> Married without children: Married with children

Durkheim argued that members of each group on the left are more socially isolated than those on the right. For example, married couples without children have fewer ties to bind them together than married couples with children.

Durkheim believed he had found a causal relationship between social isolation and suicide – the higher the level of social isolation, the greater the likelihood of suicide.

Adapted from Durkheim, 1970

Item B *Understanding suicide*

From an interpretivist view, suicide is a meaning which people give to certain deaths. The job of the sociologist is to discover why particular deaths are defined as suicides. From observations of inquests and discussions with coroners, the British sociologist J. Maxwell Atkinson believes that coroners have a picture of a typical suicide and a typical suicide victim. Road deaths are rarely seen as suicides whereas deaths by drowning, hanging, gassing and drug overdose are more likely to be interpreted as suicides. The typical suicide victim is often seen as a lonely, friendless, isolated individual with few family ties.

Adapted from Atkinson, 1978

Item C *A typical suicide?*

The Maniac Father and The Convict Brother Are Gone – The Poor Girl, Homeless, Friendless, Deserted, Destitute, and Gin Mad, Commits Self Murder.

(from a series of illustrations entitled 'The Drunkard's Children' drawn by George Cruikshank in 1848)

questions

1 How do Items A and B illustrate positivism and interpretivism?

2 Explain Item C from a) Durkheim's and b) Atkinson's view.

Behaviour can be directly observed and quantified – for example, number of visits to the opera in one year. Meanings cannot be directly observed, they can only be interpreted, for example the meanings that direct people to go to the opera.

Positivist sociology attempts to measure behaviour by translating it into numbers. This makes it possible to use statistical tests to measure the strength of relationships between various factors. This may indicate causal relationships – that one factor causes another.

Some research methods are more likely to produce data in a numerical form. Questionnaires are an example. It is fairly easy to translate the answers to a questionnaire into numbers. And some existing data is available in a numerical form – for example, official statistics.

Positivist sociology attempts to explain human behaviour by discovering cause and effect relationships. It requires data in the form of numbers for this purpose. Some research methods are designed to do this and, as a result, tend to be favoured by positivist sociologists.

Dividing sociologists into interpretivists and positivists is a simplistic and rough and ready division. However, it's a useful starting point for understanding different approaches to research. A flavour of this difference can be seen from Activity 4.

2.3 Ethical issues

Ethical considerations can have an important influence on the research process.

Ethics are moral principles – beliefs about what is right and wrong. In terms of research, ethics are the moral principles which guide research. Sociological associations in many countries have a set of ethical guidelines for conducting research. Sociology departments in universities usually have an ethics committee to ensure that research conducted by members of the department is in line with these guidelines.

There is a growing awareness that those who participate in research have rights and that researchers have responsibilities and obligations. For example, should participants be informed about the purpose of the research and what their participation involves? Should researchers make every effort to ensure that participants come to no physical or psychological harm? Is it ever justifiable to deceive participants about the purpose of the research? These are some of the ethical questions researchers should consider.

Informed consent Many researchers argue that those they are studying should be given the opportunity to agree or refuse to participate in the research. This decision should be 'informed' – information must be made available on which to base a decision to participate or not. Researchers should therefore provide information about the aims of the research, what the conduct of the research involves, and the purposes to which the research will be put.

Deception This means that information is withheld from participants and/or they are provided with false information. They may be unaware they are participating in a research study. They may be misled about the purpose of the study and the events that may take place during the research.

Clearly, participants cannot give informed consent if they are deceived. Is deception ever justifiable? Some researchers argue that deception is justified if there is no other way of gathering data. This means using a research method such as *covert (hidden) observation* so that people are unaware they are participating in research. Or, it means misleading participants about aspects of the research. For example, Humphreys (1970) gathered further information about some of the gay men in his research by calling on their homes and pretending to be conducting a health survey.

Privacy Researchers generally agree that participants' privacy should be respected. The problem here is that most research intrudes into people's lives. It has been argued that if participants consent to take part in research, then they accept this. However, they may be unaware of the extent of the intrusion. With hindsight, they may see it as an invasion of privacy.

Certain research methods, which are generally considered ethical, may result in an invasion of privacy. Take the case of the informal, unstructured interview – it often develops into a friendly chat between researcher and participant. In this relaxed atmosphere, participants may reveal all sorts of personal and private matters which they may later regret.

Confidentiality It is generally agreed that the identity of research participants should be kept secret. According to the British Sociological Association's *Statement of Ethical Practice* (1996), confidentiality must be honoured 'unless there are clear and overriding reasons to do otherwise'. It has been argued that when people in powerful positions misuse their power, then there may be a case for naming names (Homan, 1991).

key terms

Interpretivism An approach which focuses on the meanings and definitions which guide and direct behaviour.
Positivism An approach which attempts to explain behaviour in terms of cause and effect relationships.
Participant observation A research method where the researcher joins the activities of those they are observing.
Covert observation Hidden observation. Participants are unaware that they are being observed as part of a research project.
Ethics Moral principles – beliefs about what is right and wrong.

Protection from harm There is general agreement that research participants should be protected from harm. This includes any harmful effects of participating in the actual research process and any harmful consequences of the research.

Publication of research findings may harm those who have been studied. For example, a study by Jason Ditton of workers in a bread factory revealed all sorts of fiddles and petty thefts. As Ditton himself recognised, management may well clamp down on such practices after publication of his book (Ditton, 1977).

Ethics and the research process As noted earlier, all researchers have values which define what is right and wrong. To some extent, these ethical values will affect every stage of the research process. If, for example, researchers see poverty, male domination, racial discrimination, or private education as ethically wrong, then they may choose to study these topics in order to reveal the wrongs and discover ways to right them.

summary

1. The choice of research topic may be influenced by the
   - values of the researcher
   - values of society
   - type of funding
   - availability of data
   - theoretical position of the researcher.

2. The choice of research methods may be influenced by practical, theoretical and ethical considerations.

3. There are two main approaches to research in sociology – interpretivism and positivism. Each approach tends to favour particular research methods.

4. The research process is influenced by ethical considerations. Most sociologists believe that participation in research should be based on informed consent, that participants should be protected from harm, that their privacy should be respected and their confidentiality assured.

activity5 ethics and research

Item A *The National Front*

Nigel Fielding conducted a study of the National Front, which many, including Fielding, considered to be a vicious, racist organisation concerned with White supremacy. Part of his research involved attending local meetings of the Front, during which he concealed his real reason for being there. In order to avoid suspicion he contributed to discussions, appearing to be sympathetic to the Front's beliefs.

Adapted from Fielding, 1981

Item B *Missing lessons*

Val Hey studied friendship between girls. Her research was based on observation in two schools. She would sometimes give the girls small gifts and even excuses to miss lessons in exchange for cooperating in her research.

Adapted from Hey, 1997

Item C Illegal drug use

In their study of illegal drug use, Howard Parker and his colleagues found that some of the responses to their questionnaires revealed that individuals were not coping with their drug use. The researchers had to decide whether to offer help and advice or maintain the confidentiality they had promised.

Adapted from Parker et al., 1998

Smoking cannabis

questions

1 Why do you think Fielding chose to study the National Front?

2 Discuss the ethical issues involved in his research methods.

3 Do you think Hey (Item B) was justified in helping the girls truant from lessons? Explain your answer.

4 How would you have dealt with the problem faced by Parker in Item C? Give reasons for your decision.

(In the end, the researchers decided to treat each case individually.)

Unit 3 Experiments

keyissues

1 What are the main types of experiments?

2 Why are experiments rarely used by sociologists?

3.1 Laboratory experiments

For most people the word experiment conjures up a picture of white-coated researchers in a laboratory using scientific equipment to prove or disprove something. This is quite a good starting point for understanding the experimental method.

The main aspects of the experimental method can be illustrated by the following example. This experiment was conducted to test the *hypothesis* or supposition that, 'The speed of a boat depends on the shape of its hull'.

Controlling variables In order to discover the effect of hull shape on speed it is necessary to identify and control all the variables or factors which might affect speed. This is difficult to do outside a laboratory since variables such as wind strength and temperature cannot be controlled. In a laboratory, it is possible to control such variables and keep them constant so that hull shape is the only factor which

varies – from oval, to triangular, to rectangular, etc. In this way it is possible to find out how hull shape affects speed.

Quantifying results The results of experiments are usually quantified – presented in the form of numbers. Thus the speed of a model boat in the laboratory can be measured in centimetres per second using a metre rule and a stopwatch. Using a standard objective system of measurement is important as it reduces reliance on the judgement of the investigator and is therefore more likely to produce reliable data. And, it allows other researchers to *replicate* or repeat experiments and directly compare the results.

Correlation and causation If changes in one variable (eg, the shape of the hull) are matched by changes in another variable (eg, the speed of the boat) then there is a *correlation* between the two variables. But this does not mean that one causes the other. However, being able to control variables in a laboratory does help us to judge whether the correlation is causative rather than coincidental. In the case of the boat, the only apparent change is in hull shape so any change in speed is likely to result from this.

Laboratory experiments and people Laboratory experiments have been very successful in the natural sciences such as physics and chemistry. However, many sociologists have serious doubts about their application to human beings. This is partly because people act in terms of their definitions of situations. They are likely to define laboratories as artificial situations and act accordingly. As a result, their actions may be very different from their behaviour in the 'real' world. An attempt to get round this is the *field experiment*, an experiment which takes place in people's everyday situations.

activity6 laboratory experiments

Item A Imitative aggression

A group of nursery school children watched an adult mistreating a Bobo doll – a large inflatable rubber doll – by punching it, kicking it and hitting it with a mallet. The experimenter, Albert Bandura, then exposed this group and another group who had not watched the violence to the following 'frustrating experience'.

The children were shown a room full of exciting toys and given the impression they could play with them. They were then told they could not play with them. They were then taken, one by one, to a room of unattractive toys which included a Bobo doll and a mallet. As Bandura had predicted, those who had earlier watched the mistreatment of the Bobo doll were more likely to imitate this behaviour and show aggression towards the doll.

Adapted from Bandura, 1973

Imitating adults – attacking a Bobo doll.

Item B The real world

Can the results of laboratory experiments be applied to the real world? For example, does the Bobo doll experiment suggest a link between violence in films and violence in real life? Unlike people, Bobo dolls are designed to be knocked around, they invite violent behaviour. As such, they are hardly suitable for an investigation into imitative aggression. Critics of experiments argue that the many differences between the laboratory situation and real life undermine any attempts to apply research findings to the claim that films promote aggressive or violent behaviour by imitation.

Adapted from Williams, 1981

Described as 'sickeningly violent, appallingly funny and arrestingly accomplished', Reservoir Dogs became a cult movie in the mid-1990s (Chronicle of the Cinema, 1995).

questions

1 What hypothesis is being tested in Item A?

2 Do you agree with the views outlined in Item B? Give reasons for your answer.

3.2 Field experiments

Field experiments are conducted in normal social situations such as the classroom, the factory and the street corner. The following example was devised to test the effect of social class on interaction between strangers (Sissons, 1970). An actor stood outside Paddington Station in London and asked people for directions. The actor, place and request were kept the same but the actor's dress varied from a businessman to a labourer. The experiment indicated that people were more helpful to the 'businessman'. It could therefore be argued that people were responding to what they perceived as the actor's social class. However, there are other possibilities. For example, the actor may behave more confidently in his role as businessman and people might respond to his level of confidence rather than level of class.

Lack of control Field experiments are always going to be inexact and 'messy'. It is impossible to identify and control all the variables which might affect the results. For example, it is difficult, if not impossible, to control the social class of the people asked for directions in the above experiment. Most of them may have been middle class. If so, they may have been more helpful to the 'businessman' because he seemed 'more like them'.

The Hawthorne effect Whether in the laboratory or in more normal social contexts, people are often aware they are participating in an experiment. And this in itself is likely to affect their behaviour. This particular *experimental effect* is often known as the *Hawthorne effect* since it was first observed during a study at Hawthorne Works of the Western Electricity Company in Chicago in the late 1920s. The researchers conducted an experiment to discover whether there was a relationship between the workers' productivity and variables such as levels of lighting and heating and the frequency of rest periods. The researchers were puzzled as the results appeared to make little or no sense. For example, productivity increased whether the temperature in the workplace was turned up or down. The only factor which appeared to explain the increase in productivity was the workers' awareness that they were part of an experiment – hence the term Hawthorne effect.

Experimenter bias People act in terms of how they perceive others. They will tend to respond differently if the

key terms

Hypothesis A statement that can be tested about the relationship between two or more variables.

Variables Factors which affect behaviour. Variables can vary or change, eg temperature can increase or decrease.

Replication Repeating an experiment or research study under the same conditions.

Correlation A measurement of the strength of the relationship between two or more variables.

Laboratory experiment An experiment conducted in specially built surroundings.

Field experiment An experiment conducted in everyday social settings.

Experimental effect Any unintended effect of the experiment on the participants.

Hawthorne effect Changes in the behaviour of participants resulting from an awareness that they are taking part in an experiment.

Experimenter bias The unintended effect of the experimenter on the participant.

experimenter is young or old, male or female, Black or White and so on. People also tend to act in terms of how they think others expect them to act. This might explain the results in the experiment involving the actor dressed as a businessman and a labourer. He might be conveying two different expectations and this may affect the responses to his request for directions. For example, he may expect more help in his role as businessman and unintentionally convey this to the participants. The unintended effect of the experimenter on those being studied is known as *experimenter bias*.

Ethical questions Is it right to experiment on human beings? This depends partly on the nature of the experiment. Nearly everybody would reject the medical experiments performed on inmates against their will in Nazi concentration camps. However, fewer people would object to the actor asking directions outside Paddington Station. Should people be told they are the subject of an experiment? Yes, according to the British Psychological Society, unless it's absolutely necessary to deceive them, and then they must be told immediately afterwards (British Psychological Society, 1998).

summary

1. There are two main types of experiments – laboratory experiments and field experiments.

2. Experiments are often designed to test hypotheses.

3. Experiments are usually intended to measure the strength of relationships between two or more variables.

4. Ideally, laboratory experiments allow the researcher to control all the important variables.

5. Laboratory experiments have been criticised for creating artificial situations. Critics argue that as a result, findings from laboratory experiments may not apply to everyday social situations.

6. Field experiments help to avoid artificiality, but they do not provide the same control of variables.

7. Both laboratory and field experiments have been criticised for experimental effects. As a result, their findings may be low in validity.

activity7 asking directions

Same man...

different response

questions

1 Suggest reasons for the different responses pictured above.

2 Using this example, outline some of the problems with field experiments.

Unit 4 | Social surveys

keyissues

1 What is a social survey?

2 What types of sample are used for social surveys?

4.1 What is a social survey?

Survey data The National Readership Survey tells us that in 2000, *The Sun* was the most popular daily newspaper in Britain – read by 20% of adults. The International Passenger Survey tells us that Spain was the most popular overseas holiday destination in 2000 – visited by 28% of UK residents who had a holiday abroad. And the British Gambling Prevalence Survey informs us that the National Lottery Draw was the most popular gambling activity in Britain in 1999, with 65% of people aged 16 and over participating. (All figures from *Social Trends*, 2002.)

Definition The above information comes from *social surveys*. A social survey involves the systematic collection of the same type of data from a fairly large number of people. Social surveys are usually designed to gather information on the same variables – eg, age and cinema attendance – from those participating in the survey. This often means asking everybody the same set of questions.

4.2 Sampling

Nearly all social surveys are based on a *sample* of the population to be investigated. 'Population' is the term given to everybody in the group to be studied. The

population might be adult males, female pensioners, manual workers, 16-19 year old students, parents with dependent children and so on. A sample is a selection of part of the population. Samples are necessary because researchers rarely have the time and money to study everybody in the population. For example, if their research was based on women aged 16 and over in the UK, it would cover over 23 million people.

Most researchers try to select a sample which is *representative* of the population. This means that the sample should have the same characteristics as the population as a whole. Thus, if a researcher is studying the attitudes of British women, the sample should not consist of 1000 nuns, 1000 women over eighty or 1000 divorced women since such groups are hardly representative of British women. With a representative sample, *generalisations* are more likely to be true – findings from the sample are more likely to be applicable to the population as a whole.

Sample design and composition

Sampling unit Who should be included in a sample? In many cases it is fairly easy to define a *sampling unit* – ie, a member of the population to be studied. Dentists, males between 30 and 40 years of age, females who own their own businesses, people with one or more GCE A levels, can be defined without too many problems. However, other groups are not so easy – how would you define a semi-skilled manual worker or a person living in poverty? Who would you include in a population of 'criminals'? Do you limit the population to those convicted of a crime? Or do you include everybody who has ever broken the law, in which case you would include nearly every adult in the UK?

Sampling frame Once the research population has been defined, the sample is selected from a *sampling frame* – a list of members of the population to be studied. In some cases an appropriate sampling frame is readily available, eg the Electoral Register for a study of voting behaviour. In other cases researchers may have to rely on listings, such as the Postcode Address File or telephone directories, which may or may not be suitable for their purposes. And all listings have drawbacks – not everyone is included, they are often out of date, certain groups are likely to be over or under-represented, eg the poor are less likely to appear in telephone directories. Sometimes, those who have data needed for a sampling frame are unwilling to release it. This happened to Howard Newby (1977) when the Ministry of Agriculture refused to supply information for his study of Suffolk farmworkers. Newby had to use the *Yellow Pages* for his first sampling frame. Many farmworkers were absent from this directory and those included were probably unrepresentative of the group.

The design and composition of the sample will partly depend on the type of sample used. Some of the more common types will now be outlined.

Types of sample

Random samples A *random sample* gives every member of the sampling frame an equal chance of being selected. Every name is given a number and then a list of random numbers is used to select the sample. This avoids bias in selection. If researchers choose who to include and who to leave out, they may select a sample which supports their hypothesis.

Systematic samples This form of sampling systematically selects people from the sampling frame by choosing every 5th, 10th, 20th, or whatever, sampling unit. This method was used by Young and Willmott (1957) in their first study of Bethnal Green (see page 51). They selected every 10th name from the borough's electoral register.

Neither random nor systematic samples necessarily produce representative samples. Few sampling frames cover everybody in the research population. For example, on electoral registers certain groups are unrepresented (those not old enough to vote) or under-represented (the unemployed).

Even if the sampling frame covers the entire research population, a representative sample is not guaranteed. Simply because it *is* random, a random sample may select, for example, a disproportionate number of Labour voters from an electoral register. However, the larger the sample the less likely this will be. Systematic sampling can lead to an unrepresentative sample if the sampling frame is organised systematically. For example, a list of married couples in which husband follows wife would

lead to an all male sample if every 10th person was selected.

Stratified samples Stratified samples offer a solution to the problem of representativeness. The population is divided into separate *strata* in terms of one of more characteristics, eg age, gender, ethnicity, class. A sample is then drawn which reflects those characteristics. Thus if the aim is to reflect gender divisions in the UK, 51% of the sample will be randomly selected from the female stratum and 49% from the male stratum. In terms of gender, the sample will be representative of the population as a whole.

A stratified sample can only be selected if researchers have sufficient information. In some cases, this is fairly easy to obtain. For example, the distribution of age in the UK population can be obtained from census data and this can then be mirrored in the sampling frame. In other cases, the necessary information is difficult or impossible to obtain. Religion provides an example. How do we get accurate information on the distribution of atheists, agnostics, Catholics, Protestants, Muslims, Hindus and so on in the population as a whole? And even if we can discover this, available sampling frames such as electoral registers may be no use at all since they provide no information about religious belief and practice.

Quota samples A market researcher stands on a street corner looking for likely 'victims'. She has to find twenty women between the ages of 30 and 45 to answer a questionnaire on magazine readership. She fills her quota with the first twenty women passing by who a) fit the required age group and b) agree to answer her questions. The sample selection is not random – it is not randomly selected from a sampling frame. The researcher simply fills her quota from the first available bodies. This method is known as *quota sampling*. It is 'a method of stratified sampling in which the selection within strata is non-random' (Moser & Kalton, 1971).

Quota sampling is often used for opinion polls and market research. It has its advantages – it is simpler, quicker and cheaper than stratified random sampling. However, it is less likely to produce a sample which is representative of the research population. For example, where and when a quota is filled can make significant differences to the sample. Stopping people on the street during weekday working hours would exclude many people in paid employment. And the fact that researchers can choose who they interview can bias the sample still further. Faced with two young men one 'smart' and 'pleasant' looking, the other just the opposite, researchers would probably choose the former. In quota sampling, people in the same strata do not have an equal chance of being selected.

Snowball and volunteer samples Sometimes researchers have great difficulty obtaining people for their samples. First, lists for a sampling frame might not be available. Second, the research population might be so small that normal sampling methods would not supply the numbers needed. Third, members of the research population might not wish to be identified. Think of the problems in locating the following: burglars, heroin users, collectors of ancient Greek coins, gay men, members of a Masonic Lodge. One possibility is to use a network of like-minded or like-situated individuals. This is the basis of *snowball sampling*, so-called because of its similarity to rolling a snowball.

Snowballing works like this. The researcher finds someone who fits the bill. They are asked to find another person who fits and so on. In this way a network of members of the research population is built up and this forms the basis for the sample.

Snowballing has the obvious advantage of creating a sampling frame where other methods may fail. However, it is unlikely to provide a representative sample since it is not random and relies on personal recommendation.

Volunteer samples provide an alternative to snowballing. Advertisements, leaflets, posters, radio or TV broadcasts, newspaper or magazine articles announce the research and request volunteers for the sample. Annette Lawson (1988) wrote a newspaper article about her study of adultery. She used the article to obtain a volunteer sample by asking readers who had experienced adultery to complete a questionnaire. Five hundred and seventy-nine readers responded to her request.

Volunteer sampling has much the same advantages and disadvantages as snowballing. In addition, volunteer samples are *self-selected* which may systematically bias the sample in a particular direction. For example, those who volunteer may have a particular reason for doing so.

4.3 Responding to surveys

Response rates It's one thing creating a representative sample, it's quite another getting everybody in the sample to participate in the survey. The *response rate* – the percentage of the sample that participates – varies widely. For example, Shere Hite's *The Hite Report on the Family* (1994) based on questionnaires in magazines had a mere 3% response rate,

whereas everybody Ann Oakley (1974) asked to take part in her research on housework agreed to do so.

There are many reasons for non-response. They include:

1 Failure to make contact because people have moved, are on holiday, in prison, working away from home or simply out when the researcher calls.

2 Contact is made, but the interview cannot be conducted because the person is ill, deaf, experiencing some personal tragedy or can't speak English.

3 The person refuses to participate. Reasons may include no time, no interest, sees no point in the research, is suspicious of, dislikes, or is embarrassed by the researcher.

Problems of non-response Does non-response make the sample unrepresentative? Does it bias the sample and produce systematic error? Often the answer is we don't know since little or nothing is known about those who do not participate. Sometimes information on non-participants does become available. This happened in the surveys attempting to predict the 1992 General Election result. Opinion polls underestimated the Conservative vote by 8.5%. Over half of this underestimate was due to those who refused to participate – they were much more likely to vote Conservative. This produced an unrepresentative sample and in large part accounted for the failure to predict the election result (*Horizon*, BBC TV, 1994).

Evidence such as this suggests that non-response can be a serious problem.

summary

1. Social surveys are designed to provide information about particular populations.

2. They are based on samples which aim to represent the research population as a whole.

3. Whatever type of sample is used, there is no guarantee that it will be representative.

4. A high level of non-response can result in an unrepresentative sample.

key terms

Social surveys Systematic collection of the same type of data from a particular population.
Sample A selection from the research population.
Sampling unit A member of the research population.
Sampling frame A list of members of the research population.
Random sample A sample which gives every member of the sampling frame an equal chance of being selected.
Systematic sample A systematic selection of people from the sampling frame, eg every 10th member.
Stratified sample A sample which attempts to reflect particular characteristics of the research population. The population is divided into strata in terms of age, gender etc, and the sample is randomly drawn from each stratum.
Quota sample A stratified sample in which selection from the strata is not random.
Snowball sample Members of the sample select each other.
Volunteer sample Members of the sample are self-selected, eg they choose to respond to a questionnaire printed in a magazine.
Response rate The percentage of the sample that participates in the research.

activity8 sampling

Item A A stratified random sample

We wish to study the career plans of university students and have sufficient funds to interview 125. Before selecting the sample, the sampling frame is stratified into departments, eg Physics and Chemistry, and years, eg students in their first year of study. There are 5,000 students in the university and the sample of 125 is one fortieth of this total. The example below shows the numbers of students randomly selected from years 1, 2 and 3 in the Physics department.

Adapted from Arber, 1993

Stratification by department and year

Department	Year	Number in year	Number in sample
Physics	1	120	3
	2	100	3
	3	100	2
Total		320	8

Item B A volunteer sample

Shere Hite's (1994) report on family life in three Western societies received a great deal of publicity. Some of its 'findings' were dramatic. More than one in four women 'have no memory of affection by their father'. Four out of ten fathers frighten their sons with their violent tempers. And 31% of girls and young women 'report sexual harassment or abuse by a male family member'.

Hite's findings were based on 3028 completed questionnaires. Her sample was a self-selected volunteer sample. Hite distributed 100,000 questionnaires, mainly in

Will the readership of Penthouse provide a representative sample?

magazines such as *Penthouse* in America, *Women Against Fundamentalism* in Britain and *Nouvelles Questions Feminists* in France. Her statistics come from the 3% who responded. She claims that self-selected samples are acceptable as long as the study is large enough.

Adapted from Kellner, 1994

questions

1 Why do you think the researchers in Item A decided to use a stratified random sample?

2 According to one critic, Hite's 'findings' are rubbish (Kellner, 1994). Discuss this claim with reference to a) her sampling procedure and b) the response rate.

Unit 5 Questionnaires

keyissues

1 What are questionnaires?

2 What are their advantages and disadvantages?

5.1 What are questionnaires?

Questionnaires are lists of questions. They are the main method for gathering data in social surveys. They are sometimes handed to or posted to the respondent – the person answering the questions – and he or she is asked to fill them in. This is known as a *self-completion questionnaire*. They are sometimes read out by an interviewer who records the answers. This is known as an *interview questionnaire* or a *structured interview*.

Comparable data In theory questionnaires produce data

which can be directly compared. Everybody is answering exactly the same questions and are therefore responding to the same thing. Any differences in the answers will therefore reflect real differences between the respondents.

This is fine in theory. However, it's easier said than done. As we shall see, the same questions worded in exactly the same way can mean different things to different people. And in the case of the structured interview there is the problem of *interviewer bias* – the effect an interviewer may have on respondents' answers. Imagine how the age, gender and personality of an interviewer might affect your answers on a sensitive subject such as sexual behaviour.

Quantifiable data Questionnaires are usually designed to generate data which can be easily quantified – put into numbers. Here is an example from *British Social Attitudes: the 17th Report* (Jowell et al., 2000). It shows the percentage of respondents who chose each option. Constructing questions in this way makes it easy to quantify the results.

A frank scene in a film shows a man and woman having sex. How would you feel about this being shown on one of the regular television channels?

	% agreeing
Should not be allowed to be shown at all	23
Only after midnight	18
Only after 10pm	35
Only after 9pm	18
Only after 8pm	3
Allowed to be shown at any time	2

Numerical data lends itself to statistical techniques. It makes it possible to discover whether or not there is a correlation – a statistical link – between two or more variables.

Operationalising concepts Questionnaires are designed to measure things. And to do this, those 'things' must be *operationalised*, ie put in a form which allows them to be measured. How, for example, do you measure the strength of religious belief? The example below is from the 1998

Belief in God, Britain, 1998 (%)

I don't believe in God.	10
I don't know whether there is a God and I don't believe there is any way to find out.	15
I don't believe in a personal God but I do believe in a Higher Power of some kind.	14
I find myself believing in God some of the time but not at others.	14
While I have doubts, I feel that I do believe in God.	23
I know God really exists and I have no doubts about it.	21
Don't know and no answer.	3

From Jowell et al., 1998

British Social Attitudes Survey. It is an attempt to measure people's belief in God. Respondents were asked to choose the statement which best fits their beliefs.

Operationalising concepts is difficult, especially when sociologists themselves cannot agree on their meaning. For example, how do we operationalise concepts such as poverty and social class? Often concepts are operationalised in different ways in different studies which means the results are difficult, if not impossible, to compare. And the problem of comparability becomes even greater when we attempt to discover what respondents really mean when they answer questions. This problem will be looked at shortly.

Coding answers Answers to questions are *coded*. This means they are classified into various categories. When concepts, such as belief in God, are operationalised, the questionnaire can be pre-coded. The responses to the Belief in God questionnaire are pre-coded into seven categories. The researcher simply has to count the number of people who choose each category. Quantifying the data is easy.

It is more difficult to code a written answer. Consider the following.

Question   Do you believe in God?

Answer   It depends what you mean by God. Do you mean a God that just exists apart from this world? Or, do you mean a God that controls what happens in this world? Sometimes, I think I believe in the first type of God.

This answer is difficult to code. Researchers usually have a list of categories in terms of which written answers are coded. Often, however, written answers don't fit neatly into a particular category. For example, the above answer would not fit neatly into any of the categories in the Belief in God questionnaire.

Written answers are sometimes difficult to code. As a result, they are difficult to quantify.

5.2 Types of questions

Closed questions There are two main types of questions used in questionnaires – closed and open. In *closed questions*, the range of responses is fixed by the researcher. The respondent usually has to select one answer from two or more given alternatives. The questions above on sex on television and belief in God are examples of closed questions. Here is a different example in which the respondent is asked to rank the alternatives provided.

> **Which do you feel are the most important factors in choosing a university? Please rank the following in order of importance to you. Number them from 1 = most important, to 7 = least important.**
>
> Closeness to a town or city
> Good academic reputation
> Good chance of getting a job after graduation
> Attractive campus
> Good social facilities
> Good accommodation
> Availability of real ale
>
> From Newell, 1993

Closed questions are relatively easy, quick and cheap to classify and quantify. They are pre-coded in the sense that the categories are set and the respondent simply has to choose one or rank some. However, the researcher has chosen the available responses and in this respect is imposing his or her choice of alternatives on the respondent. Look at the question above on choosing a university. Can you think of any 'important factors' not given? There is a way round this problem by adding 'other, please specify' which asks the respondent to add, in this case, any other reasons for choosing a university.

Open questions An *open question* asks the respondent to answer a question in their own words. Open questions give the respondent more freedom, but coding the responses can be difficult and time consuming. In many cases it might be difficult to fit responses into a particular category.

Most researchers see closed questions as suitable for simple, factual data such as age, gender and income level. Open questions are usually seen as more suitable for data on attitudes and values where respondents are required to express how they feel. An open question allows them to say things in their own way.

5.3 Types of questionnaires

Self-completion questionnaires

Self-completion questionnaires can be left with respondents either to be picked up later or posted back to the researcher. *Postal questionnaires*, as their name suggests, are mailed to respondents with a request to mail them back to the researcher. Usually most of the questions in self-completion questionnaires are closed and pre-coded.

Self-completion questionnaires have the following advantages and disadvantages.

Advantages

- Inexpensive – no interviewers to pay, cheap to classify results.
- As a result, often possible to survey a large sample.
- Fast and efficient analysis possible with pre-coded closed questions. Answers can be easily quantified and entered straight on to computers.

- Postal questionnaires allow a geographically dispersed sample to be contacted easily and cheaply.
- No interviewer bias – the interviewer does not influence the respondent's answers.

Disadvantages

- A relatively low response rate – often well below 50% for postal questionnaires. This may destroy the representativeness of the sample.
- Respondents may not understand the questions or follow the instructions.
- Answers may be incomplete, illegible or incomprehensible.
- Closed questions may seriously limit what respondents want to say.

Structured interviews

In a structured interview the interviewer reads out the questions and records the responses in writing, on audio-tape or on a portable computer.

Advantages

- Response rate usually much higher than for postal questionnaires.
- Interviewers can explain the purpose of the research, clarify questions and ask for further details. This can result in more information.
- Respondents who cannot read and write can be included in the survey.

Disadvantages

- More expensive – interviewers are usually paid.
- Cost increases if sample spread over a wide area.
- Interviewer bias.

5.4 Questions and answers

Constructing a questionnaire is not easy. The researcher must make sure that questions are clear and unambiguous. Where possible, words and phrases should be simple and straightforward. Leading questions, eg 'Don't you agree that ...' should be avoided as they direct the respondent to a particular answer. Questions should be meaningful and relevant – there's not much point in asking people if they've enjoyed their holiday abroad if they've never been out of the country. And, most importantly, the questions must mean the same thing to all respondents. If they mean different things respondents are, for all intents and purposes, answering different questions. And this means that their answers cannot be directly compared.

Researchers sometimes use a *pilot study* to iron out problems with questionnaires. They test the questions on a relatively small number of people who share the characteristics of the main sample. A pilot study can be invaluable for removing ambiguity and misunderstanding. Yet all the preparation in the world cannot completely remove the basic problems of questions and answers.

What do answers mean? Are respondents telling the truth? Yes and no. Are they giving the answers they think the researcher wants? Sometimes. Do all respondents understand the questions? Not always. Do the questions mean the same to all respondents? Probably not. Do respondents' answers reflect their behaviour in everyday life? Maybe. Given all this, what appears to be a precise, reliable and efficient research method – the social survey – may be nothing of the sort.

Creating an impression Everybody plays the game of 'impression management'. They try to manage the impression of themselves which others form. This can shape their responses to a questionnaire and more particularly to a structured interview. Consider the following example.

Survey after survey has shown a high level of church attendance in the USA, far higher than for any comparable Western industrial society. Yet figures produced by the churches tell a somewhat different story. For example, surveys conducted by Gallup suggested that 35% of Episcopalians (a type of Christians) in the USA had been to church in the last 7 days, yet figures from the churches indicated that only 16% actually did so. Why the discrepancy? It appears that many respondents were concerned with giving the 'right' answer to the interviewer – they wished to appear upright, decent and respectable and regular church attendance was, to many, a way of giving this impression (Bruce, 1995).

Examples such as this suggest that researchers must know as much as possible about what questions and answers mean to respondents. Only then can they write appropriate questions and be in a position to interpret the answers.

Words and meanings For a questionnaire to do its job, questions have to have the same meaning for all respondents. The following example from the USA illustrates how easy it is for a question to be interpreted differently. A survey of reading habits produced the unexpected result that working-class respondents read more books than middle-class respondents. This result was largely due to the interpretation placed on the word 'book'. Unlike most middle-class respondents, those from the working-class included magazines in their definition of books.

This illustrates that the more researchers know about those they study, the better the questions they ask and the better their interpretation of the answers.

5.5 Theoretical considerations

Positivism Two research traditions – positivism and interpretivism – were introduced on pages 146-147. As noted, positivists tend to favour 'hard', quantitative data. Positivist sociologists attempt to measure behaviour by translating it into numbers. This makes it possible to use

key terms

Self-completion questionnaire A questionnaire completed by the respondent.
Structured interview/interview questionnaire A questionnaire read out by an interviewer who also records the answers.
Operationalise Translating concepts into a form which can be measured.
Coding Classifying answers into various categories.
Closed questions Questions in which the range of responses is fixed by the researcher.
Open questions Questions which allow the respondent to answer in their own words.
Postal questionnaire A questionnaire mailed to respondents with a request to mail it back after completion.
Pilot study A preliminary study designed to identify any problems with the main study.

statistical tests to measure the strength of relationships between variables. This may indicate causal relationships – that one variable causes another.

It is fairly easy to translate the answers to a questionnaire into numbers. This is particularly so with closed questions. As a result, positivists tend to favour questionnaires as a method of producing data.

Interpretivism By contrast, interpretivists are concerned with the meanings which guide and direct human actions. Many interpretivists would reject questionnaires as a means of discovering meanings. They argue that questionnaires, particularly those with closed questions, fail to give people the freedom to talk about their behaviour as they see it.

summary

1. Questionnaires are the main method for collecting data in social surveys.
2. In theory, questionnaires provide directly comparable data.
3. Closed questions are pre-coded. They produce data which is easy to quantify.
4. Answers to open questions can be difficult to code and quantify.
5. Self-completion questionnaires and structured interviews each have their advantages and disadvantages.
6. It can be difficult to discover what respondents' answers actually mean.

activity9 asking questions

Item A *On the toilet*

A study based in Bristol asked nearly 2,000 people to fill out a questionnaire on how many times they went to the toilet during the week and the shape, size, consistency and texture of their faeces. They were required to tick whether it was 'like a sausage or snake but with cracks on its surface' or 'fluffy with ragged edges' and so on.

Adapted from O'Connell Davidson & Layder, 1994

Item B *Non-existent videos*

The Video Recording Bill was passed by the Conservative government in 1984. Its aim was to place strict controls on 'video nasties'. Survey evidence was used to support the bill. Children were given a list of video titles and asked to indicate which they had seen. Forty per cent claimed to have seen at least one of the video nasties on the list.

Later, Guy Cumberbatch presented children with a list of fictitious titles such as 'I vomit on your cannibal apocalypse'. Sixty-eight per cent claimed to have seen at least one of these non-existent videos.

Adapted from Harris, 1984

Have you watched this video?

Item C *Saying one thing, doing another*

In the early 1930s, Richard LaPiere, a social psychologist at Stanford University, travelled 10,000 miles across the USA with a young Chinese-American couple. At the time, there was widespread prejudice against Asians and there were no laws preventing racial discrimination in public accommodation. They visited 250 hotels, restaurants and campsites and only once were they refused service. After the trip, LaPiere sent a letter to all the places they had visited asking, 'Will you accept members of the Chinese race as guests in you establishment?' 92% said 'no', 7% said 'uncertain, depends on the circumstances' and only 1% said 'yes'.

Adapted from LaPiere, 1934

questions

1 Read Item A. Comment on the accuracy of the data which this questionnaire might produce.

2 What problems do Items B and C raise for interpreting answers to questionnaires?

Unit 6 *Interviews*

keyissues

1 What are the main types of interviews?
2 What are their advantages and disadvantages?

6.1 Types of interviews

Structured interviews As outlined in the previous unit, structured interviews are simply questionnaires which are read out by the interviewer who then records the respondent's answers. The same questions are read out in the same order to all respondents.

Semi-structured interviews Each interview usually has the same set of questions, but in this case the interviewer has the freedom to 'probe'. Respondents can be asked to clarify their answers, to provide examples, and to develop what they've said.

Unstructured interviews By comparison, unstructured interviews are more like an everyday conversation. They are more informal, open-ended, flexible and free flowing. Questions are unlikely to be pre-set, though researchers usually have certain topics they wish to cover. This gives the interview some structure and direction.

Group interviews The interviews discussed so far involve two people – an interviewer and a respondent or interviewee. Group interviews involve the interviewer and a group of respondents – usually between 8 and 10 people. In some group interviews, the respondents answer questions in turn. In others, known as *focus groups*, participants are encouraged to talk to each other. They are guided rather than led or directed by the interviewer – for example, they are asked to discuss particular questions or topics.

Structured interviews – advantages and disadvantages

Why use different types of interviews? Each type has its strengths and weaknesses. Structured interviews have many of the advantages and disadvantages of questionnaires. They are particularly suitable for simple, straightforward, 'factual' information such as a respondent's age, gender, educational qualifications and occupation.

Structured interviews are seen as more likely to produce comparable data – since all respondents answer the same questions this should allow researchers to directly compare their responses and identify similarities and differences. Quantifiable data is more likely since questions can be structured to provide yes/no answers or choices between

given alternatives. And, as structured interviews are more formal than other types, there may be less chance of interviewer bias.

However, structured interviews can place strict limitations on respondents' answers. This is particularly true of closed questions which force respondents to choose between pre-set alternatives. This prevents respondents from answering in their own words and in their own way.

Semi-structured interviews – advantages and disadvantages

This type of interview has many of the advantages of the structured interview. In addition, it allows the interviewer to probe – to jog respondents' memories, and ask them to clarify, spell out and give examples of particular points. This can add depth and detail to answers.

However, this gain is accompanied by a loss of standardisation and comparability (May, 2001). Although the basic questions are pre-set, probes are not, which results in non-standard interviews. This means that each interview is somewhat different. As a result, the data is not strictly comparable since, to some extent, interviewees are responding to different questions.

Group interviews – advantages and disadvantages

Focus groups are becoming increasingly common in sociological research. They have been used to study the effects of long-term imprisonment, victims of crime, conflicts within organisations and changes in working practices among steel workers (May, 2001; Walklate, 2000).

The results of focus group interviews are sometimes different from those of individual interviews. This does not mean that one is 'right' and the other 'wrong'. Interaction within groups affects people's opinions. Since much of our lives is spent in groups, it is important to obtain data from this source (May, 2001).

Some researchers find focus groups provide a rich source of qualitative data. In her study of victims of crime, Sandra Walklate (2000) claims that without the use of focus groups, many of the shades of meaning and subtleties of people's views would be lost.

Unstructured interviews advantages

Unstructured interviews are often seen to have the following advantages.

Sensitive groups Some groups are less likely than others to provide information for researchers. They might be suspicious of outsiders, hostile towards them, afraid of them or simply uncomfortable in their presence. An unstructured interview can allay these feelings as it provides an opportunity for understanding and trust to develop between interviewer and interviewee. This can be seen from the following example. Postal surveys were used in London to find out why people did not apply for welfare benefits to which they were entitled. The response rate was very low, due partly to fear and suspicion, a reaction often found amongst the frail and the elderly. Research indicated that a one-to-one interview was the most effective way of gaining information, in large part because interviewers were able to put respondents' minds at rest (Fielding, 1993).

Sensitive topics Unstructured interviews are also seen as particularly suitable for sensitive topics. Respondents may be more likely to discuss sensitive and painful experiences if they feel that the interviewer is sympathetic and understanding. Unstructured interviews provide the opportunity for developing this kind of relationship. Joan Smith's (1998) study about the family background of homeless young people produced detailed and in-depth information using unstructured interviews.

Respondent's viewpoint Structured and semi-structured interviews give respondents few opportunities to develop their answers and direct the interview into areas which interest them. The researcher has constructed the questions and, in the case of closed questions, the range of possible answers. In these respects the researcher has decided what's important.

An unstructured interview offers greater opportunity for respondents to take control, to define priorities and to direct the interview into areas which they see as interesting and significant. In this way, they have a greater chance to express their own viewpoints. And this can lead to new and important insights for the researcher.

Validity and depth If respondents feel at ease in an interview situation they will be more likely to open up and say what they really mean. Unstructured interviews can provide this opportunity. They are therefore more likely to produce valid data and to produce richer, more vivid and more colourful data. They also allow interviewers more opportunity to pursue a topic, to probe with further questions, to ask respondents to qualify and develop their answers. Because of this, the resulting data may have more depth.

Meanings and attitudes Many researchers see unstructured interviews as particularly suited to discovering meanings, values, attitudes, opinions and beliefs. People often take these for granted and find it difficult to spell them out. For example, what exactly are people's religious beliefs; what does music really mean to them; what do they really think about the welfare state? Unstructured interviews can explore such areas without the limitations of pre-set questions.

Meanings and opinions are not simple and clear-cut. There are shades of meaning. Opinions are not cut and dried, they are hedged with qualification. A skilled interviewer can encourage and enable people to spell out this complexity. Structured interviews with pre-set questions are unlikely to capture this range of meaning. However, not everybody agrees with this view. The British Social Attitudes Survey uses a very detailed structured interview and a self-completion questionnaire to discover attitudes on a range of issues.

Unstructured interviews – disadvantages

Interviewer bias Interviewer bias is unavoidable. To some extent the interviewer will affect the responses of the interviewee.

Interviewers are people with social characteristics – they have a nationality, ethnicity, gender, social class, age group and so on. They also have particular personalities – they may be shy or outgoing, caring or uncaring, aggressive or unaggressive. These social and psychological characteristics will be perceived in certain ways by interviewees and will have some effect on their responses. In some cases this may systematically bias the results.

A number of American studies have examined the effect of the social characteristics of interviewers and respondents. J. Allan Williams Jr (1971) claims that the greater the status difference between interviewer and respondent, the less likely respondents are to express their true feelings. He found that African-Americans in the 1960s were more likely to say they approved of civil rights demonstrations if the interviewer was Black rather than White.

Social desirability In general, people like to present themselves in a favourable light. This can result in respondents emphasising socially desirable aspects of their behaviour and attitudes in the presence of interviewers. As noted in the previous unit, Episcopalians in the USA tend to exaggerate the frequency of their attendance at church in order to appear upright and respectable (see page 158).

Respondents tend to be open about and even exaggerate aspects of their behaviour which they see as socially desirable, and to conceal or minimise aspects seen as undesirable.

Validity Do respondents tell lies? Is their memory hazy or faulty? Is what they say in interviews different from what they have done or will do? In some cases the answer is yes to all these questions. An instance has been given above in the case of church attendance. Voting intention is a case where people's intentions expressed in interviews and their actions at a later date are sometimes different. And there is evidence that some people tell downright lies, for example when recounting their sexual activity to an interviewer (O'Connell Davidson & Layder, 1994).

Item B *In the classroom*

The following extract is taken from David Hargreaves's study of an all-boys secondary school in England. He sat at the back of the classroom to observe lessons. Later, he talked to some of the boys about the behaviour of the teachers. This is what they said.

'When you're in he tries to act calmly as though he's a little angel and all that.'

'They put on a show for you. They put the good act on, smiles and all that.'

'Like if Mr O's getting mad 'cos someone's ripped a book or something, but if you're in he seems to drop it. If you weren't there, he'd get real mad.'

Adapted from Hargreaves, 1967

Item C *In the pub*

Dick Hobbs's research involved much heavy drinking in pubs and he experienced some of the dangers of 'going native'. He writes: 'I often had to remind myself that I was not in a pub to enjoy myself but to conduct an enquiry and repeatedly woke up the following morning with an incredible hangover facing the dilemma of whether to bring it up or write it up'.

Adapted from Hobbs, 1988

Item D *Backstage*

As part of his research, Rubenstein completed police training and rode as an 'armed observer' in patrol cars in Philadelphia – and perhaps that degree of involvement has helped to produce what will surely become a classic. His *City Police* is an insider's view of backstage police behaviour. In microscopic detail, Rubenstein takes us into the policeman's world. The information he collected on violence and corruption could only have been gained by a trained observer who was accepted by the policemen.

Adapted from Punch, 1979

questions

1   Item A points to one of the main problems of participant observation. What is this problem and how is it usually dealt with?

2   What are the advantages and disadvantages of participant observation indicated by Items B, C and D?

Unit 8 *Secondary sources*

keyissues

1   What are the main secondary sources of data?

2   What are the advantages and disadvantages of using these sources?

Primary data So far, this chapter has been mainly concerned with *primary data* – data produced by researchers using methods such as questionnaires, interviews and observation. Primary data is new data that did not exist before the research began.

Secondary data There is a vast range of existing information which is available for sociological research. It includes letters, diaries, novels, autobiographies, legal documents, parish records, official statistics, newspapers, magazines, television and radio programmes, recorded music, films, photographs and paintings. These sources of information are known as *secondary sources* and the data itself as *secondary data*.

This unit looks at a number of secondary sources and assesses the usefulness of secondary data.

8.1 Official statistics

Sources of official statistics

Official statistics are numerical data produced by national and local government bodies. They may be a by-product of the normal workings of a government department. For example, the claimant count measure of unemployment – a measure of unemployment based on the number of people who claim unemployment-related benefit – is a by-product of administering the benefit system. Or official statistics may result from research designed to produce them – for example, the Labour Force Survey collects information on unemployment from a quarterly survey of 60,000 households.

Official statistics cover a wide range of behaviour including births, deaths, marriage and divorce, the distribution of income and wealth, crime and sentencing and work and leisure. The following are among the main sources of official statistics.

1 **Government departments** Departments such as Education and Skills and the Home Office regularly request information from organisations such as local tax offices, social services departments, hospitals, job centres and police stations. This information is then processed and much of it published.

2 **Surveys** The Office for National Statistics is the government agency responsible for compiling and analysing many of the UK's economic, social and population statistics. Surveys are a major source of statistical data. Every ten years the Office for National Statistics carries out the Census of the Population which covers every household in the UK. Each head of household must, by law, complete a questionnaire that deals with family composition, housing, occupation, transport and leisure. Other large scale surveys include the annual General Household Survey based on a detailed questionnaire given to a sample of nearly 12,000 people and the New Earnings Survey based on a 1% sample of employees drawn from Inland Revenue PAYE records.

Using official statistics

Official statistics provide a vast array of quantitative data. However, sociologists cannot accept them at face value – they must use them only with care and caution. It is essential to bear the following points in mind.

How are official statistics constructed? Sociologists must know how official statistics are constructed in order to assess the quality of the data they provide. The example of unemployment statistics shows why.

As noted earlier, there are two main sources of data for unemployment statistics – the benefit system and social surveys. And there are two main definitions of unemployment – the claimant count definition which uses data from the benefit system, and the International Labour Organisation definition which uses data from the Labour Force Survey. Although both measures show broadly the same levels of and trends in unemployment, there are differences.

Sociologists using official statistics on unemployment should be aware of how these statistics have been constructed. This applies to all official statistics, no matter what the topic.

Who decides what statistics are collected and published? Official statistics are government statistics. Elected representatives and government officials decide what information is important and useful and, on this basis, what data to collect and publish. And, maybe more importantly, they decide what *not* to collect and publish.

These decisions may be 'political'. They may reflect the concerns and priorities of government rather than a desire to provide sound and reliable information. For example, Muriel Nissel, the first editor of *Social Trends*, an annual publication of the Office for National Statistics has written, 'From time to time, there has been great pressure on directors of statistics in departments to withhold or modify statistics, particularly in relation to employment and health, and professional integrity has forced some to threaten resignation' (Nissel, 1995).

Are official statistics politically biased? Does the actual construction of statistics reflect government interests? Are they shaped to present the government of the day in a favourable light? The following evidence suggests that in some cases this might happen.

According to the Labour Party, Conservative governments changed the method used to count unemployment over 30 times between 1982 and 1992. And in practically every case, these changes resulted in a drop in the official level of unemployment (Denscombe, 1994). At best, some would argue, this is politically convenient, at worst it is outright fiddling to present the government in a better light.

Do official statistics provide valid measures?

Do official statistics really measure what they claim to measure? For example, do the annual crime statistics produced by the Home Office provide an accurate measurement of crime? Even the Home Office accepts that the answer is no. Similar criticisms can be made for a range of official statistics from unemployment and suicide to the distribution of income and wealth.

The problem of validity was examined with reference to suicide statistics in Activity 4. It is looked at again in terms of crime statistics in Activity 12.

Advantages of official statistics Despite the above warnings, official statistics can be very useful for sociological research. They have the following advantages.

- Published statistics are readily available and cost little or nothing to use.
- Care is taken to select representative samples and sample sizes are often large. Surveys as large as the General Household Survey are usually outside sociologists' research budgets.
- Many government surveys are well planned and organised with detailed questionnaires or interview schedules. As such, they meet the standards of sociological research.
- Surveys are often conducted regularly, for example on a fortnightly, monthly, annual or ten yearly basis. This can allow for comparisons over time and the identification of trends.
- Sometimes official statistics are the only major source of information on a particular topic.

Perspectives on official statistics

A positivist view From this perspective (see pages 146-147), official statistics are a potentially valuable source of quantitative data. They have their faults but, in may cases, they provide measures of behaviour that can be used to investigate possible cause and effect relationships.

An interpretivist view From this perspective (see page 146), official statistics are not 'facts', they do not represent some objective reality 'out there' in the real world. Instead, they are definitions and meanings in terms of which people construct social reality. The job of the sociologist is to discover these meanings and how they are constructed. For example, an interpretivist sociologist would not use suicide statistics to explain why people commit suicide. Instead, they would ask why certain kinds of death are defined as suicide. In this sense, suicide is a meaning (see page 146).

Take crime statistics. The question is not whether they are accurate or inaccurate. A crime is simply a meaning given to an event. And the job of the sociologist is to understand how this meaning is constructed.

A Marxist view From a Marxist viewpoint, official statistics are an aspect of ruling class ideology. Generated by government departments and agencies, official statistics derive from questions asked by, information processed by, and results either suppressed or made public by a state which represents the interests of the capitalist class. As such, they provide information which helps to maintain and justify the power of capital and disguise the reality of exploitation and oppression.

key term

Official statistics Statistics produced by local and national government, government agencies and organisations funded by government.

summary

1. Sociologists using official statistics should be aware of how those statistics have been constructed.

2. Decisions on what statistics to collect and publish may be politically biased.

3. In some cases, official statistics fail to produce valid measures.

4. Official statistics can provide valuable data for sociological research.

5. Positivists see official statistics as a potentially valuable source of quantitative data. Interpretivists see official statistics as meanings in terms of which people construct their social reality. Marxists see official statistics as an aspect of ruling class ideology.

activity 12 crime statistics

Item A Ethnicity and crime

African Caribbeans make up around 1.5% of the UK population. In the mid-1990s, they formed nearly 12% of the prison population.

The police rely on the public to report crimes to them. Evidence indicates that White people are more likely to report Black rather than White suspects. In London, Black males aged 16 to 24 were ten times more likely to be stopped by police under stop and search powers. If arrested for the same offence, young Black males were more likely to be charged than their White counterparts. And if found guilty of the same offence, Black people were more likely to be sent to prison.

Research indicates that statistics which link ethnicity and crime result from a series of decisions based on prejudice and discrimination. This is why so many Black people end up in prison.

Adapted from May, 2001

Stop and search

Item B *The social construction of crime statistics*

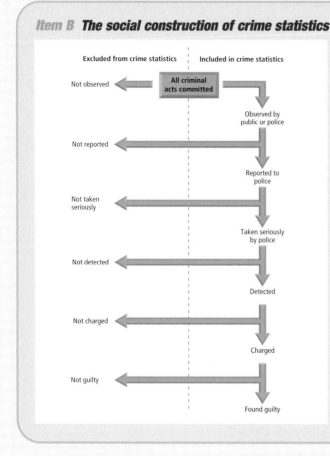

Excluded from crime statistics | Included in crime statistics

All criminal acts committed

Not observed ← → Observed by public or police

Not reported ← → Reported to police

Not taken seriously ← → Taken seriously by police

Not detected ← → Detected

Not charged ← → Charged

Not guilty ← → Found guilty

questions

1. a) What are the statistics in Item A actually measuring?
   b) Do they indicate a link between ethnicity and crime?
2. Look at Item B.
   a) Why does it suggest that crime statistics must be treated with caution?
   b) Item B assumes that there are such things as 'criminal acts' which are either included in or excluded from official statistics. Criticise this view.

8.2 Documents

The term documents covers a wide range of written and recorded material. It includes letters, diaries, memoirs, autobiographies, novels, newspapers, advertisements, posters, photographs and radio and television broadcasts.

This section looks at some of the ways sociologists have analysed documents. Ray Pawson (1995) distinguishes three main types of analysis, 1) formal content analysis 2) thematic analysis 3) textual analysis.

Formal content analysis

This method attempts to classify and quantify the content of a document in an objective manner. Say you were interested in the portrayal of gender roles in children's fiction published during the last five years. You could take a sample of the books and analyse each in terms of the same pre-set categories. For example, which activities are shared by girls and boys and which are limited to one or the other. The results are then quantified and interpreted. If, for example, preparing food and taking care of younger brothers and sisters is limited to girls, then it could be argued that gender roles remain distinct.

Critics accept that formal content analysis can often effectively measure simple straightforward aspects of content – see the example in Activity 13, Item A. However, they argue that it says little about the meaning of a document, either in terms of its meaning to the audience or the meaning the producer intends to communicate.

Thematic analysis

This approach looks for the motives and ideologies which are seen to underlie documents. For example, a news broadcast may reflect the interests of powerful groups in society. The job of the researcher is to uncover this underlying ideology. The Glasgow University Media Group combined content and thematic analysis in their analysis of TV news broadcasts in the 1970s and 80s. They made a strong case that there is a pro-management, anti-union bias in the reporting of industrial disputes.

However, there are a number of problems with thematic analysis. Who is to say that the sociologist's interpretation of the underlying ideology is correct? And if it is correct, does the existence of such ideology matter? Readers of *The Sun*, for instance, may see through or ignore or be unaware of its right-wing views. This may well explain why a significant minority of *Sun* readers regularly vote Labour.

Textual analysis

Rather than looking for underlying ideologies, this method involves a close examination of the 'text' of a document to see how it encourages a particular reading and creates a particular impression. Ray Pawson (1995) gives the following example from a newspaper headline, GIRL GUIDE, 14, RAPED AT HELLS ANGELS CONVENTION. This is an example of the 'innocent victim'/'wicked perpetrator' pair which creates the impression of two extremes, one good, the other evil. It is one of the many tricks of the trade used to convey particular messages.

As with thematic analysis, the problem with textual analysis is reading things into the text which may have little or nothing to do with the intentions of the producers or the interpretations of the audience.

Audience research

Some researchers argue that the focus of document research should be the audience. From this viewpoint, the audience is not made up of passive consumers who are brainwashed by underlying ideologies or swayed by textual 'tricks of the trade'. Instead, it sees audiences actively negotiating the meaning of messages with the outcome of negotiation ranging from acceptance to indifference to opposition (Pawson, 1995).

The news game But finding out how audiences respond is far from easy. Jenny Kitzinger's use of the 'news game' provides a novel and interesting alternative to the methods examined so far. Small 'audience groups' averaging three people from different social backgrounds were given a set of 13 photographs taken from TV news items and documentaries about AIDS. The groups were asked to select pictures and use them to write a news report on AIDS. Kitzinger (1993) concluded from this exercise that audiences are selective in their interpretation of news. They highlight certain views and modify or oppose others. They are able to 'read between the lines' of news reports, to uncover dominant themes and to construct alternative accounts which draw on their personal experience and political beliefs. This gives some indication of the variety and complexity of audience responses.

The 'news game' was first used by Greg Philo to study audience response to the media and the miners' strike of 1984/85. It represents an important change of direction – from the document, to the document in relation to the audience.

Audience understandings In more recent research, Greg Philo and David Miller (2002) examined BBC and ITN TV news broadcasts of the Israeli/Palestinian conflict. The broadcasts focused on images of violence and the bleak prospects for peace. The researchers' audience sample included 300 young people aged 17-22. The responses of this sample show how TV news affected their knowledge and understanding of the conflict.

News broadcasts made little reference to the history and background of the Israeli/Palestinian conflict. Broadcasts referred to 'occupied territories' but provided no explanation of what they were. Only 9% of the young people sampled knew it was Israelis occupying Palestinian land, 71% had no idea what the term meant, and 11% actually thought it was the Palestinians occupying Israeli land. Broadcasts showed Palestinians burning the American flag and mentioned their distrust of American peace proposals. There was little or no mention of why. For example, there was hardly a reference to the fact that the USA supplied some three billion dollars of aid to Israel

each year, much of it in military hardware. When asked to explain Palestinian distrust of the Americans, 66% of the sample had no idea, 24% thought America 'supported' Israel and only 10% mentioned money and arms (Philo & Miller, 2002).

This study shows the importance of audience research. Sociology is the study of people in society. When researchers examine 'documents' such as TV news, a major concern is how they affect members of society. And this requires researchers to discover the meanings people give to those documents and the understandings they draw from them. To do this they must 'ask the audience'.

Historical documents

For studying the past, historical documents are often the major and sometimes the only source of information. Max Weber's classic study *The Protestant Ethic and the Spirit of Capitalism* could not have been written without a range of historical documents. For example, he illustrates the spirit of capitalism with quotes from two books by Benjamin Franklin, *Necessary Hints to Those that would be Rich* (1736) and *Advice to a Young Tradesman* (1748). Weber builds a strong case for the religious basis of the capitalist work ethic by quoting from the speeches and writings of ministers such as John Calvin (1509-1564).

Geoffrey Pearson's *Hooligan: A History of Respectable Fears* (1983) provides a more recent example of the use of historical documents. Pearson looks back to Victorian England and forward to today to show that 'for generations Britain has been plagued by the same fears and problems'. He looks at 'hooliganism' – street crime and violence – the moral panics it generates and its 'discovery' time and time again as something new, in contrast to the 'good old days'. Pearson builds up a substantial case for this argument with a range of historical documents which include newspapers, magazines such as *Punch* and *The Teacher's World*, contemporary novels and government reports.

Using historical documents Historical documents are often a long way from the objectivity which sociologists strive for. They are usually biased, prejudiced, one-sided and concerned with putting over a particular point of view. However, as long as researchers take them for what they are, historical documents provide a rich and valuable source of data. Thus Lord Ashley's announcement in the

House of Commons in 1843 that, 'the morals of the children are tenfold worse than formerly' (quoted in Pearson, 1983) cannot be seen as a balanced assessment of juvenile morality. However, for Pearson's study of 'respectable fears', it is a very useful piece of data since it exemplifies a fear that has recurred throughout the past two centuries.

Historical documents bring their own problems of interpretation because they are from a different era, a different culture, and those who produced them are often dead. Add to this the fact that interpretation relies heavily on the researcher's viewpoint and background and it is clear that there is plenty of room for disagreement. For example, J. Berger argued that a number of paintings from the 17th and 18th centuries showed how art patrons at the time were very concerned with material possessions. He saw this concern as linked to the rise of capitalism. However, as Berger himself notes, this interpretation was hotly disputed by an art critic (discussed in Macdonald & Tipton, 1993).

Assessing historical documents John Scott (1990) provides four 'quality control criteria' for assessing documents which are particularly applicable to historical documents.

Authenticity The first refers to authenticity. Is the document genuine or a forgery? As the famous 60 volume *Hitler Diaries* which surfaced in 1983 showed, forgeries can fool even top historians. Or, is the document an original or a

copy? For example, the writings of Roman historians have been copied and recopied by hand. How true to the originals are the copies?

Credibility Is the author of the document 'sincere' or does he or she distort the evidence in order to mislead the reader? There are plenty of examples of distortion, deceit and outright lies in documents. Former US President Nixon denied all knowledge of the illegal break-in at the Democratic Party's headquarters which became known as the Watergate Affair. This lie appeared in TV and radio broadcasts by Nixon and his officials, and in White House press releases.

Representativeness To what extent is the document representative? For example, is a newspaper article typical of the articles which appear in that particular newspaper? The question of representativeness is particularly important in the case of historical documents as many have been lost or destroyed. Those that remain may be untypical. For example, a study of witchcraft in 17th century New England was based on court records relating to 114 suspects. The researcher believes that these surviving records are only the 'tip of the iceberg', a 'tip' which may well be unrepresentative (discussed in O'Connell Davidson & Layder, 1994).

Meaning What does a document mean? This ranges from

activity13 *analysing documents*

Item A Content analysis

Television programmes containing reference to or depiction of disability

Genre	Number of programmes	Percentage of total programmes	Number with disability	Percentage of total with disability
News	221	27	54	42
Current affairs	28	4	0	0
Documentary	155	19	21	16
Magazine	70	9	20	16
Informational	59	7	4	3
Debate	15	2	2	2
Religious	9	1	2	2
Quiz	24	3	3	2
Music/dance	38	5	0	0
Educational	5	0.6	2	2
Game show	44	5	0	0
Chat show	24	3	4	3
Sport	36	4	1	1
Special broadcast	46	6	12	9
Special interest programme	3	0.4	3	2
Other	27	3	0	0
Total	804	99	128	100

From Cumberbatch & Negrine, 1992

Item B Newspaper headlines

These headlines refer to men and women infected with the AIDS virus through blood transfusions, and mother to child transmission in the womb.

From Kitzinger, 1993

the literal meaning of the text – can the researcher 'literally' understand it, eg can the researcher read a text in Anglo Saxon English – to higher level interpretations of meaning and significance. As the previous section on analysing documents has indicated, questions of meaning will never be settled.

Item C First World War posters

Item D The Israeli/Palestinian conflict

Palestinian boy with a slingshot hurling stones at a Jewish settlement in the occupied territories

questions

1 a) What does Item A tell us?

   b) What further information might be useful?

2 Analyse the headlines in Item B using thematic and textual analysis.

3 What use might a sociologist studying gender make of the posters in Item C?

4 a) What additional information would you need in order to understand what's going on in Item D?

   b) Do you think most young people in the UK have this information? Explain your answer.

summary

1. There are three main methods for the analysis of documents – formal content analysis, thematic analysis and textual analysis. In each case, the analysis is conducted by the researcher.

2. In recent years, the focus has moved towards audience research. The emphasis here is on how audiences interpret documents.

3. For studying the past, historical documents are often the major and sometimes the only source of information.

4. Historical documents are usually biased and one-sided but this does not necessarily detract from their usefulness.

5. Historical documents can be assessed in terms of their authenticity, credibility, representativeness and meaning.

activity14 historical documents

Item A The diaries of a cabinet minister

Richard Crossman was an MP and cabinet minister in the Labour government of 1964-1970. His political diaries were published after his death in 1975.

Memory is a terrible improver – even with a diary to check the tendency. And it is this which makes a politician's autobiography so wildly unreliable. But if I could publish a diary of my years as a minister without any editorial improvements, as a true record of how one minister thought and felt, I would have done something towards lighting up the secret places of British politics and enabling any intelligent elector to have a picture of what went on behind the scenes between 1964 and 1970.

Of course the picture which this diary provides is neither objective nor fair – although as a lifelong political scientist I have tried to discipline myself to objectivity. In particular, I have tried to avoid self-deception, especially about my own motives; the tendency to attribute to others my own worst failings; and the temptation to omit what might make me look silly in print. I have been urged by many to remove all the wounding passages about colleagues or officials. I have not done so because it would make the book untrue, and I hope that when some of them find me intolerably unfair, they will recall the follies and illusions I faithfully record about myself. A day-by-day account of a Government at work, as seen by one participant, is bound to be one-sided and immensely partisan. If it isn't, it too would fail to be true to life.

Adapted from Crossman, 1975

Item B Images of Africans

The crest of Sir William Hawkins, an English sea captain who made a fortune from the slave trade in the 16th century.

A bill of sale

This advert for Pears soap was actually painted on a rock in the Sudan by invading British forces.

questions

1 With some reference to Item A, suggest why diaries might be preferable to autobiographies as a source of information.

2 a) Provide a sociological interpretation of the pictures in Item B.

   b) Critically assess your interpretation.

Unit 9 Types of research

keyissues

1 Why use different types of research?

2 What are their strengths and weaknesses?

This chapter has already looked at three types of research – experiments, social surveys and ethnography. This unit looks at several more.

9.1 Life histories

As their name suggests, *life histories* are accounts of people's lives which they tell to researchers.

Something of the flavour and significance of life histories can be obtained from a brief discussion of *Cheyenne Memories*, the life history of John Stands In Timber (1884-1967) as told to the anthropologist Margot Liberty. He was a member of the last generation who experienced the traditional way of life of the Cheyenne Indians during the 19th century.

The Cheyenne were a non-literate society, so oral accounts are particularly important. Stands In Timber's account of his life and the history and culture of his people is given from the Cheyenne point of view. In Margot Liberty's words, 'John has given us the history of the Cheyennes as they themselves recall and interpret it' (1967). Much of the material is new, that which isn't confirms, complements and amplifies 19th century ethnographic accounts.

Advantages Life histories have illuminated many areas of social life. For example, *The Polish Peasant in Europe and America*, a five volume work first published from 1918 to 1920, included an extensive life history of a Polish peasant which provided many valuable insights into the experience of migration from Poland to the USA (Thomas & Znaniecki, 1958). *The Jack Roller* (Shaw, 1930) is a story, written in his own words and from his own point of view, of a young American 'jack roller', the 1930s equivalent of today's 'mugger'. It is this first-hand account of people's experience of their life as they see it which many researchers regard as the main value of the life history. It can provide insights and information which are not obtainable from any other source, as Stands In Timber's life history shows. It can give a picture of the process and development of social life over time. It can also serve as a basis for confirming or questioning other interpretations and accounts. And it can direct researchers into new areas and encourage them to ask new questions.

Disadvantages However, as the title *Cheyenne Memories* suggests, the life history is heavily dependent on people's memory which is inevitably patchy and selective. To some extent, it will also reflect their attitudes and opinions. Some would see this as a serious criticism of the life history. For example, Stands In Timber has been criticised by other members of his tribe for being too pro-Crow – the Crow are traditional enemies of the Cheyenne.

A further criticism concerns the researcher. There is a temptation for researchers to lead as life histories are recounted, particularly when areas of interest to them are touched upon. For example, Margot Liberty (1967) writes, 'My tendency was at first to press him for stories. I soon found it far better to trust his own instinct. Where he did not volunteer material freely he usually had little to say'.

While accepting many of the criticisms of life histories, supporters argue that they are far outweighed by the valuable information that a good life history can provide.

9.2 Case studies

A case study is a study of one particular case or instance of something. It may be a study of a particular school, factory or hospital, or a study of a single individual such as a manual worker, a mother with dependent children, or a retired person. The life history is an example of a case study. Using examples from the previous section, it is the study of one Cheyenne Indian or one Polish peasant.

Case studies have a number of advantages.

- By focusing on a particular case, they can provide a richer and more detailed picture than research based on large samples.
- This may result in new insights and fresh ideas.
- Case studies can provide useful information for a larger research project. For example, the experiences of one retired person could be used in a questionnaire in order to discover how far they apply to other retired people.
- There is a better chance of a questionnaire or interview being relevant and meaningful if it is based, at least in part, on a case study.
- Theories can be tested to see whether they apply in particular situations. Sociologists at Lancaster University tested the theory of secularisation (the idea that religion is becoming less important in modern societies) by conducting a case study of religion in a single town – Kendal in the Lake District.

Some of the advantages of case studies can be seen from Macbeath and Mortimore's (2001) study of school effectiveness. They used case studies of a small number of schools in addition to a large-scale social survey. The case studies helped them identify key themes to explore in their survey, allowed them to check that their survey findings held true in particular schools, and added depth to their quantitative data.

Case studies have sometimes been criticised as limited

and unrepresentative. Since they are one-off instances, they cannot be used as a basis for generalisation. However, this is their strength. They are a valuable warning to rash and sweeping generalisations. A single case study can call into question the findings of a much larger study.

activity15 bullying – a case study

The only thing that prevented me from enjoying my first year at high school was one person in my class who started to bully me. This led to several other people following his example and my life became sheer misery. At first, I was upset but able to cope with it, then I became angry and distressed. I couldn't sleep for worrying about the next day. It would be name-calling, stone-throwing and threatening. It all got too much and I decided to tell my Mum and Dad. We all agreed that I had to tell the teacher. The next day, though worried, I did.

The teacher was very sympathetic and said it must stop. We had lunch meetings to discuss the problems. The bullies were very surprised that they were included instead of being punished. We discussed my feelings at being bullied and we would agree on some plan of action so that I would get support from my friends. Once the bullies realised that they were being included, the bullying ceased.

Adapted from Donnellan, 1994

question

Using examples from this activity, suggest some advantages of the case study approach.

9.3 Longitudinal studies

How can you show what a person looks like? One way is to produce a photograph. This is similar to most sociological research which consists of a snapshot, a one-off investigation of an aspect of social life. Another way of showing what a person looks like is to produce a series of photographs taken at different points in their lifetime. This shows how their appearance changes and develops. The equivalent in sociology is the longitudinal study which examines the same group of people over a fairly long period of time.

As the following example shows, longitudinal studies can provide important insights. Each year from 1991 to 1995, 1125 young people in Merseyside and Greater Manchester filled in a confidential questionnaire about their attitudes to and use of illegal drugs. At the start of the research, members of the sample were aged 14, by the end, aged 18. The study was carried out by a team of sociologists led by Howard Parker (1998). Parker was interested in the extent of illegal drug use within this age group and whether sensational media reports about widespread drug abuse were accurate. The questionnaire was concerned with the types of drugs taken, reasons for the first use of drugs, how drug use changed over time and why some people refused to take drugs.

Parker's team found that cannabis was the most frequently used illegal drug. It was also the first drug that most of the sample experimented with. Working-class young people were more likely to experiment at an early age, though by 18 the middle class had caught up. There were few differences between boys and girls. By aged 18, 20-25% of the sample were regular users.

Advantages As these findings suggest, the strength of the longitudinal study is its ability to examine developments over time. By studying the same group, ie by keeping the same sample, the researcher can be sure that any changes in attitudes and behaviour are not simply due to changes in the makeup of the sample.

Disadvantages But keeping the same group is one of the main difficulties with longitudinal studies. The National Child Development Study has attempted to follow the lives of every child born in Britain between 3rd and 9th March 1958. Follow-up surveys were conducted in 1965, 1969, 1974, 1981, 1991 and 1999 to trace developments in health, education, family life, career and so on, and to try to establish links between these changes and factors such as class, gender and ethnicity. The survey began with 17,400 children but by 1999 researchers were able to contact only 11,400 members of the original sample.

Reasons for this *sample attrition* included death, emigration, refusal to participate and failure to trace. The result is not just a smaller sample but, in all probability, a less representative one.

Researchers are aware of this and attempt to minimise the problem of sample attrition. This can be seen from the lengths that some go in order to trace members of an original sample. Parker's team sent letters, follow-up letters, further reminders and even Christmas cards to their sample. If none of these worked they actually went from door to door tracking their 'lost' respondents. The National Child Development Study has adopted a similar approach, contacting relatives, visiting workplaces and searching telephone directories and electoral registers. As this suggests, longitudinal studies can cost a great deal of time and money. Few organisations have the resources to fund an investigation which continues for twenty years or more.

9.4 The comparative method

Comparative studies make comparisons between different societies, between different groups within the same society, and between societies and groups over time.

Durkheim's study of suicide is an example of a comparative study (see page 146). He compared suicide rates in different European societies, eg Italy, England, France and Denmark, at different time periods, eg 1866-70, 1871-75, 1874-78. He also compared suicide rates for different groups within society, eg rates for Protestants compared to Catholics, city dwellers compared to rural dwellers, and married compared to unmarried people.

The comparative method helps sociologists to investigate what causes what. For example, Durkheim's study suggested that religion may be a factor affecting the suicide rate. His figures indicated that the suicide rate for

activity16 Britain and France

Item A Similarity – production technology

Fawley oil refinery, Hampshire

Item B Difference - nationality

Britain and France

Duncan Gallie compared workers in oil refineries in Britain and France. Would the same kind of production technology – in this case the technology used in oil refineries – lead to the same kind of behaviour at work? Gallie found important differences between British and French workers, for example there were far more strikes in the French refineries.

Adapted from Gallie, 1978

question

How might the comparative method be useful for explaining behaviour at work?

Protestants *within* particular societies was higher than the rate for Catholics. The same applied to comparisons *between* societies – the suicide rate for Protestant countries was significantly higher than the rate for Catholic societies.

A natural laboratory The comparative method is the nearest most sociologists get to the laboratory method of the natural sciences. Unlike laboratory experiments, variables in the real world cannot be systematically manipulated and controlled. However, it is possible to find 'natural' laboratories which allow the influence of variables to be estimated.

Europe provided a natural laboratory for Durkheim. He found a statistical link between suicide rates and religion between European societies, within those societies, and over different time periods.

Cross-cultural studies Is social inequality universal – ie, is it found in every society? Is a division of labour based on gender natural – ie, is it natural to have male jobs and female jobs? These are important questions, particularly for those concerned about social inequality. Cross-cultural studies – studies based on a number of different cultures – help to answer this type of question. For instance, if cross-cultural evidence indicated that, in some societies, gender has little or no influence on job allocation, then this suggests that any influence of gender on the division of labour is based on culture rather than nature.

Evaluation The comparative method has some obvious strengths. It provides a natural laboratory for researchers to estimate the influence of variables. It allows researchers to look at the effect of culture on behaviour.

But cross-cultural research has inbuilt problems. How, for example, can a Western researcher understand non-Western cultures? When he or she compares marriage in various cultures, are they comparing like with like? Does marriage mean the same thing in different societies, does it involve the same rights and responsibilities? Despite these problems, the comparative method holds considerable promise (May, 2001).

9.5 Triangulation and methodological pluralism

The types of research outlined in this unit may draw data from various research methods and various sources. For example, a case study might be based on participant observation or interviews, on primary or secondary data, on quantitative or qualitative data. Sometimes, different kinds of data and research methods are combined within a single study.

Triangulation Some researchers combine different research methods and different types of data in order to check the validity and reliability of their findings. This is known as *triangulation*. For example, if participant observation and

activity17 methodological pluralism

Our research on victims of crime was based on method-ological pluralism. This approach favours neither qualitative or quantitative research methods. It is a position which recognises that different research techniques can uncover different layers of social reality and that the role of the researcher is to look for confirmations and contradictions between those different layers of information.

So, for example, for the first stage of our data-gathering process we walked our two research areas with police officers, we frequented the public houses, and we engaged in in-depth interviews with a variety of people working in the localities.

Then, on the basis of this information, we produced a criminal victimisation survey questionnaire and conducted a survey in each area, and, on the basis of this experience, moved into focus group discussions with survey participants. So, as a research process, we were always moving between quantitative and qualitative data looking for ways of making sense of the different layers of social reality which were being revealed to us.

Adapted from Walklate, 2000

Victims of crime – burgled during their wedding

question

According to this extract, what are the main advantages of methodological pluralism?

interviews produce conflicting findings, this raises questions about the validity of the data. This often leads to further research to re-examine the original findings.

Methodological pluralism Other researchers combine different research methods and different types of data in order to build up a fuller picture of social life. This approach is known as *methodological pluralism*.

It recognises that each method and type of data has its particular strengths and weaknesses. Combined they are seen to produce a more comprehensive and rounder picture of social reality. And their combination can also provide new insights and new directions for research.

Some of the strengths of methodological pluralism can be seen from Eileen Barker's (1984) study of the Moonies – the Unification Church. She conducted in-depth interviews, each lasting 6-8 hours, with a number of Moonies. The interviews dealt with their background, why they became a Moonie, their life in the church and the meaning of religion as they saw it. Barker also lived as a participant observer in several centres with the Moonies at various times during the six years of her research. This enabled her to gain the trust of many members of the church, resulting in information which would not have been given to an outsider. Two years after the start of her research, she constructed a large (41 page) questionnaire based on her findings from interviews and observation. This provided information from a larger sample and was intended to reveal 'social patterns, trends and tendencies and gain a more reliable understanding of regularities between variables – of "what goes with what" '.

Barker claims that combining different methods of investigation gave her a much fuller picture than any one method or data source could have provided.

key terms

Life history An account of an individual's life as told to a researcher.
Case study A study of one particular case or instance of something.
Longitudinal study A study of the same group of people at various times over a period of years.
Sample attrition The reduction in size of a sample during a longitudinal study.
Comparative studies Studies which make comparisons between different societies and different groups within the same society.
Cross-cultural studies Studies based on a number of different cultures. Studies which compare different cultures.
Triangulation Combining different research methods and different types of data in order to check the validity and reliability of findings.
Methodological pluralism Combining different research methods and different kinds of data in order to build up a fuller picture of social life.

summary

1. Life histories provide a first-hand account of people's life experience as they see it. This can result in valuable insights. However, life histories are dependent on people's memory which is often patchy and selective.

2. Case studies focus on a particular case. This can provide a rich and detailed picture. A single case study can call into question the findings of a much larger study.

3. The main strength of the longitudinal study is its ability to examine developments over time. The main problem is sample attrition – the steady loss of sample members.

4. The comparative method provides a 'natural laboratory' within which the influence of variables can be estimated. It allows researchers to examine the effect of culture on behaviour. The main difficulty for researchers is understanding different cultures.

5. Triangulation provides a check on the validity and reliability of research findings.

6. Methodological pluralism builds up a fuller picture of social life.

5 Coursework – the Research Proposal

Introduction

Take a moment to think of a topic or issue in sociology that has caught your interest. Maybe it's the growing success of girls in education. Imagine you could design your own research to discover more about this. What exactly would you want to find out? One idea could be to investigate whether girls do more homework than boys. How would you go about doing this research – a qualitative study involving unstructured interviews, or a number-crunching questionnaire? And what problems would you face? Would students really be honest about their homework? If some theories are right, boys might be reluctant to admit they did a lot of homework for fear of being seen as a swat.

AQA AS level coursework provides the opportunity to design your own *Research Proposal*. You are asked to explain the aim of your research, identify some key background material, plan and justify the main method to be used and anticipate the problems you might face in carrying out the research.

The Research Proposal is worth 30% of your AS marks and, if you go on to do A2, it makes up 15% of the final grade.

One advantage of writing the proposal is that it allows you to develop some really interesting ideas for research, safe in the knowledge that you don't actually have to carry them out! You may decide that the best way of testing your chosen hypothesis would be to interview a thousand carefully selected people all on the same day. As an AS student you would never be able to do that, but you can plan it as if it were possible in an ideal world. Many students however, prefer to choose something that is realistic for them to carry out. Taking this approach means that the Research Proposal can be used as the basis for the A2 coursework project where you are asked to actually carry out the research.

chaptersummary

▶ **Unit 1** provides an overview of the requirements of the Research Proposal.

▶ **Unit 2** looks at the first part of the Research Proposal – the Aim/Hypothesis section.

▶ **Unit 3** explains the Context and Concepts section.

▶ **Unit 4** outlines the Main Research Method and Reasons section.

▶ **Unit 5** explains the final section – Potential Problems.

Unit 1 General advice

keyissues

1 What do I need to know?

2 How should I present my coursework?

3 What ethical guidelines do I need to follow?

1.1 The specification

Examining boards produce *specifications* which provide detailed guidance about the content and assessment of courses. The AQA specification for AS Sociology lays down the key concepts and issues that you need to be familiar with for your coursework. These are explained fully in the Methods chapter and are outlined below.

● Quantitative and qualitative research methods and types/sources of data

● Questionnaires, interviews, observation and experiments

● Documents and official statistics

● Primary/secondary and quantitative/qualitative data

● Positivist and interpretivist approaches

● The relationship between theory and methods

- Practical, ethical and theoretical considerations and how they affect choice of topic, methodology and planning
- The strengths and limitations of different types of data and research methods.

Obviously these cannot all be covered in the 1200 words you have available for your coursework. Marks are gained according to how well you select concepts and issues from the list above, how clearly these are explained, and how effectively they are used to discuss your Research Proposal.

1.2 The format

The format for the Research Proposal is quite specific and needs to be followed to the letter. The four sections are:

		Word limit	Marks
1	Hypothesis/Aim	100	8
2	Context and Concepts	400	20
3	Main Research Method and Reasons	400	20
4	Potential Problems	300	12
Total		**1200**	**60**

The word count is particularly important. Get as close as you can to the word limit for each section. When it says 100 don't feel tempted to stop after 80. Remember those other 20 words might help you get the full marks for the section. However, going over 100 words indicates that you have not been succinct – that is you have not said exactly what you mean in the minimum number of words.

It is essential that each section of the Research Proposal meets its own word limit. If only 50 words are used in the first section, don't think that there are now 50 'spare' to use in later sections. By doing so, you have wasted potential in the first section and failed to be succinct in the later section containing the extra words.

1.3 Ethical guidelines

Ethics refer to beliefs about what is right and wrong. Sociologists follow a set of ethical rules or guidelines when they conduct research and students writing Research Proposals are no exception. You gain marks for awareness of the particular ethical issues raised in your research. Ethical issues in research are discussed in detail on pages 147-148. Some of the key points which apply to the Research Proposal are outlined below.

Protection from harm Researchers should make every attempt to avoid harm to others, especially the young and vulnerable. Apply the golden rule – do as you would be done by. Plan to do research that you would not object to being carried out on yourself. But remember too, that everybody is not the same – for example, some people may

be more sensitive about privacy than you.

Try not to hurt people's feelings. Sometimes even quite innocent questions can have unforeseen repercussions. For example, if you are interviewing women about their attitudes to having children, be aware that miscarriages and still-births do occur and are traumatic for those involved. A question about children could bring back very upsetting memories. Similarly, a question about marital status, apparently harmless, may well upset someone who has recently been divorced. It is not suggested that you avoid such questions, merely that you are aware that they may have consequences that you have not anticipated.

Informed consent Anyone asked for information should know why that information is needed. Only then can they give informed consent. Self-completion questionnaires will need an introductory passage explaining the aims of the research and the uses to which responses will be put. Interviewers will need to explain this to respondents. It should be made clear that participants can withdraw from the research at any time they wish. No attempt should be made to deceive anyone, although the aims of the research can be set out in fairly general terms. For example, 'I am conducting research about boys and girls in the classroom' would normally be enough.

Any form of covert (hidden) research poses particular problems for informed consent and its justification will need to be argued very carefully. It may be best to avoid covert methods entirely.

Privacy and confidentiality Participants in research should have their privacy and confidentiality respected. People and organisations should not usually be referred to by their real names. For example, the names of schools and colleges where research takes place should be changed.

Illegality Any research that uncovers illegal activities, or asks respondents to reveal illegal activities, raises serious ethical concerns. The Police and Criminal Evidence Act makes it clear that every citizen has what is known as a duty of disclosure. This means that when they believe that a crime may have taken place, or might be about to take place, they should inform the relevant authorities.

Many researchers appear to ignore this but, since some proposals involve research which may well uncover

key terms

Research Proposal The AS coursework task set by AQA. Students have to design their own piece of sociological research.

Specification The detailed guidance about the content and assessment of a course provided by an examining board.

Ethical guidelines The guidelines concerned with the rights and wrongs of conducting research.

Informed consent Participants agreeing to take part in research after being provided with full and accurate information about the aims and conduct of the study.

crimes, you should be aware of what you are doing. If you decide you are going to study teenage leisure patterns, do you really want to discover how many people are breaking the law with regard to alcohol use, illegal drugs and underage sex? If you don't, you'll need to ensure that questions exclude references to such illegal activities.

This issue is a very tricky one so you are strongly advised to talk about problems of illegality with your teacher.

summary

1. Your research proposal should be organised under the following headings.
   - Hypothesis/Aim
   - Context and Concepts
   - Main Research Methods and Reasons
   - Potential Problems

2. A very precise format and specific word limits are provided by the exam board. You need to follow these exactly.

3. Ethical issues should be taken into account wherever they are relevant.

activity1 ethics and research

Researcher

Let me ask you a few probing questions.

What is your name?

What is the most serious illegal act you've ever committed?

question

Identify as many ethical problems as you can in the approach to research shown in the cartoon and questions.

Unit 2 Hypothesis/Aim

keyissues

1 What are aims and hypotheses?

2 How are they developed for research?

In the Hypothesis/Aim section, you identify the issue to be investigated, explain why you are interested in it and develop a single aim or hypothesis that will act as the starting point for research.

The word limit is 100 and there are eight marks available.

2.1 Keep it simple, keep it small

The first section of the Research Proposal requires you to develop a research hypothesis or an aim. A *hypothesis* is a 'hunch' that something is true. It is an 'educated guess' which is usually based on existing evidence. It takes the form of a statement such as 'older people place more value on the extended family than younger people'. The researcher then goes on to collect evidence to see whether or not the hypothesis is supported.

An *aim* represents a broader starting point and is a general intention to investigate something. An aim is more likely to be used in situations where the researcher is unsure of what they are likely to discover.

Your aim or hypothesis should be simple, clear and not too broad. Say your aim was to investigate gender differences which might explain why girls are achieving better exam results than boys. This is a very broad aim which could be developed into a variety of research projects. For the purposes of your coursework, it is better to focus on something more specific and more manageable – for example, gender differences in one of the following.

- Time spent on homework
- Attitudes towards teachers
- Ambitions for future employment
- Value placed on exam results
- Support from parents
- Peer group attitudes towards education.

Once the focus has been narrowed, it is easier to translate aims into hypotheses. For example, each of the above areas for investigation can be translated into the following hypotheses. Girls do better than boys because they:

- Spend more time on homework
- Have a more positive attitude towards teachers
- Are more ambitious when it comes to employment
- Place a higher value on educational qualifications
- Receive more support from their parents
- Get more encouragement from their peers to achieve at school and college.

2.2 The mark scheme

The Hypothesis/Aim section is probably the most important part of your proposal. Word for word it is the most valuable in terms of marks. And if you get your aim or hypothesis right, the rest should follow logically.

The mark scheme provides descriptions of different standards of work. The highest level of achievement is described as follows.

The candidate demonstrates a very good ability to identify and define a relevant sociological focus. A clear, precise and appropriate hypothesis or aim that enables the research issue to be successfully progressed is offered. All reasons given are appropriate.

We can look at each aspect of this description in turn.

Identify and define a relevant sociological focus The key word here is sociological – it is after all a sociology exam. If the topic is included somewhere in the specification, then you can be certain that it is acceptable. If it is not, then consult your coursework supervisor and take their advice. *Identify* means to name the focus of interest, whilst *define* refers to the process of reducing the general area to manageable proportions, sifting out the part that you will study.

A clear, precise and appropriate hypothesis or aim that enables the research issue to be successfully progressed is offered Make sure the method you choose will actually allow you to test your hypothesis or cover the aim you have stated. Some hypotheses are so large and unwieldy that they could never be tested.

All reasons given are appropriate There could be a range of reasons for selecting your area of study. They may be personal – something about you or your life makes the issue interesting to you. Alternatively, they could be

activity2 aims and hypotheses

Item A Football supporters

Item B A student's work

I am very interested in looking at the connection between hair colour and examination results. As far as I know, there is no research on this subject. However, I think blondes have more fun and will therefore do better in exams. I believe there is a system of positive discrimination whereby blondes are treated more favourably by teachers. By looking at what goes on in the classroom, I should be able to see if this is true.

questions

1 Using the picture in Item A as a starting point, develop two aims and two hypotheses for research.
2 Read the Hypothesis/Aim section from a Research Proposal in Item B. Identify its strengths and weaknesses.

theoretical – you want to test one sociological theory against another. Perhaps a previous piece of research from ten or twenty years ago needs updating. It could simply be that something in the course has puzzled you and you want to find out whether or not it is true. Whatever the reasons for your choice, you will need to explain them clearly at this point.

key terms

Hypothesis A starting point for research. A hunch or educated guess that something is true. Hypotheses are presented as statements.

Aim A general intention to find out about something.

summary

1. The Hypothesis/Aim section is worth 8 marks and should be no longer than 100 words.
2. In this section you need to:
    - Identify a sociological issue that you intend to study
    - Develop an aim or hypothesis
    - Explain the reasons behind your choice.

Unit 3 *Context and Concepts*

key issues

1 What is a Context?

2 What are Concepts?

3 How are Context and Concepts used in the Research Proposal?

There are two parts to the Context and Concepts section.
- **The context** Two brief summaries of relevant pieces of material which could be used as a background to research.
- **The concepts** Two or three brief definitions of sociological terms which are relevant to the chosen research, along with reasons for their inclusion.
  The word limit is 400 and there are 20 marks available.

3.1 Context

Sociologists always review relevant background material before beginning their own research. For example, if they were researching divorce they would examine studies on the subject by other sociologists, they would bring themselves up to date with the latest divorce statistics, and they may draw on novels or plays for insights into divorce.

In terms of coursework, your summaries of two relevant pieces of background material will give you a taste for this process. The background material which forms the context for research can come from anywhere – sociological studies, historical documents, statistics, a film, anything. All that is required is that they are relevant to your proposal and that you describe them briefly, showing how they will serve as background material. This is sometimes quite difficult to do within the word limit, so you have to make sure that you emphasise only those parts which relate directly to the research.

3.2 Concepts

Concepts are terms used by sociologists to help describe and explain social life. Social class, gender and ethnicity are examples of commonly used concepts. Some concepts will be necessary for your proposal. For example, if you are considering the effect of social class on educational attainment then two key concepts are educational attainment and social class.

As part of your Research Proposal, you are asked to define two or three relevant concepts. In the above example, this means defining social class and educational attainment – what are they and how will you measure them?

You are also asked to give reasons for their inclusion in the proposal. For example, why use the concept of social class in a study of educational attainment?

3.3 The mark scheme

The top band description:

The candidate demonstrates a very good knowledge and understanding of appropriate material. Two relevant pieces of material are accurately and concisely presented, providing a clear context for the proposed hypothesis or aim. The two or three concepts identified are pertinent, precisely defined and appropriately developed.

'Appropriate material' is directly concerned with the area your proposal is covering. If you are looking at the family, material on schools may well be irrelevant. If you are looking at single-parent family life in Britain there may be more relevant background material than an episode of *EastEnders*. When the mark scheme talks of two pieces it means two, no more and no less if you want to get into the top band.

'Concisely presented' refers to the ability to summarise material to maximise its relevance to your research aim. If you want to use a table of statistics, for example, you should describe only the figures and trends that shed light on your aim or hypothesis.

summary

1. The Context and Concepts section is worth 20 marks and should be no longer than 400 words.
2. You need to summarise two pieces of secondary data and explain how they act as relevant background material for your research.
3. You need to define two or three sociological concepts that are important for your research.
4. The relevance of the concepts needs to be explained.

key terms

Context Items of secondary data that help throw light on the aim or hypothesis.
Concepts Sociological words or expressions that help understand society.

activity3 context and concepts

Item A Gender and earnings

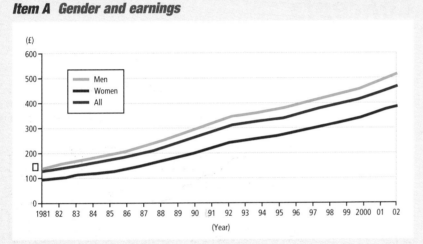

Average gross weekly earnings of full-time employees by gender, Great Britain 1981-2002

Adapted from *Labour Market Trends*, December 2002

Item B Thinking about gender

How are men and women to think about their maleness and their femaleness in this century, in which so many of our ideas must be made new? Have we overdomesticated men, denied their natural adventurousness? Have we cut women off from closeness to their children, taught them to look for a job, instead of for the touch of a child's hand, for status in a competitive world? In educating them both the same, have we done something disastrous to both men and women alike, or have we only taken one further step in the recurrent task of building more and better on our original human nature?

Adapted from Mead, 1949

questions

1 Item A is an example of the type of material that could be used as background information for a Research Proposal on gender and income. Describe the main patterns shown in the graph. Write no more than 100 words.

2 a) Identify and define three concepts in Item B.
  b) Suggest how they might be measured.

Unit 4 Main Research Method and Reasons

keyissues

1 What research methods are available?
2 Why choose a particular method?

In the Main Research Method and Reasons section you need to identify and describe your main research method and give reasons for choosing this method. The word limit for this section is 400 and there are 20 marks available.

4.1 Main method

First, you need to choose the *main method* for your research. For example, you may choose participant observation, structured interviews, or content analysis.

Select the method which is most appropriate for testing your hypothesis or investigating your aim.

Next, you need to give a brief description of your main method including details of how you would apply this method in your research. For example, if you plan to conduct a large-scale social survey, you should include a short discussion on the size and type of sample and the type of questionnaire or interview you will use. And you should indicate how you are going to operationalise (put in a form that can be measured) the key concepts selected in the Context and Concepts section. For example, you could indicate how you would operationalise the concept of social class by giving a couple of questions you would ask.

Always consider the practicalities, strengths and weaknesses of your chosen method. For example, if your research calls for a large representative national sample on which to test a hypothesis, then participant observation is not recommended. It would probably take years to complete the research and cost a fortune.

Particular methods are associated with different theoretical positions. Participant observation and unstructured interviews are linked to interpretivist sociology while large-scale social surveys are often favoured by those from the positivist tradition. The theoretical influence on your research may be worth mentioning at this point.

4.2 Reasons

Choice of method will depend on your research proposal. It is difficult to lay down hard and fast rules, but certain methods tend to be more appropriate than others for certain types of research. If the aim of the research is to compare or generalise from large samples, then methods that provide quantitative data may be more appropriate. On the other hand, if your aim is to collect really rich and detailed information from a small sample, then more qualitative approaches such as unstructured interviews may work best. Practical factors such as access to a sample may also draw you to certain methods.

Ethical considerations will also influence your choice of method. For example, many sociologists try to avoid covert or secret observation as it prevents those observed from giving informed consent.

4.3 The mark scheme

The top band description for the Main Research Method and Reasons section reads as follows.

> *The candidate demonstrates a very good knowledge and understanding of the chosen method. All reasons for the choice are relevant and developed. All details on the implementation of the proposed methodology are appropriate, clear and accurate and succinctly presented. The chosen method is appropriate to the hypothesis or aim.*

If your answer is 'yes' to the four questions below, then you have a good chance of being in that top mark band.

1 Is my choice the best method to use for this proposal?

2 Have I described the method clearly, including its basic theoretical background?

3 Have I given reasons for my choice, including any ethical ones?

4 Are all the practical details clearly expressed?

key terms

Main method The key research method that you will use to investigate your aim or hypothesis.
Reasons Your reasons for choosing that method.

activity4 choosing a method

Aim: To examine the representation of females in girls' magazines.

question

Suggest what method would be most appropriate for investigating this aim. Give reasons for your choice.

summary

1. The Main Research Method and Reasons section is worth 20 marks and should be no longer than 400 words.

2. You need to:
   - Provide a brief description of the main method you think is best to investigate your aim or test your hypothesis.

- Explain the practical, ethical and theoretical reasons for your choice.
- Describe how you will carry out the research including sampling and the operationalising of key concepts.

Unit 5 Potential Problems

keyissues

1 What problems might be met in carrying out your research?

2 At 300 words, the Potential Problems section is shorter than the previous two sections and is worth 12 marks. It is designed to encourage you to ponder on problems that might arise if the research is carried out.

5.1 The mark scheme

You need to discuss a) the practical problems of carrying out the actual research and b) the problem of whether the method chosen can succeed in investigating the aim or testing the hypothesis.

Top mark band:

The candidate demonstrates a very good ability to identify potential problems in carrying out the proposed research. Appropriate, accurate and succinct reasons are offered and explained. There are clear links between the identified problems and the research hypothesis or aim. The candidate demonstrates very good sociological insight.

5.2 Potential Problems

All research proposals contain a range of possible problems.

Practical difficulties These may include some of the following.

- Can a sample be found?
- Is the sample representative of the group to be studied?
- Do the questions mean the same thing to all the research participants?
- Will the questions be answered honestly?
- Do the researchers have the time and money to conduct the research?

Ethical problems Research always involves ethical considerations. Ethical problems may include some of the following.

- How will the participants be asked for their consent?
- How can their privacy and anonymity be assured?
- How can the researcher ensure that participants come to no physical, social or psychological harm?

Theoretical problems Research which develops from a positivist tradition is often based on quantitative data derived from questionnaires given to large samples. Will such methods uncover the complexities of people's views and experiences?

Research based on an interpretivist approach tends to use small samples and to search for the meanings underlying people's actions. Will such small-scale research manage to see the big picture? Is it possible to generalise from such small samples?

activity5 potential problems

Hypothesis Young people vandalise property because they feel cut off from society.

Main method Unstructured interviews

question

Suggest what potential problems may be involved in this piece of research.

Conclusion

Once you have identified something as a problem, explain why it is a problem. Remember this section is only about finding problems, not about solving them. Identifying problems and reasons why they are problems get the marks, solutions score nothing.

Throughout the Potential Problems section, you should link everything to your original aim or hypothesis. To what extent will the potential problems you have identified affect the realisation of your aim or the testing of your hypothesis?

References

Abraham, J. (1995). *Divide and school: Gender and class dynamics in comprehensive education.* London: Falmer.

Allan, G. & Crow, G. (2001). *Families, households and society.* Basingstoke: Palgrave.

Allan, G. (1985). *Family life.* Oxford: Blackwell.

Allen, I. & Dowling, S.B. (1999). Teenage mothers: Decisions and outcomes. In S. McRae (Ed.), *Changing Britain: Families and households in the 1990s.* Oxford: Oxford University Press.

Althusser, L. (1972). Ideology and ideological state apparatus: Notes towards an investigation. In B.R. Cosin (Ed.), *Education, structure and society.* Harmondsworth: Penguin.

Anderson, M. (1971). Family, household and the industrial revolution. In M. Anderson (Ed.), *Sociology of the family.* Harmondsworth: Penguin.

Appleyard, D. (2002). *Out of love.* London: Black Swan.

Arber, S. (1993). Designing samples. In N. Gilbert (Ed.), *Researching social life.* London: Sage.

Ariès, P. (1962). *Centuries of childhood.* London: Jonathan Cape.

Atkinson, J.M. (1978). *Discovering suicide.* London: Macmillan.

Ball, S.J. (1981). *Beachside Comprehensive.* Cambridge: Cambridge University Press.

Ball, S.J. (2003). *Class strategies and the education market: The middle classes and social advantage.* London: RoutledgeFalmer.

Ballantine, J. & Spade, J. (2001). *Schools and society.* Belmont: Wadsworth.

Bandura, A. (1973). *Aggression: A social learning analysis.* Englewood Cliffs, NJ: Prentice Hall.

Barker, E. (1984). *The making of a Moonie.* Oxford: Blackwell.

Barley, N. (1995). *Dancing on the grave.* London: Abacus.

Bathurst, B. (2002). It isn't clever and it isn't fun. *The Guardian,* 30 September.

Baxter, J. & Western, M. (1998). Satisfaction with housework: Examining the paradox. *Sociology, 32,* 101-120.

Beattie, J. (1964). *Other cultures: Aims, methods and achievements in social anthropology.* London: Routledge & Kegan Paul.

Beck, U. (1992). *Risk society: Towards a new modernity.* London: Sage.

Beck U. (1997). *The reinvention of politics.* Cambridge: Polity Press.

Becker, H.S. (1971). Social-class variations in teacher-pupil relationship. In B.R. Cosin, I.R. Dale, G.M. Esland & D.F. Swift (Eds.), *School and society.* London: Routledge.

Beck-Gernsheim, E. (2002). *Reinventing the family.* Cambridge: Polity.

Bedell, G. (2002). One step beyond. *OM,* October 6.

Benston, M. (1972). The political economy of women's liberation. In N. Glazer-Malbin & H. Y. Waehrer (Eds.), *Woman in a man-made world.* Chicago: Rand McNally.

Beresford, P., Green, D., Lister, R. & Woodard, K. (1999). *Poverty first hand: Poor people speak for themselves.* London: CPAG.

Berger, P. (1966). *Invitation to sociology.* Harmondsworth: Penguin.

Bernades, J. (1997). *Family studies: An introduction.* London: Routledge.

Bernstein, B. (1973). *Class, codes and control.* London: Paladin.

Berthoud, R. & Beishon, S. (1997). People, families and households, In Modood, T. et al. (Eds.), *Ethnic minorities in Britain: Diversity and disadvantage.* London: Policy Studies Institute.

Berthoud, R., McKay, S. & Rowlingson, K. (1999). Becoming a single mother. In S. McRae (Ed.), *Changing Britain: Families and households in the 1990s.* Oxford: Oxford University Press.

Bourdieu, P. & Passeron, J. (1977). *Reproduction in education, society and culture.* London: Sage.

Bowles, S. & Gintis, H. (1976). *Schooling in capitalist America.* London: Routledge & Kegan Paul.

Brazier, C. (1995). African village. *New Internationalist,* June.

British Psychological Society. (1998). *Code of conduct, ethical principles and guidelines.* Leicester: British Psychological Society.

British Sociological Association. (1996). *Statement of ethical practice.* Durham: British Sociological Association.

Brown, P., Halsey, A.H., Lauder, H. & Wells, A. (1997). The transformation of education and society: An introduction. In A.H. Halsey et al. (Eds.), *Education: Culture, economy, society.* Oxford: Oxford University Press.

Bruce, S. (1995). Religion and the sociology of religion. In M. Haralambos (Ed.), *Developments in Sociology, Volume 11.* Ormskirk: Causeway Press.

Buckingham, D. (2000). *After the death of childhood: Growing up in the age of electronic media.* Cambridge: Polity.

Bukatko, D. & Daehler, M.W. (2001). *Child development: A thematic approach* (4th ed.). Boston: Houghton Mifflin Company.

Burgess, R. (1983). *Experiencing comprehensive education.* London: Methuen.

Bush, T., Coleman, M. & Glover, D. (1993). *Managing autonomous schools: The grant-maintained experience.* London: Paul Chapman.

Chagnon, N. (1968). *Yanomamo.* New York: Holt, Rinehart & Winston.

Charles, N. & Kerr, M. (1988). *Women, food and families.* Manchester: Manchester University Press.

Cheal, D. (1999). The one and the many: Modernity and postmodernity. In G. Allan (Ed.), *The sociology of the family: A reader.* Oxford: Blackwell.

Chester, R. (1984). Divorce. In E. Butterworth & D. Weir (Eds.), *The new sociology of modern Britain.* Glasgow: Fontana.

Chitty, C. (1997). Choose…education? *Sociology Review,* April.

Chitty, C. (2002). *Understanding schools and schooling.* London: RoutledgeFalmer.

Chubb, J. & Moe, T. (1997). Politics, markets and the organisation of schools. In A.H. Halsey et al. (Eds.), *Education: Culture, economy, society.* Oxford: Oxford University Press.

Cicourel, A.V. (1976). *The social organisation of juvenile justice.* London: Heinemann.

Cockett, M. & Tripp, J. (1994). *The Exeter family study: Family breakdown and its impact on children.* Exeter: Exeter University Press.

Coffey, A. (2001). *Education and social change.* Buckingham: Open University Press.

Cohen, P. (1984). Against the new vocationalism. In I. Bates et al. (Eds.), *Schooling for the dole?* London: Macmillan.

Coleman, D. & Chandola, T. (1999). Britain's place in Europe's population. In S. McRae (Ed.), *Changing Britain: Families and households in the 1990s.* Oxford University Press.

Collins, R. (1972). Functional and conflict theories of educational stratification. In B.R. Cosin (Ed.), *Education, structure and society.* Harmondsworth: Penguin.

Commission for Racial Equality (1992). *Set to fail? Setting and banding in secondary schools.* London: Commission for Racial Equality.

Connolly, P. (1998). *Racism, gender identities and young children.* London: Routledge.

Coote, A. & Campbell, B. (1982). *Sweet freedom.* London: Pan.

Crossman, R.H.S. (1975). *The diaries of a cabinet minister.* London: Jonathan Cape.

Crow, G. & Hardy, M. (1992). Diversity and ambiguity among lone-parent households in modern Britain. In C. Marsh & S. Arber (Eds.), *Families and households.* London: Macmillan.

Cumberbatch, G. & Negrine, R. (1992). *Images of disability on television.* London: Routledge.

Davies, S. (1995). Reproduction and resistance in Canadian high schools: An empirical examination of the Willis thesis. *British Journal of Sociology, 46,* 4.

Delphy, C. & Leonard, D. (1992). *Familiar exploitation*. Cambridge: Polity.

Demack, S., Drew, D. & Grimsley, M. (2000). Minding the gap: Ethnic, gender and social class differences in attainment at 16, 1988-95. *Race, Ethnicity and Education, 3*, 117-143.

Dennis, N. & Erdos, G. (2000). *Families without fatherhood* (3rd ed.). London: Institute for the Study of Civil Society.

Dennis, N., Henriques, F. & Slaughter, C. (1956). *Coal is our life*. London: Eyre & Spottiswoode.

Denscombe, M. (1994). *Sociology update 1994*. Leicester: Olympus Books.

Devine, F. (1992). *Affluent workers revisited: Privatisation and the working class*. Edinburgh: Edinburgh University Press.

DfEE (1997). *Excellence in schools*. London: HMSO.

Ditton, J. (1977). *Part-time crime*. London: Macmillan.

Donnellan, C. (Ed.) (1994). *The rights of the child*. Cambridge: Independence.

Douglas, J.W.B. (1964). *The home and the school*. London: MacGibbon & Kee.

Douglas, M. (Ed.), (1964). *Man in society: Patterns of human organisation*. London: Macdonald & Co.

Duncombe, J. & Marsden, D. (1993). Love and intimacy. *Sociology, 27*, 221-241.

Duncombe, J. & Marsden, D. (1995). 'Workaholics and whingeing women': Theorising intimacy. *Sociological Review, 43*, 150-169.

Dunham, C. (1992). Brotherly love. *Observer Magazine*, 18 October.

Dunne, G. (1997). *Lesbian lifestyles: Women's work and the politics of sexuality*. London: Macmillan.

Durkheim, E. (1970). *Suicide: A study in sociology*. London: Routledge.

Edgell, S. (1980). *Middle-class couples*. London: George Allen & Unwin.

Edholm, F. (1982). The unnatural family. In E. Whitelegg et al. (Eds.), *The changing experience of women*. London: Martin Robertson/Open University.

Elias, N. (1978). *The civilising process, volume 1*. Oxford: Basil Blackwell.

Employment Department Group & Radio One (1991). *Action special 91*. London: HMSO.

Engels, F. (1972). *The origin of the family, private property and the state*. London: Lawrence & Wishart.

Epstein, D., Elwood, J., Hey, V. & Maw, J. (Eds.) (1998). *Failing boys? Issues in gender and achievement*. Buckingham: Open University Press.

Ferri, E., Bynner, J. & Wadsworth, W. (2003). *Changing Britain, changing lives*. London: Institute of Education.

Festinger, L. et al. (1964). *When prophecy fails*. New York: Harper Torchbooks.

Fielding, N. (1981). *The National Front*. London: Routledge & Kegan Paul.

Fielding, N. (1993). Qualitative interviewing. In N. Gilbert (Ed.), *Researching social life*. London: Sage.

Finch, J. & Mason, J. (1993). *Negotiating family responsibilities*. London: Routledge.

Finn, D. (1987). *Training without jobs*. London: Macmillan.

Firth, R. (1963). *We the Tikopia: A sociological study of kinship in primitive Polynesia*. Palo Alto: Stanford University Press.

Fitzgerald, B. (1999). Children of lesbian and gay parents: A review of the literature. *Marriage & Family Reviews, 29*, 57-75.

Fletcher, R. (1966). *The family and marriage in Britain*. Harmondsworth: Penguin.

Fortes, M. (1950). Kinship and marriage among the Ashanti. In A.R. Radcliffe Brown & D. Forde (Eds.), *African systems of kinship and marriage*. London: Oxford University Press.

Foster, P. (1990). *Policy and practice in multicultural and antiracist education*. London: Routledge.

Frankenberg, R. (1966). *Communities in Britain*. Harmondsworth: Penguin.

French, J. (1986). Gender and the classroom. *New Society*, 7 March.

Gaine, C. & George, R. (1999). *Gender, 'race' and class in schooling: A new introduction*. London: Falmer.

Gallie, D. (1978). *In search of the new working class*. Cambridge: Cambridge University Press.

Gershuny, J. (1992). Change in the domestic division of labour in the UK, 1975-1987: Dependent labour versus adaptive partnership. In W. Abercrombie & A. Warde (Eds.), *Social change in contemporary Britain*. Cambridge: Polity Press.

Gewirtz, S., Ball, S.J. & Bowe, R. (1995). *Markets, choice and equity in education*. Milton Keynes: Open University Press.

Ghee, C. (2001). Population review of 2000: England and Wales. *Population Trends, 106*, 7-14.

Giddens, A. (1991). *Modernity and self-identity*. Cambridge: Polity.

Giddens, A. (1992). *The transformation of intimacy: Sexuality, love and eroticism in modern societies*. Cambridge: Polity Press.

Giddens, A. (2001). *Sociology* (4th ed.). Cambridge: Polity Press.

Gillborn, D. (1990). *'Race', ethnicity and education: Teaching and learning in multi-ethnic schools*. London: Unwin Hyman.

Gillborn, D. & Drew, D. (1992). 'Race', class and school effects. *New Community, 18*, 4.

Gillborn, D. & Mirza, H.S. (2000). *Educational inequality: Mapping race, class and gender*. London: OFSTED.

Gillborn, D. & Youdell, D. (2001). The new IQism: Intelligence, 'ability' and the rationing of education. In J. Demaine (Ed.), *Sociology of education today*. Basingstoke: Palgrave.

Gittins, D. (1993). *The family in question* (2nd ed.). Basingstoke: Macmillan.

Goffman, E. (1968). *Asylums*. Harmondsworth: Penguin.

Goffman, E. (1969). *The presentation of self in everyday life*. Harmondsworth: Penguin.

Goldthorpe, J.H., Lockwood, D., Bechofer, F. & Platt, J. (1969). *The affluent worker in the class structure*. Cambridge: Cambridge University Press.

Goulborne, H. (1999). The transnational character of Caribbean kinship in Britain. In S. McRae (Ed.), *Changing Britain: Families and households in the 1990s*. Oxford: Oxford University Press.

Graham, H. (1987). Being poor: Perceptions and coping strategies of lone mothers. In J. Brannen & G. Wilson (Eds.), *Give and take in families*. London: Allen & Unwin.

Griffin, J.H. (1960). *Black like me*. New York: Signet.

Halfpenny, P. (1984). *Principles of method*. York: Longman.

Hall, E.T. (1973). *The silent language*. New York: Doubleday.

Hall, R., Ogden, P.E. & Hill, C. (1999). Living alone: Evidence from England and Wales and France for the last two decades. In S. McRae (Ed.), *Changing Britain: Families and households in the 1990s*. Oxford: Oxford University Press.

Hall, S. (1997). *Representations: Cultural representations and signifying practices*. London: Sage Publications with Open University.

Halsey, A.H., Floud, J. & Anderson, C.A. (1961). *Education, economy and society*. New York: Free Press.

Halsey, A.H., Heath, A. & Ridge, J.M. (1980). *Origins and destinations: Family, class and education in modern Britain*. Oxford: Clarendon.

Halsey, A.H., Lauder, H., Brown, P. & Wells, A. (1997). *Education: Culture, economy, society*. Oxford: Oxford University Press.

Haralambos, M. (1994). *Right on: From blues to soul in Black America*. Ormskirk: Causeway Press.

Hargreaves, D.H. (1967). *Social relations in a secondary school*. London: Routledge & Kegan Paul.

Harris, M. (1984). The strange saga of the Video Bill. *New Society*, 26 April, 140-142.

Haskey, J. (1994). Stepfamilies and stepchildren in Great Britain. *Population Trends, 76*, 17-28.

Haskey, J. (2001). Cohabitation in Great Britain: Past, present and future trends – and attitudes. *Population Trends, 103*, 4-19.

Haskey, J. (2002). One-parent families – and the dependent children living in them – in Great Britain. *Population Trends, 109*, 46-57.

Hetherington, E.M. (2002). *For better or for worse: Divorce reconsidered*. New York: Harper & Brothers.

Hey, V. (1997). *The company she keeps*. Milton Keynes: Open University Press.

Hill, A. (2002). Who needs you, baby? *The Observer*, 21 July.

Hobbs, D. (1988). *Doing the business*. Oxford: Oxford University Press.

Hoebel, E.A. (1960). *The Cheyennes*. New York: Holt, Rinehart & Winston.

Homan, R. (1991). *The ethics of social research*. Harlow: Longman.

Hopkins, N. (2000). Tide of violence in the home: Domestic attacks occur every six seconds. *The Guardian*, 26 October.

Hornsby-Smith, M. (1993). *Gaining access*. In N. Gilbert (Ed.), *Researching social life*. London: Sage.

Humphreys, L. (1970). *Tearoom trade: Impersonal sex in public places*. Chicago: Aldine.

Iannucci, A. (1995). Play your card right. *The Guardian*, 2 May.

Ireson, J. & Hallam, S. (2001). *Ability grouping in education*. London: Sage.

Jackson, D. (1998). Breaking out of the binary trap: Boys' underachievement, schooling and gender relations. In D. Epstein et al. (Eds.), *Failing boys? Issues in gender and achievement*. Buckingham: Open University Press.

Jowell, R., Curtice, J., Park, A., Brook, L., Thomson, K. & Bryson, C. (Eds.), (1998). *British and European social attitudes in the 15th report: How Britain differs*. Aldershot: Ashgate.

Jowell, R., Curtice, J., Park, A., Thomson, K., Jarvis, L., Bromley, C. & Stratford, N. (Eds.), (2000). *British social attitudes the 17th report: Focusing on diversity*. London: Sage.

Keddie, N. (1973). Classroom knowledge. In N. Keddie (Ed.), *Tinker, tailor ... the myth of cultural deprivation*. Harmondsworth: Penguin.

Kellner, P. (1994). The figures are Shere Nonsense. *The Sunday Times*, 27 February.

Kerr, M. (1958). *The people of Ship Street*. London: Routledge & Kegan Paul.

Kiernan, K. & Mueller, G. (1999). Who divorces? In S. McRae (Ed.), *Changing Britain: Families and households in the 1990s*. Oxford: Oxford University Press.

Kirton, A. (1998). Labour and education: The story so far. *S magazine*, September.

Kitzinger, J. (1993). Understanding AIDS. In J. Eldridge (Ed.), *Getting the message: News, truth and power*. London: Routledge.

Kluckhohn, C. (1951). The concept of culture. In D. Lerner & H.D. Lasswell (Eds.), *The policy sciences*. Stanford: Stanford University Press.

Kulick, D. (1998). *Travesti – Sex, gender and culture among Brazilian transgendered prostitutes*. Chicago: University of Chicago Press.

Kurz, D. (1995). *For richer, for poorer: Mothers confront divorce*. London: Routledge.

Labov, W. (1973). The logic of nonstandard English. In N. Keddie (Ed.), *Tinker, tailor ... the myth of cultural deprivation*. Harmondsworth: Penguin.

Lacey, C. (1970). *Hightown Grammar*. Manchester: Manchester University Press.

Langham, S. (2000). Feminism and the classroom. *Sociology Review*, November.

LaPiere, R.T. (1934). Attitudes vs. actions. *Social Forces, 13*, 230-237.

Laslett, P.K. (1965). *The world we have lost*. London: Methuen.

Laslett, P.K. (1977). *Family life and illicit love in earlier generations*. London: Methuen.

Lawson, A. (1988). *Adultery: an analysis of love and betrayal*. Oxford: Blackwell.

Leach, E.R. (1967). *A runaway world?* London: BBC publications.

Lee, D. & Newby, H. (1983). *The problem of sociology*. London: Hutchinson.

Lee, D., Marsden, D., Rickman, P. & Dunscombe, J. (1990). *Scheming for youth: A study of YTS in the enterprise culture*. Milton Keynes: Open University Press.

Lee, N. (2001). *Childhood and society: Growing up in an age of uncertainty*. Buckingham: Open University Press.

Lees, S. (1986). *Losing out: Sexuality and adolescent girls*. London: Hutchinson.

Leonard, M. (2000). Back to the future: The domestic division of labour. *Sociology Review*, November, 26-28.

Lévi-Strauss, C. (1956). The family. In H. L. Shapiro (Ed.), *Man, culture and society*. London: Oxford.

Lewis, J. (2001). Women, men and the family. In A. Sheldon (Ed.), *The Blair effect: The Blair government 1997-2001*. London: Little, Brown and Company.

Lewis, O. (1951). *Life in a Mexican village: Tepoztlan restudied*. Urbana IL: University of Illinois Press.

Liebow, E. (1967). *Tally's Corner*. Boston: Little Brown.

Lister, R. (1996). Back to the family: Family policies and politics under the Major government. In H. Jones & J. Millar (Eds.), *The politics of the family*. Aldershot: Avebury.

Lobban, G. (1974). Data report on British reading schemes. *The Times Educational Supplement*, 1 March.

Long Lance, Chief Buffalo Child (1956). *Long Lance*. London: Corgi Books.

Lynch, K. (1989). *The hidden curriculum: Reproduction in education, a reappraisal*. London: Falmer.

Mac an Ghaill, M. (1988). *Young, gifted and Black: Student-teacher relations in the schooling of Black youth*. Milton Keynes: Open University Press.

Mac an Ghaill, M. (1992). Coming of age in 1980s England: Reconceptualising black students' schooling experience. In D. Gill, B. Mayor & M. Blair (Eds.). *Racism and education: Structures and strategies*. London: Sage.

Mac an Ghaill, M. (1994). *The making of men: Masculinities, sexualities and schooling*. Buckingham: Open University Press.

Macbeath, J. & Mortimore, P. (2001). *Improving school effectiveness*. Buckingham: Open University Press.

Macdonald, K. & Tipton, D. (1993). Using documents. In N. Gilbert (Ed.), *Researching social life*. London: Sage.

Machin, S. (2003). Unto them that hath ... *Centrepiece, 8*, 4-9.

MacInnes, J. (1998). Manly virtues and masculine vices. *Living Marxism*, November.

Mahony, P. (1998). Girls will be girls and boys will be first. In D. Epstein et al. (Eds.), *Failing boys? Issues in gender and achievement*. Buckingham: Open University Press.

Mair, L. (1971). *Marriage*. Harmondsworth: Penguin.

Malinowski, B. (1927). *Sex and repression in savage society*. London: Routledge.

Mansfield, P. & Collard, J. (1988). *The beginning of the rest of your life?* Basingstoke: Macmillan.

Mars, G. (1982). *Cheats at work: An anthropology of workplace crime*. London: Allen & Unwin.

May, T. (2001). *Social research: Issues, methods and process* (3rd ed.). Buckingham: Open University Press.

McGlone, F., Park, A. & Roberts, C. (1999). Kinship and friendship: Attitudes and behaviour in Britain, 1986-1995. In S. McRae (Ed.), *Changing Britain: Families and households in the 1990s*. Oxford: Oxford University Press.

McKenzie, J. (2001). *Changing education: A sociology of education since 1944*. Harlow: Pearson Education.

McMahon, A. (1999). *Taking care of men: Sexual politics in the public mind*. Cambridge: Cambridge University Press.

McRae, S. (1999). Introduction: Family and household change in Britain. In S. McRae (Ed.), *Changing Britain: Families and households in the 1990s*. Oxford: Oxford University Press.

Mead, M. (1949). *Male and female*. London: Gollanz.

Mirza, H. (1992). *Young, female and Black*. London: Routledge.

Modood, T., Berthoud, R., Lakey, J., Nazroo, P., et al. (1997). *Ethnic minorities in Britain: Diversity and disadvantage*. London: Policy Studies Institute.

Morgan, P. (1999). *Farewell to the family: Public policy and family breakdown in Britain and the USA*. London: The IEA Health and Welfare Unit.

Moser, C.A. & Kalton, G. (1971). *Survey methods in social investigation* (2nd ed.). London: Heinemann.

Murdock, G.P. (1949). *Social structure*. New York: Macmillan.

Murray, C. (1990). *The emerging British underclass.* London: Institute of Economic Affairs.

Murrary, C. (2001). *Underclass + 10: Charles Murray and the British underclass, 1990-2000.* London: Civitas.

Neale, B. & Smart, C. (1997). Experiments with parenthood? *Sociology, 31,* 201-219.

Newark, P. (1980). *The illustrated encyclopedia of the old West.* London: André Deutsch.

Newby, H. (1977). In the field: Reflections on a study of Suffolk farm workers. In C. Bell & H. Newby (Eds.), *Doing sociological research.* London: Allen & Unwin.

Newell, R. (1993). Questionnaires. In N. Gilbert (Ed.), *Researching social life.* London: Sage.

Nissel, M. (1995). Vital statistics. *New Statesman, 27* January.

O'Brien, M. (2000). Family life. In M. Haralambos (Ed.), *Developments in Sociology Volume 16.* Ormskirk: Causeway Press.

O'Connell Davidson, J. & Layder, D. (1994). *Methods, sex and madness.* London: Routledge.

O'Hagan, S. (2003). From sinner to saint. *The Observer,* 12th January.

Oakley, A. (1974). *The sociology of housework.* London: Martin Robertson.

Okely, J. (1983). *The traveller-gypsies.* Cambridge: Cambridge University Press.

Page, R. (2002). New Labour and the welfare state. In M. Holborn (Ed.), *Developments in Sociology, Volume 18.* Ormskirk: Causeway Press.

Pahl, J. (1989). *Money and marriage.* Basingstoke: Macmillan.

Parker, H., Aldridge, J. & Measham, F. (1998). *Illegal leisure: The normalisation of adolescent recreational drug use.* London: Routledge.

Parsons, T. (1951). *The social system.* New York: Free Press.

Parsons, T. (1961). The school class as a social system. In A. H. Halsey et al. (Eds.), *Education, economy and society.* New York: Free Press.

Parsons, T. & Bales, R.F. (1955). *Family, socialisation and interaction process.* New York: The Free Press.

Pawson, R. (1995). Methodology. In M. Haralambos (Ed.), *Developments in Sociology, Volume 5.* Ormskirk: Causeway Press.

Pearson, G. (1983). *Hooligan: A history of respectable fears.* London: Macmillan.

Philo, G. & Miller, D. (2002). Circuits of communication and power: Recent developments in media sociology. In M. Holborn (Ed.), *Developments in Sociology, Volume 18.* Ormskirk: Causeway Press.

Pilkington, A. (2003). *Racial disadvantage and ethnic diversity in Britain.* London: Palgrave.

Platt, J. (1976). *Realities of social research.* London: Chatto & Windus.

Pleck, J. (1985). *Working wives, working husbands.* London: Sage.

Plummer, G. (2000). *Failing working-class girls.* Stoke on Trent: Trentham Books.

Postman, N. (1983). *The disappearance of childhood.* London: W.H. Allen.

Punch, M. (1979). Observation and the police. In M. Hammersley (Ed.), *Social research: Philosophy, politics and practice.* London: Sage.

Reay, D. (1998). *Class work: Mothers' involvement in their children's primary schooling.* London: UCL Press.

Redfield, R. (1930). *Tepoztlan: A Mexican village.* Chicago: University of Chicago Press.

Rist, R. (1970). Student social class and teacher expectations: The self-fulfilling prophecy in ghetto education. *Harvard Educational Review, 40.*

Rodgers, B. & Pryor, J. (1998). *Divorce and separation: The outcomes for children.* York: Joseph Rowntree Foundation.

Rosenthal, R. & Jacobson, L. (1968). *Pygmalion in the classroom.* New York: Holt, Rinehart & Winston.

Royle, E. (1997). *Modern Britain: A social history 1750-1997.* London: Hodder Headline.

Saunders, P. (2000). Afterward: Family research and family policy since 1992. In N. Dennis & G. Erdos *Families without fatherhood* (3rd ed.). London: Institute for the Study of Civil Society.

Scanzoni, J., Polonko, K., Teachman, J. & Thompson, L. (1989). *The sexual bond.* Newbury Park: Sage.

Scase, R. (2000). *Britain in 2010.* Oxford: Capstone Publishing.

Scott, J. (1990). *A matter of record.* Cambridge: Polity Press.

Sewell, T. (1997). *Black masculinities and schooling.* Stoke on Trent: Trentham Books.

Sharpe, S. (1976). *Just like a girl: How girls learn to be women.* Harmondsworth: Penguin.

Sharpe, S. (1984). *Double identity.* Harmondsworth: Penguin.

Sharpe, S. (1994). *Just like a girl: How girls learn to be women: The 70s to the 90s.* Harmondsworth: Penguin.

Shaw, C. (1930). *The Jack Roller.* Chicago: University of Chicago Press.

Sissons, M. (1970). *The psychology of social class.* Milton Keynes: Open University Press.

Smith, D. & Tomlinson, S. (1989). The school effect: A study of multi-racial comprehensives. London: Policy Studies Institute.

Smith, J., Gilford, S. & O'Sullivan, A. (1998). *The family background of homeless young people.* London: Family Policy Studies Centre (now available through the Joseph Rowntree Foundation).

Smith, T. & Noble, M. (1995). *Poverty and schooling in the 1990s.* London: CPAG.

Social Trends (2002). London: The Stationery Office.

Social Trends (2003). London: The Stationery Office.

Spender, D. (1983). *Invisible women: The school scandal.* London: Women's Press.

Stacey, J. (1996). *In the name of the family: Rethinking family values in the postmodern age.* Boston MA: Beacon Press.

Stainton Rogers, W. & Stainton Rogers, R. (2001). *The psychology of gender and sexuality.* Buckingham: Open University Press.

Stainton Rogers, W. (2001). Constructing childhood, constructing child concern. In P. Foley, J. Roche & S. Turner (Eds.), *Children in society: Contemporary theory, policy and practice.* Basingstoke: Palgrave.

Stands In Timber, J. & Liberty, M. (1967). *Cheyenne memories.* New Haven, Yale University Press.

Stanworth, M. (1983). *Gender and schooling.* London: Hutchinson.

Strathdee, R. (2003). Labour market change, vocational education and training, and social class. In M. Holborn (Ed.), *Developments in Sociology, Volume 19.* Ormskirk: Causeway Press.

Sugarman, B. (1970). Social class, values and behaviour in schools. In M. Craft (Ed.), *Family, class and education.* London: Longman.

Sukhnandan, L. & Lee, B. (1998). *Streaming, setting and grouping by ability.* Slough: NFER.

Thomas, W.I. & Znaniecki, F. (1958). *The Polish peasant in Europe and America.* New York: Dover.

Tizard, B. & Phoenix, A. (1993). *Black, white or mixed race.* London: Routledge.

Turnbull, C. (1961). The forest people. London: Jonathan Cape.

Vogler, C. & Pahl, J. (1994). Money, power and inequality within marriage. *Sociological Review, 42,* 263-288.

Walford, G. (1993). Researching the City Technology College Kingshurst. In R. Burgess (Ed.), *Research Methods.* London: Nelson.

Walklate, S. (2000). Researching victims. In R.D. King & E. Wincup (Eds.), *Doing research on crime and justice.* Oxford: Oxford University Press.

Weale, S. (2002). The right to choose. *The Guardian,* 2 December.

Weber, M. (1958). *The Protestant ethic and the spirit of capitalism.* New York: Charles Scribner's Sons.

Weeks, J., Heaphy, B. & Donovan, C. (1999a). Partners by choice: Equality, power and commitment in non-heterosexual relationships. In G. Allan (Ed.), *The sociology of the family: A reader.* Oxford: Blackwell.

Weeks, J., Heaphy, B. & Donovan, C. (1999b). Families of choice: Autonomy and mutuality in non-heterosexual relationships. In S. McRae (Ed.), *Changing Britain: Families and households in the 1990s*. Oxford: Oxford University Press.

Westwood S. & Bhachu, P. (1988). Images and realities. *New Society*, 6 May.

White, L. (1998). Boys will be boys – and failures. *The Sunday Times*, 11 January.

Whyte, W.F. (1955). *Street corner society* (2nd ed.). Chicago: University of Chicago Press.

Williams, B. (1981). *Obscenity and film censorship*. Cambridge: Cambridge University Press.

Williams, J.A. Jr. (1971). Interviewer-respondent interaction. In B.J. Franklin & H.W. Osborne (Eds.), *Research Methods*. Belmont: Wadsworth.

Willis, P. (1977). *Learning to labour: How working-class kids get working-class jobs*. Farnborough: Saxon House.

Willmott, P. (1986). *Social networks, informal care and public policy*. London: Policy Studies Institute.

Wright, C. (1986). School processes – An ethnographic study. In S.J. Eggleston, D. Dunn & M. Angali (Eds.), *Education for some*. Stoke on Trent: Trentham Books.

Wright, C. (1992). Early education: Multiracial primary school classrooms. In D. Gill, B. Mayor & M. Blair (Eds.), *Racism and education*. London: Sage.

Young, M. & Willmott, P. (1957). *Family and kinship in East London*. London: Routledge & Kegan Paul.

Young, M. & Willmott, P. (1973). *The symmetrical family*. London: Routledge & Kegan Paul.

Author index

Subject index